Mark G. Henninger is Assistant Professor of
Philosophy, Loyola University of Chicago.

D1606477

Relations

Relations
Medieval Theories 1250–1325

MARK G. HENNINGER, SJ

CLARENDON PRESS · OXFORD
1989

Oxford University Press, Walton Street, Oxford OX2 6DP

Oxford New York Toronto
Delhi Bombay Calcutta Madras Karachi
Petaling Jaya Singapore Hong Kong Tokyo
Nairobi Dar es Salaam Cape Town
Melbourne Auckland

and associated companies in
Berlin Ibadan

Oxford is a trade mark of Oxford University Press

Published in the United States
by Oxford University Press, New York

British Library Cataloguing in Publication Data
Henninger, Mark G.
Relations: medieval theories 1250–1325
1. European philosophy, 500–1500
189
I. Title
ISBN 0-19-824444-4

Library of Congress Cataloging in Publication Data
Henninger, Mark Gerald, 1948–
Relations: medieval theories, 1250–1325
Mark G. Henninger.
Bibliography: p.   Includes index.
1. Relation (Philosophy)—History. 2. Philosophy, Medieval.
I. Title.
B738.R44H46   1989   111—dc19   88-32666
ISBN 0-19-824444-4

Photoset by Rowland Phototypesetting Ltd
Bury St Edmunds, Suffolk
Printed and bound in
Great Britain by Biddles Ltd,
Guildford and Kings's Lynn

To my parents,
David and Aileen

Acknowledgements

I should like to acknowledge the debt of gratitude I owe to the Jesuits of the Detroit Province of the Society of Jesus for their unwavering support, both personal and financial. In particular I thank Edmund Miller for his candid and constant friendship during many years, John O'Malley for his outstanding example as a humane scholar and priest, and John McManamon, colleague, friend, and brother. In addition I am most grateful for the exceptionally warm and active support that I received during my research from my Jesuit brothers at Loyola University of Chicago, at the Collegio S. Roberto Bellarmino in Rome, at Loyola-Marymount University in Los Angeles, and at the Jesuit Novitiate at Santa Barbara.

I am also very happy to acknowledge Marilyn McCord Adams, my director during my studies at the University of California in Los Angeles, for her high standards, hard work, and lasting personal example. For reading earlier drafts of parts of this book I thank Allan Wolter, Clifford Kossel, Gordon Wilson, Raymond Macken, and Jerome Brown. Finally, I thank the American Philosophical Society for their generous grant, Loyola University of Chicago for my research leave 1987–8, and my colleagues in the philosophy department there for their warm and constant encouragement.

M.G.H.

Contents

1

Introduction

IN the thirteenth and early fourteenth centuries many thinkers argued for different theories concerning the ontological status of relations, for relations were of prime theological and philosophical importance. The doctrine of the Trinity is the most outstanding theological example. Christian thinkers followed Augustine in speaking of the three divine persons as constituted in some way by their relations to one another. As the writings of Aristotle became available to the West in the thirteenth century, many sought to understand more clearly the doctrine of the Trinity by adapting some of Aristotle's thoughts on relations. In addition, this theological doctrine reinforced a realism in some philosophical theories of relation: the belief that the Trinity of persons, constituted by relations, is real and not simply a product of our mind persuaded some that more mundane relations, as colour similarity and equality in height, are not reducible simply to our way of comparing the things related.

Purely philosophical concerns raised questions about the type of being to be accorded relations. For example, as today so then some 'nominalist/conceptualists', as Henry of Harclay and William of Ockham, used similarity relations in their accounts of universals. The realists' charge that these accounts render universal concepts arbitrary and subjective can be evaluated only after determining whether the similarity relations obtaining between co-specific and co-generic individuals are themselves arbitrary and subjective. Other questions concerning relations come to mind. How can one explain the relatedness of the intellect and will to their objects? Are these faculties in some way 'relational' by nature? What could this mean? Furthermore, some thinkers explained key parts of their ontologies and epistemologies in terms of relations. Henry of Ghent taught that a creature's actual existence is a relation to God as efficient cause, and Duns Scotus used his own theory of relations in discussing abstractive and intuitive cognition.

1. The Problem of the Ontological Status of Relations

The basic task of describing clearly the way relations exist was particularly intractable. Key sources of difficulty were logical and semantic differences between statements containing 'relative' terms and those containing only 'absolute' terms. It is, in fact, from the medieval thinkers by way of J. S. Mill that we inherit this useful distinction.[1] In the statement 'Duns Scotus is taller than William of Ockham', Scotus' being, or being truly characterized as, taller than Ockham depends not only on a property of Scotus, i.e. his height, but also on a property of Ockham, i.e. his height. This is not the case in the statement 'Duns Scotus is white'.

Since Plato, statements containing relative terms have puzzled philosophers. Many of these thinkers assumed a subject–attribute analysis of all affirmative statements according to which all statements ascribe an attribute to the individual denoted by the grammatical subject. In 'Duns Scotus is white', the attribute of being white is ascribed to Scotus. But in 'Duns Scotus is taller than William of Ockham' complications arise immediately on a subject–attribute analysis. What precisely is ascribed to Scotus: the attribute of being tall, being taller than, or being taller than William of Ockham? What role is 'William of Ockham' to play? Further, from the statement 'Duns Scotus is taller than William of Ockham' we can validly infer that 'William of Ockham is shorter than Duns Scotus'. How is this type of inference involving relative terms to be handled in the traditional Aristotelian subject –predicate logic?

For centuries this type of analysis was the standard view, and it regulated, consciously or not, the best minds. Bertrand Russell argued that it was the chief source of Leibniz's metaphysical doctrines.[2] It was not until the nineteenth century that the

---

[1] J. S. Mill, *A System of Logic Ratiocinative and Inductive*, ed. J. M. Robson, in *Collected Works of John Stuart Mill*, vol. 7 (Toronto and Buffalo, 1973), bk. 1, chap. 2, no. 7: 'Every relative name which is predicated of an object, supposes another object (or objects), of which we may predicate either that same name or another relative name which is said to be the *correlative* of the former' (p. 42). Also W. van O. Quine, *Word and Object* (New York and London, 1960), n. 22, pp. 105–10.

[2] B. Russell, *A Critical Exposition of the Philosophy of Leibniz*, 2nd edn. (London, 1937), pp. 9–15. Russell and N. Rescher have taken Leibniz's doctrine on relation to imply the reducibility of relational propositions to non-relational ones. J. Hintikka and H. Ishiguro

inadequacies of this type of analysis became clear and alternatives were explored. Such sustained work on the logic of relations began with De Morgan and continued with Peirce, Schroeder, and Russell.[3] With his analysis of statements in terms of functions and arguments, Frege provided (among other things) a clear notation for relational statements. Certainly sentences ascribing an attribute to a subject can be symbolized, as 'Romeo is an Italian' = Ir. But sentences with relations involving two or more terms can also be easily symbolized, as 'Romeo loves Juliet' = Lrj, and 'Verona is between Padua and Brescia' = Bvpb. With such polyadic functions the logical form of these statements became clear, and with logical constants, variables, and quantifiers there developed a powerful and rich logic of relations.

Advances in the logic of relations, however, did not resolve the problem of their ontological status. Are relations completely mind-dependent, or do they have some extra-mental being? How is their way of existing different from, say, that of physical objects? Are they 'concrete' or 'abstract' entities? If concrete, are they reducible to their relata? If so, *how* are they reducible? If abstract, what specific type of abstract objects are they? Are they special kinds of sets or classes, e.g. sets of ordered pairs, triplets, n-tuples? Are they propositional functions of two or more variables? Recently R. M. Martin has suggested that mathematical entities exist in the same way as relations, and these latter can be analysed in terms of 'ordinal individuals'.[4]

2. The Late Medieval Debate over Relations

The disagreement that marks contemporary discussion over the ontological status of relations also characterized the debate of

disagree. See the essays in *Leibniz: A Collection of Critical Essays*, ed. H. G. Frankfurt (New York, 1972); and more recently D. Wong, 'Leibniz's Theory of Relations', *The Philosophical Review* 89 (1980), pp. 241–56. For newly released letters and manuscripts on Russell's views on Leibniz, see W. H. O'Briant, 'Russell on Leibniz', *Studia Leibnitiana* 11 (1979), pp. 159–222.

[3] For helpful insights into this history, see R. R. Dipert, 'Peirce, Frege, the Logic of Relations, and Church's Theorem', *History and Philosophy of Logic* 5 (1984), pp. 49–66.
[4] R. M. Martin, 'On the Metaphysical Status of Mathematical Entities', *The Review of Metaphysics* 39 (1985), pp. 3–21.

the thirteenth and early fourteenth centuries. According to the present state of research, it seems that until the second decade of the fourteenth century there was still widespread agreement among scholastics that relations exist independently of the mind. The difficulty that most troubled these thinkers was not whether relations are extra-mental, but what type of extra-mental status to accord them. In answering this latter question, they frequently asked whether a relation was identical with the things related and if not, how it is distinct. In their terminology, they asked: is a real categorical relation distinct from its foundation? To understand this formulation is to understand the terms of the medieval debate over relations. Such an understanding is also necessary to appreciate what happened in the second decade of the fourteenth century that changed and deepened the medieval debate. For this, a few preliminary remarks are necessary.

2.1. Relation as Accident

The principal assumption of the late medieval controversy over relation is that a real relation is an Aristotelian accident.[5] The participants in this discussion agreed that a relation's ontological status, whatever else it may be, must be explained in terms of its being in, 'inhering in', a subject. This fact is crucial for understanding the debate. It is at the root of the strangeness most find in medieval theories of relation. Today we might talk of one symmetrical relation R of colour similarity between two pieces of white chalk, *a* and *b*. But for the medievals, if there are two really distinct substances, there must be two really distinct accidents.

---

[5] For a historical overview of the problem of relation, see J. Weinberg, 'The Concept of Relation: Some Observations on its History', in *Abstraction, Relation, and Induction: Three Essays in the History of Thought* (Madison and Milwaukee, 1965), pp. 61–119. For the problem of relation before Aristotle, see ibid., pp. 61–7. While some maintain that Plato was not aware of the problems concerning relations and/or did not develop a theory of relation, both H.-N. Castañeda and M. Matthen agree that Plato did have a theory of relational statements, though they disagree on what it was. See H.-N. Castañeda, 'Plato's *Phaedo* Theory of Relations', *Journal of Philosophical Logic* 1/3–4 (1972), pp. 467–80; 'Plato's Relations, Not Essences or Accidents, at *Phaedo* 102 b2–d2', *Canadian Journal of Philosophy* 7 (1978), pp. 39–53; 'Leibniz and Plato's *Phaedo* Theory of Relations and Predication', in *Leibniz: Critical and Interpretive Essays*, ed. M. Hooker (Manchester, 1982); M. Matthen, 'Plato's Treatment of Relational Statements in the *Phaedo*', *Phronesis* 27 (1982), pp. 90–100; M. McPherran, 'Matthen on Castañeda and Plato's Treatment of Relational Statements in the *Phaedo*', *Phronesis* 28 (1983), pp. 298–306.

Being an accident, a relation is not an entity that somehow hovers between the two things related or, in Aristotelian terms, inheres in both. Like Liebniz,[6] Ibn Sīnā (d. 1037) makes this point in his discussion of relations: 'Therefore in no way may you think that one accident is in two subjects.'[7] In the chalk example, one relation of colour similarity R of *a* to *b* is based on an accident, the quality of whiteness in *a*. A numerically distinct relation of similarity R' of *b* to *a* is based on a numerically distinct accident of whiteness inhering in *b*. There are two relations, one in each of the things related. Furthermore, each relation is based upon another accident, in this case that of whiteness, which in its turn inheres in the substance. Since such relations are accidents in the category of relation, they are called 'categorical relations'. Because categorical relations depend upon entities of other categories as their foundations, Aristotle calls relations the least of all extra-mental realities.[8]

If *a* is really related to *b*, then *a* is called the subject of the relation R (of, say, colour similarity) to *b*, the term. Inhering in *a* is an accident of whiteness *c*, which is called the foundation for the relation R. Conversely, if *b* is also really related to *a*, *b* is the subject of the co-relation R' of similarity to the term *a*. The whiteness *d* in *b* is the foundation of the co-relation R'. At times the scholastics referred to *a* and *b* as the extremes or relata of the relations.

The medievals often conceived of a categorical real relation, then, as existing in one relatum and 'pointing to' or 'being toward' the other. This peculiar property of being toward, its *esse-ad*, distinguishes relations from substances and other accidents. In this debate, much tension springs from the need to do justice

[6] See Leibniz, *Philosophical Papers and Letters*, trans. and ed. L. E. Loemker, Synthese Library, 2nd edn. (Dordrecht, 1969), p. 609, for Leibniz's often quoted passage: 'I do not believe that you will admit an accident that is in two subjects at the same time. My judgment about relations is that paternity in David is one thing, sonship in Solomon another, but that the relation common to both is a merely mental thing whose basis is the modifications of the individuals.' The effect of this doctrine on Leibniz's theory of relational propositions is controversial; see n. 2 above. For Leibniz's medieval connection through the late scholastic Suarez (1548–1617), see L. B. McCullough, 'Leibniz and Traditional Philosophy', *Studia Leibnitiana* 10 (1978), pp. 254–70.

[7] Avicenna, *Liber de Philosophia Prima sive Scientia Divina* I–IV, ed. S. Van Riet in *Avicenna Latinus* (Louvain and Leiden, 1977), tract. 3, chap. 10: 'Igitur nullo modo putes quod unum accidens sit in duobus subiectis . . .' (p. 177: 93).

[8] Aristotle, *Metaphysics* XIV, c. 1 (1088ᵃ20–7).

to both of these characteristics: a relation's alleged reality as
an Aristotelian accident (*esse-in*) and its peculiar character of
involving somehow more than the subject (*esse-ad*).

2.2 Types of Real Relations

The influence of Aristotle was felt in other ways. The scholastics
base their discussion of relation on a passage in his *Metaphysics*
book five, a lexicon of philosophical terms. In chapter fifteen,[9]
Aristotle draws distinctions between three kinds of 'relatives'
or relata based on differing foundations. These kinds can be
characterized as numerical, causal, and psychological.

This threefold division strikes the modern reader as odd. For
example, the first class consists of relatives of a numerical nature,
'as double to half, and treble to third, and in general that which
contains something else many times to that which is contained
many times in something else, and that which exceeds to that
which is exceeded'.[10] If this is taken as referring to numerical
relations expressed by 'greater than', 'equal to', 'a multiple of',
etc., so far so good. But strangely enough, in addition to strictly
numerical relations, Aristotle includes in this class relations
such as specific identity, qualitative similarity, and quantitative
equality:

For all refer to unity. (i) Those things are the same whose substance is
one; (ii) those are similar whose quality is one; (iii) those are equal whose
quantity is one; and one is the beginning and measure of number, so that
all these relations imply number, though not in the same way.[11]

Many scholastics understood Aristotle as stating in (i) that the
relations of identity in species of two humans are founded on their
respective specific natures. They took him as teaching in (ii) that
the relations of similarity of two objects are founded on their
respective qualities (e.g. whiteness) and in (iii) that the relations of
equality of two objects are founded on their respective quantities
(e.g. five pounds). Further, the relations of specific difference,

---

[9] Aristotle, *Metaph.* V, c. 15 (1029^{b}25–1021^{b}11).
[10] Ibid. (1020^{b}25–8); trans. W. D. Ross in *The Basic Works of Aristotle*, ed. R. McKeon
(New York, 1941), p. 768.
[11] Ibid. (1021^{a}10–14).

dissimilarity, and inequality are founded on the specific natures, qualities, and quantities which in these cases are not 'one'.

Causal relations comprise the second class. Their foundations are the accidents of action and passion and active and passive potencies.[12] As examples he gives the relation of what heats to what is heated and the relation of what can cut to what can be cut. Finally, Aristotle's third class consists of relations involving the 'measure and the measured'. As an example he gives the relation between the known (the measure) and the knower (the measured). The former is described by a relative term, 'the known', only because the knower is really related to it.[13]

Like many scholastics, Aquinas believed Aristotle taught that relations in this third class are non-mutual, and relations in the first and second classes are mutual. Mutual relations R and R′ must both be real, while with non-mutual relations, R is real and R′ is of reason. The difference between these latter two types of relation can be grasped in terms of their causes. A relation of reason is caused and depends for its existence on the activity of some mind. A real relation is caused and depends for its existence on some real extra-mental foundation in the subject of the relation.

On this last point, Aquinas is clear and representative of the tradition. He held that a relation R of a to b is real only if a and b are really distinct extra-mental things, and there is a real extra-mental foundation in a for R. Aquinas also held that a relation R of a to b is of reason only if either (i) a and/or b is not real, or (ii) a and b are not really distinct, or (iii) there is no real foundation in a for R.[14] Aquinas gives as an example of (i) the relations between some concepts, as the concept of man is related to the concept of animal as species to genus.[15] Another example he gives is our relation of temporal priority to non-existent future generations.[16] He gives as an example of (ii) the relation of self-identity,[17] and for (iii) the problematical example of the relation of a column's being to the right of an animal.[18]

---

[12] Ibid. (1021ª15–27).   [13] Ibid. (1021ª27–ᵇ2).

[14] Thomas Aquinas, *Summa Theologica* I, q. 13, a. 7, corp.; *In I Sent.*, d. 26, q. 2, a. 1, corp.; d. 30, q. 1, a. 3, ad 3; d. 33, q. 1, a. 1, corp. and ad 4.

[15] *Summa Theol.* I, q. 13, a. 7, corp.; q. 28, a. 1, corp.

[16] *In I Sent.*, d. 26, q. 2, a. 1, corp.

[17] Ibid.; *De Potentia*, q. 7, a. 11, ad 3; *Summa Theol.* I, q. 13, a. 7, corp.

[18] *Summa Theol.* I, q. 13, a. 7, corp.

Many of those teaching that relations of Aristotle's third (psychological) class are non-mutual held that the knower is really related to the extra-mental thing known and the known thing is related only by reason to the knower. The knower and the known are really distinct, and there is a real foundation in the knower for the knower's relation to the thing known, the foundation being the real act of knowing in the knower. Hence there is a real relation in the knower toward the known. But, as discussed in Chapter Two, Section Six, there is no corresponding foundation in the thing known, and without this real foundation there can be no real relation to the knower in the thing known.

This third class of psychological, non-mutual relations is extremely important since most scholastics used it as a model for explicating the nature of the relations between God and creatures. The view became common, though not universal, that although creatures are really related to God, God is related to them only by a relation of reason. The question of the relations between God and creatures was often discussed in the first book of the scholastics' commentary on the *Sentences* of Peter Lombard, around distinction thirty. This became the *locus classicus* for their philosophical discussions of relation.

2.3. A Key Text of Aristotle

In the thirteenth and early fourteenth centuries many in the debate used the considerable authority of Aristotle to support their theories by citing a passage from his *Physics*: 'In respect of Substance there is no motion, because Substance has no contrary among things that are. Nor is there motion in respect of Relation: for it may happen that when one correlative changes, the other can truly be said not to change at all, so that in these cases the motion is accidental.'[19] Some scholastics use this to argue against those who hold that a real relation is some entity really distinct from its foundation. They claim Aristotle here teaches that *a* could begin to be really related to *b* with no change in *a*, but only in *b*. But if *a* does not change, it acquires no really distinct entity.

This argument was used by many others both before and after

---

[19] Aristotle, *Physics* V, c. 2 (225^b11–13) (Oxford trans.). See also Aristotle, *Metaph.* XIV, c. 1 (1088^a29–35); Mill, *System*, p. 44.

the medieval controversy. As transmitted to the West and interpreted by Sextus Empiricus, Plotinus, and Simplicius, the Stoics
were taken to believe that all relations are subjective and do not
have any existence outside the mind.[20] According to Sextus
Empiricus, one reason for their view was the belief that *a* is not
changed internally by becoming (or ceasing to be) related to *b*.[21]
This assumption is found in another who denied the extra-mental
reality of relations, John Locke: 'And if either of those things [i.e.
relata] be removed or cease to be, the Relation ceases and the
Denomination consequent to it, though the other receive in it self
no alteration at all.'[22] In the medieval debate, it was the passage of
Aristotle cited above that was the focus for discussion of this
intuition. In this way, the passage became central to the scholastics' disputes over relations, forcing them to think through the
implications of their theories.

In passing I should mention another argument that has a long
and distinguished history connected with the controversy over
relations: the charge of an infinite regress of relations. Earlier
in the Middle Ages, some orthodox Muslim theologians, the
Mutakallimūn, seem to have held that relations were purely
subjective.[23] They argued that positing a relation as an extra-
mental entity leads to an infinite regress. According to Fakhr

[20] Sextus Empiricus, *Adversus Dogmaticos Libros Quinque* (= *Adv. Mathem.* VII–XI), ed.
H. Mutschmann in *Sexti Empirici Opera*, vol. 2 (Bibliotheca Scriptorum Graecorum et
Romanorum Teubneriana, 1801; Leipzig, 1914), bk. 2 *Adv. Dog.* (= bk. 8 *Adv. Math.*), p.
206: 453–4; Plotinus, *Enneads* VI, 1, 6–9, ed. P. Henry and H.-R. Schwyzer, vol. 3
(Oxford, 1982), pp. 11–18; Simplicius, *In Aristotelis Categorias Commentarium* c. 7, ed. C.
Kalbfleisch in *Commentaria in Aristotelem Graeca*, vol. 8 (Berlin, 1907), p. 173: 1–6. For the
medieval Latin translation of William of Moerbeke, see Simplicius, *In Praedicamenta
Aristotelis* c. 7 (6ᵃ36–ᵇ14), ed. A. Pattin and W. Stuyven in *Corpus Latinum Commentariorum in Aristotelem Graecorum*, vol. 5/1 (Louvain and Paris, 1971): 'Post communes autem
dubitationes et solutiones neque eas quae particulariter inducuntur praetermittamus.
"Simile enim aiunt [Stoici] nihil esse praeter id quod in utrolibet quale, quae quidem
praeexistunt ante habitudinem; habitudo autem nihil utique erit nisi quoddam nostrum
iudicium comparantium quae a seipsis sunt et dicentium 'quod hoc et hoc eamdem
magnitudinem habet et eamdem qualitatem'; et sessio autem, aiunt, et statio quod utique
erit praeter sedens et stans?"' (p. 234: 80–7).
[21] Sextus Empiricus, *Adversus Dogmaticos*, p. 206: 9–14.
[22] John Locke, *An Essay Concerning Human Understanding*, ed. P. H. Nidditch (Oxford,
1975), bk. 2, c. 25, para. 5, p. 321. Furthermore, '. . . it [relation] be not contained in the
real existence of Things, but something extraneous, and superinduced . . .' (ibid., para. 8,
p. 322).
[23] For the Mutakallimūn, see Weinberg, 'Concept of Relation', pp. 89–91.

al-Din al-Rāzī (d. 1209),[24] they argued that such an entity would be an accident and would inhere in its subject. This inherence, being itself a relation, would be another distinct entity and would itself have its own relation of inherence, etc. Arguing against any reality for relations, absolute idealists as F. H. Bradley used a form of the infinite regress argument and were criticized by Russell. As we shall see, this charge of an infinite regress becomes important in the medieval debate, being levelled against Duns Scotus by Henry of Harclay, William of Ockham, and Peter Aureoli.

To sum up: the medievals conceived of a real categorical relation (as opposed to a relation of reason) as an accident existing in a subject as foundation, and there are three basic kinds of real categorical relations: numerical, causal, and psychological. These assumptions must be kept in mind in order to understand the medievals' use of Aristotle, particularly his *Physics* text, and the charge of an infinite regress.

3. Conclusion

The diversity of theories that emerges from this medieval controversy is striking. One reason for this diversity is the variety of general ontologies the scholastics brought to the question of relation. As Thomas Aquinas' ontology differs from that of Duns Scotus and both differ from that of William of Ockham, it is to be expected that their theories of relation will reflect these differences. In this study, I relate the theories on relation to these general ontologies. Presented in this larger context, the individual theories become more perspicuous to those who are already familiar with the ontologies of particular figures. For those who are not so familiar, I believe following the course of this inquiry on relation is an excellent way to introduce oneself to the variety of ontologies.

I decided upon the historical figures to be examined with the intention of assuring a wide spectrum of competing theories. To assure this diversity, I chose such major thinkers as Thomas

---

[24] M. Horten, *Die philosophischen Systeme der spekulativen Theologen im Islam* (Bonn, 1912), pp. 2, 5–6.

Aquinas, Henry of Ghent, John Duns Scotus, and William of Ockham. Their theories of relation are explicated in terms of key elements of their opposing philosophies: Thomas's doctrine of being, Henry of Ghent's doctrine of essential being and modes of existence, Duns Scotus' realist ontology, and William of Ockham's understanding of relative terms as connotative. There are a host of other figures to be studied, and the final choice was a function of my own history and interests. As I read through the texts of the often neglected Richard of Mediavilla, Henry of Harclay, and Peter Aureoli, I was often pleasantly surprised by their originality, trenchant criticism, and detailed consideration of arguments.

English translations of these medieval texts on relations are virtually non-existent, a situation that greatly restricts the number of those able to read the primary sources. As a partial remedy, I have translated into English numerous key texts on relations from various medieval thinkers. For those trained to read scholastic Latin, however, I have adopted the following policy. When modern critical editions are readily available, as with Thomas Aquinas, Duns Scotus, and William of Ockham, I only cite the references in the notes, except when it is important to have the Latin original on hand. For those cases where such critical editions are not easily available or I have used manuscript sources, I include the Latin text in the notes.

I have tried to strike a balance between the presentation/criticism of arguments and a straight historical account. To this end I have extracted cardinal points around which the debate revolves and formulated them in theses designated as (T1), (T2), etc. With these we can pin-point where one figure differs from another, and by examining the arguments for and against the theses we can see why they differ.

Since I focus this study, with its theses and arguments, on the question of the ontological status of relations, I cannot examine the several theological and philosophical issues that depend upon a theory of relation. This would be difficult to accomplish for one figure, much less for seven. I believe, however, that I provide a map to some uncharted territory that will help others wishing to examine these issues. At the end of Chapter Two I do allow myself one example to show how an understanding of a person's theory of relation deepens our grasp of other parts of his thought.

Finally, I have come to the conclusion that in the course of the medieval discussion some scholastics began conceiving of a relation in non-traditional ways similar to those found in some early modern philosophers. There was a move from a traditional medieval view of relation as an accident in a subject toward a view of relation as a concept in a mind. This change began in the second decade of the fourteenth century. I say more on this in the conclusion. Briefly, and without making claims about subsequent historical influence, I am convinced that there was a significant change in how a relation was conceived among the thinkers I treat, among them the most influential of the late medieval period. But this makes more sense after following the actual course of the debate that I trace, beginning with Thomas Aquinas, who started writing in the 1250s, and ending with Peter Aureoli, who died in 1322.

2

Relation as Being and Ratio

THOMAS AQUINAS

THOMAS AQUINAS (1224/5–74) was among the first scholastics to wrestle with the problem of the reality of relations within
the Aristotelian framework outlined in the Introduction. As one
of the first to use Aristotle's metaphysics as a Christian theo-
logian, he did not raise, much less settle, all relevant questions,
nor did he specifically ask whether a real relation is distinct from
its foundation.[1] This explicit formulation of the problem came
later. Consequently, he is not clear on some fundamental points,
and this ambiguity has caused him to be interpreted variously by
his followers.[2] Nevertheless, in a number of his works he dealt in
depth and well with the problem, and his position has much of the
coherence characteristic of his thinking.

1. The Two Ontological Constituents
of a Real Relation

Fundamental to Thomas's theory of relation throughout his
career[3] is his view that

---

[1] See A. Krempel, *La Doctrine de la relation chez saint Thomas* (Paris, 1952); C. Kossel,
'Principles of St. Thomas's Distinction between the *Esse* and *Ratio* of Relation', *The
Modern Schoolman* 24 (1946), pp. 19–36 and (1947), pp. 93–107; id., 'St. Thomas's
Theory of the Causes of Relation', *The Modern Schoolman* 25 (1948), pp. 151–72; F.-A.
Blanche, 'Les Mots significant la relation dans la langue de saint Thomas d'Aquin', *Revue
de philosophie* 32 (1925), pp. 363–88; B. Coffey, 'The Notion of Order according to St.
Thomas Aquinas', *The Modern Schoolman* 27 (1949), pp. 1–18.

[2] See Krempel, *La Doctrine*, pp. 20–37.

[3] I agree with Krempel (*La Doctrine*, p. 11) that Thomas's basic theory of relation was
already present in his commentary on the *Sentences*. I have not found any development in
his thinking on the ontological status of categorical relations.

(T1)   In each of the nine accidental categories there is a distinc-
       tion between accidental being common to all nine cate-
       gories and the *ratio* of that particular category.[4]

First I make some preliminary remarks about these two constituents of a real relation, its accidental being and its specific
ratio. In the following sections, I explicate their ontological status.

What is meant by the first constituent, accidental being?
Following Aristotle, Thomas claims that substances exist primarily. Being what primarily exists, a substance exists through
itself or *per se*, for substantial form actualizes matter, giving it its
first act of being. On the other hand, an accidental form does not
exist *per se*, but in and through the substance by actualizing some
secondary potency in the substance to be such-and-such. An
accident, therefore, does not exist *per se* or through itself,
but receives its act of being from the substance. According to
Thomas, the substance is the cause of all its accidents.[5]

This substance–accident ontology underlies Thomas's claim
that to be an accident is to be in a subject.

(T2)   For each of the nine accidental categories, accidental
       being is to be in (to inhere in) a subject.[6]

He also holds that

(T3)   If *a* inheres in *b*, then *a* is dependent on *b*, and *a* makes a
       composition with *b*, and something is posited in *b*.[7]

Both (T2) and (T3) hold for the accidental category of relation,[8]
but only for real relations. When he speaks of relations having

---

[4] *Summa Theol.* I, q. 28, a. 2, corp. Also *In I Sent.*, d. 8, q. 4, a. 3, corp.; d. 26, q. 2, a. 1,
corp. When citing and quoting from the works of Aquinas, I use the following editions: the
Leonine edition (*Sancti Thomae Aquinatis Doctoris Angelici Opera Omnia*) for *Summa
Theologiae* I, vol. 4 (Rome, 1888); *Summa Theologiae* III, vol. 12 (Rome, 1906); *Summa
contra Gentiles* II, vol. 13 (Rome, 1918); *De Veritate*, vol. 22 (Rome, 1970–4); *De Ente et
Essentia*, vol. 43 (Rome, 1976); *Commentaria in Octo Libros Physicorum Aristotelis*, vol. 2
(Rome 1884). I have used the Parma edition (1852–73) for *De Potentia*, vol. 8; *Commentum
in Quatuor Libros Sententiarum*, vols. 6–7; *In Duodecim Libros Metaphysicorum Aristotelis
Expositio*, vol. 20.

[5] Thomas Aquinas, *De Ente et Essentia*, c. 6.

[6] See n. 4 above. More precisely, one should say that being-in pertains to an accident;
an accident is apt to be in its subject. According to many scholastics, there is at least one
case in which an accident exists without inhering in a substance as in a subject, i.e.
Eucharistic transubstantiation. See *Summa Theol.* III, q. 77, a. 1.

[7] *In I Sent.*, d. 8, q. 4, a. 3, corp.; *In I Sent.*, d. 26, q. 2, a. 1, corp.

[8] *In I Sent.*, d. 33, q. 1, a. 1, corp.; *Summa Theol.* I, q. 28, a. 2, corp.

accidental being, he is speaking only of real categorical relations which have some extra-mental being, not of relations of reason.

Further, while substance is the cause of its accidents, there is a certain order by which the accidents 'flow from' the substance. In material substances, quantity is the first accident upon which follow all other sensible accidents. The accident of a real relation is founded immediately on another accident and mediately on the substance.[9] If, then, we want to know about the accidental being of a real relation, we need to look at its causes in substance and in other accidents of the substance.

Besides accidental being, common to all nine accidental categories, Thomas claims with (T1) that we can consider what distinguishes each category from the others, i.e. the *ratio* of each particular category. What does Thomas mean here by *ratio*? In his *Sentences* commentary, he says that in one of its senses '*ratio*' means 'nothing else than that which the intellect understands of the signification of any name'.[10] Thomas explicates this notion with the theory of absolute nature. While something existing can exist in extra-mental reality or in the intellect, an essence can be considered 'absolutely' or 'in itself', that is without reference to whether it exists in extra-mental reality or in the intellect as thought. So considered, there belongs to it only what is included in the concept of the essence.[11] For example, humanity, considered absolutely, includes rationality and animality, and no reference is made to whether humanity exists either in some extra-mental person or in the intellect.

The *ratio* of something is often given by the definition of the concept signifying it. But with things that are not able to be defined, as God's attributes and the categories, the *ratio* is whatever the intellect does understand correctly by the concept signifying the reality.

Thomas claims that each of the categories strictly speaking is indefinable by genus and difference, since they are the highest genera. Still, according to (T1), each has its own *ratio*. For example, the *ratio* of the category of quantity is the measure of substance, while the *ratio* of the category of quality is the

---

[9] *In III Physica*, lect. 1. (ed. Leonine, vol. 2, pp. 102b–103a, n. 6). See also *In I Sent.*, d. 30, q. 1, a. 3, ad 3; d. 8, q. 4, a. 3, ad 4.

[10] *In I Sent.*, d. 2, q. 1, a. 3, corp. Also *In I Sent.*, d. 33, q. 1, a. 1, ad 3.

[11] *De Ente et Essentia*, c. 3 (ed. Leonine, vol. 43, p. 374a).

disposition of substance.[12] But there is an important difference between the *ratio* of the 'absolute accidents', i.e. quantity and quality, and that of the accident of relation. Although the *ratio* of an absolute accident prescinds from existence, the nature absolutely considered implies that it can only exist as inhering in a subject.[13] If *a* is an accidental form of quantity, by its very *ratio a* is the measure of a substance, and so its very *ratio* implies that it can only exist in a substance. Otherwise it would not be the measure of a substance.

But the category of relation is different.

only with those that are called 'toward-something' [i.e. relations] are there some [existing] according to reason only and not in extra-mental reality. This is not the case in other categories, for other categories, as quantity and quality, by their own *ratio* signify something inhering in something. But those that are called 'toward-something' signify by their own *ratio* only a respect toward another.[14]

In short, Thomas holds regarding accidents that

(T4)   The *ratio* of something absolute implies inherence in a subject.

(T5)   The *ratio* of something relative does not imply inherence in a subject, but only implies a respect or condition toward another.[15]

By (T5) something can be described correctly as a relation without implying that it inheres in a subject. This is particularly important for Aquinas since he wants to account for certain non-categorical relations. In Thomas's ontology, as in most Christian thinkers of the medieval period, two types of such relations are the personal relations in the Trinity, such as paternity and filiation, and relations of reason. The former are certainly not accidents in God. The latter, as beings of reason, are not the type of things that could be an accident. While not accidents, relations of reason and the personal relations in the

---

[12] *In I Sent.*, d. 8, q. 4, a. 3, corp.

[13] Ibid.; *In I Sent.*, d. 26, q. 2, a. 1, corp.; d. 30, q. 1, a. 1, corp.; *Summa Theol.* I, q. 28, a. 1, corp.; *De Pot.*, q. 7, a. 8, corp.

[14] *Summa Theol.* I, q. 28, a. 1, corp.

[15] *In I Sent.*, d. 26, q. 2, a. 1, corp. Also *Quodl.* I, a. 2; IX, a. 4; *De Veritate*, q. 1, a. 5, ad 16; *In I Sent.*, d. 20, q. 1, a. 1, corp.

Trinity are truly relations, for although they do not have the property of inhering in a subject (T2), they do have the *ratio* of a relation, i.e. a respect toward another (T5).

The subject of this study is not the Trinity nor relations of reason, but categorical real relations. In such relations, then, we need to inquire into the ontological status Thomas accords this 'respect toward another'. Still this is only part of the question. For although real relations in the Trinity and relations of reason have this condition of being toward another and do not have accidental being, Thomas claims that in categorical real relations

(T6) The respect toward another *and* the accidental being of a relation are each necessary and jointly sufficient for a real relation.[16]

To understand his position, then, one must understand each of these two ontological constituents of a real relation. One must examine the accidental being, sometimes referred to as the *esse-in* of a relation (Sections Two and Three), and the respect to another, sometimes referred to as the *esse-ad* of a relation (Section Four).

2. The Causes of Real Relations

The difference between a real relation and a relation of reason can be grasped in terms of their respective causes. A relation of reason is caused by and depends for its existence on the activity of some mind.[17] A real relation is caused by and depends for its existence on some real extra-mental foundation in the subject of the relation.

For Thomas, what counts as a cause or foundation of a real relation? He holds that the two causes of real relations in creatures are (i) quantity or what pertains to quantity, and (ii) action and passion or active and passive potencies.[18] This is the result of Thomas's reflection on the text of Aristotle in which the Philosopher classifies 'relatives' into three types: numerical,

[16] *In I Sent.*, d. 26, q. 2, a. 1, ad 3. See also *De Pot.*, q. 7, a. 8, ad 5; q. 7, a. 9, ad 7.
[17] See n. 14 of ch. 1.
[18] *De Pot.*, q. 7, a. 9, corp. *In III Phys.*, lect. 1; *In V Metaph.*, lect. 17, nn. 1001–5.

causal, and, according to some, non-mutual, e.g. the knower and the known. Instead of taking number as the foundation of the first class, Thomas takes quantity in a broad sense so that there are included not only such relations as equality and inequality, but also, under the rubric of 'what exceeds to what is exceeded', such relations as 'whiter than' and 'less hot than'. In commenting on this passage of Aristotle, Thomas groups all such relations under the rubric of those caused by 'quantity and what pertains to quantity'.[19]

Thomas holds that (i) quantity and what pertains to quantity and (ii) action and passion or active and passive potencies are the only causes of real relations.[20] He argues that one thing is related to another as it is ordered to that other:

But one thing is ordered to another either by quantity or by a power, active or passive. For only from these two is something in one [thing] extended (*attenditur*) toward [something] extrinsic [to it]. For something is measured not only by intrinsic quantity, but also by extrinsic [quantity]. And through active power each thing acts upon another and through passive [power] is acted upon by another.[21]

An absolute accident, like quantity, inheres in a subject, and it is by virtue of that accident that the subject is, say, some determinate height. The accident is thus said to be 'the intrinsic measure of the subject'. But it is also by virtue of that same accident that the subject is 'measured by' or compared to other things of a determinate quantity. Since it is by virtue of that accident that the subject is related to or 'ordered to' others, that accident is said to be the foundation and cause of the real relation of equality (or inequality).

The same is true of other accidents 'pertaining to quantity' such as quality.[22] The absolute accident of whiteness in a piece of chalk is an inherent perfection of its subject, but it is by virtue of that same accident that the subject is related to other things. The cause and foundation of the chalk's similarity (or dissimilarity) to others is its quality of whiteness.

In a similar way Thomas understands the second class of

[19] *In V Metaph.*, lect. 17, n. 1005. For more on the two causes of a relation, see Krempel, *La Doctrine*, pp. 195–233.
[20] *In V. Metaph.*, lect. 17, n. 1004; *In III Phys.*, lect. 1 (ed. Leonine, vol. 2, p. 103a, n. 6).
[21] *De Pot.*, q. 7, a. 9, corp.
[22] Ibid.; *In V Metaph.*, lect. 17, n. 1005. See Ch. 1, sect. 2.2.

relations founded on action and passion. In commenting on Aristotle's *Metaphysics*,[23] he says that this class can be taken in two ways: as the extremes are in act, as what heats to what is heated, and as the extremes are in potency, as what can heat to what can be heated. In either case, the active power of heating inheres in the fire. But it is also by virtue of that accident that the fire heats or is able to heat another, and so is related to that other. Therefore, that accident, the active power of heating, is said to be the foundation or cause of the real relation of heating or being able to heat another.

3. The Accidental Being of a Real Relation

Recall the passage of Aristotle's *Physics*, book five, chapter two: 'Nor is there motion in respect of Relation: for it may happen that when one correlative changes, the other can truly be said not to change at all, so that in these cases the motion is accidental.'[24] Thomas finds no difficulty in agreeing with the Philosopher where relations of reason or non-mutual relations are concerned.[25] In both cases one term can change, and the other term without changing can cease (or begin) to be related to it, as Aristotle claims. For example, if I cease to know an object, that object without changing in any way ceases to be related to me as known.

But Thomas states that there seems to be a difficulty with real mutual relations such as equality and similarity: 'But in those in which there is really a relation in each of the extremes it seems difficult that something be said relatively of one [a] through a change of the other [b] without any change of it [a], since nothing may newly come to something without any change of that to which it comes.'[26]

The difficulty here confronts an adherent of what I call the strongly realist position. Take, as an illustration, two pieces of white chalk, *a* and *b*. In each there inheres an accident of

[23] *In V Metaph.*, lect. 17, n. 1002.
[24] *Physics* V, c. 2 (225ᵇ11–13) (Oxford trans.).
[25] *In V Phys.*, lect. 3. For a good discussion of Thomas's handling of this passage of Aristotle, see Kossel, 'Causes of Relation', pp. 156–61.
[26] *In V Phys.*, lect. 3 (ed. Leonine, vol. 2, p. 237b, n. 8).

whiteness with its own accidental being, making by (T3) a composition with the subject. Further, there inheres in each a relation of similarity with *its* own accidental being really distinct from both the whiteness and the subject. This relation makes a further composition with its subject.[27]

An adherent of this strongly realist position will have difficulty accepting Aristotle here. For according to this position, if *a* becomes really related to *b*, *a* acquires an accident, a real relation, with its own accidental being really distinct from its foundation. But if this is so, then by

(T2)   For each of the nine accidental categories, accidental being is to be in (to inhere in) a subject

and

(T3)   If *a* inheres in *b*, then *a* is dependent on *b*, and *a* makes a composition with *b*, and something is posited in *b*

if *a* becomes really related to *b*, then something is posited in *a* and *a* is changed—which is contrary to Aristotle.

Thomas rejects this position, for he agrees with Aristotle that if you become equal in height to me, I without changing in any way become really related to you. He argues that in no way am I changed since the relation of equality to you already existed in me 'as in its root' before you changed size.

And so it is to be said that if someone through a change in him becomes equal to me while I am not changed, that equality was first in me in some way, as in its root from which it has real being. For since I have such quantity, it pertains to me that I be equal [in size] to all those who have the same quantity. So, if someone has that quantity for the first time, that common root of equality is determined to him. And so nothing comes to me for the first time from the fact that I begin to be equal to another through his changing.[28]

How are we to understand the metaphor of a root? In short, what is the ontological status of the relation of equality in me before your change in size? Is it something relative or absolute? Not the former, for there is no term. Not the latter, for what is absolute cannot be a relation. Perhaps it is a potency in the

---

[27] See n. 81 of ch. 5.
[28] *In V Phys.*, lect. 3 (ed. Leonine, vol. 2, p. 237b, n. 8).

absolute accident to be a relation. This seems closer to the metaphor of root. As certain substances are in potency to an absolute accidental form, so certain substances with an absolute accidental form are in potency to be related to others. But in the former case, when the potency is reduced to act, the subject is changed. What reason could be given for denying this in the latter case?

There is a more plausible interpretation using Thomas's own ideas on relation:

(T6) The respect to another *and* the accidental being of a relation are each necessary and jointly sufficient for a real relation.

On this interpretation, contrary to the strongly realist position, the accidental being, the *esse-in*, of a real relation is identical with the accidental being of its foundation. The relation of equality to you is already in me 'in some way', for there is already in me one of the necessary conditions for a real relation, its accidental being which is identical with the accidental being of its foundation, my size.

In discussing this question, Thomas also holds that

(T7) Something changes only if there is a change *in* it.[29]

The *esse-in*, the accidental being of the relation, is identical with the accidental being of my quantity, and that does not change. Further, I am not changed by acquiring the second necessary condition, the *esse-ad*, for (as shown in Section Four) its whole reality is to be toward another, not to be in anything.[30] Hence, Thomas can agree with Aristotle that when you grow, and I become equal in height to you, I do not change.

This explanation is illumined by another passage of Thomas in which he explains how God became human without changing. In it, Thomas distinguishes between being changed (*mutari*) and becoming (*fieri*). '"To be changed" properly is said because of a removal from a *terminus a quo*, "to become" however is said because of a drawing near to a *terminus* [*ad quem*].'[31]

---

[29] See n. 16 above. Also see *In I Sent.*, d. 30, q. 1, a. 1, corp.; *De Pot.*, q. 7, a. 9, ad 7.

[30] *De Pot.*, q. 7, a. 8, corp.; *Summa Theol.* I, q. 28, a. 2, corp.

[31] *In III Sent.*, d. 7, q. 2, a. 1, ad 1. Cf. *In I Phys.*, lect. 12.

When dealing with absolute accidents, becoming entails being changed; black *a*'s becoming white also involves *a*'s being changed. For both terms, *a*'s blackness and *a*'s whiteness, are intrinsic to *a*, and hence the attaining of one entails the removal of the other; becoming, i.e. the drawing near to the *terminus ad quem* (whiteness), entails being changed, i.e. the removal from the *terminus a quo* (blackness). But with real relations, becoming does not entail being changed precisely because it is not the case that both terms are intrinsic to the subject. Hence the drawing near to one does not entail the removal from another. The *terminus ad quem* of a real relation is the really distinct term. Hence when *a* becomes really related to *b*, *a* need not be changed, i.e. there need be no removal from a *terminus a quo* as there is in the case of an absolute accident. The same holds conversely for *a*'s ceasing to be really related to *b*.

This is not to say that since *a* is not changed in this technical sense, *a*'s becoming really related to *b* 'makes no difference' to *a*. *a* is now related in a new way to *b*, and this becoming enriches and perfects *a*.[32]

In sum, Thomas holds

(T8)   *a* comes to be or ceases to be really related to *b* through some change of the foundation that is or is in *a* and/or of the foundation that is or is in *b*.[33]

In the case at hand, your foundation (your size) changes, not mine. And so, by (T8), I am able to become really related to you by equality without my changing. In short,

(T9)   If the foundation that is or is in *a* changes, then there is a change of *a*; but if only the foundation that is or is in *b* changes, there is no change of *a*, for there is no change *in a*.[34]

Finally, the relation of equality was in me 'as in its root from which it has real being', i.e. as a cause. This is precisely the role of the foundation according to Thomas. In fact, in his *Physics*

[32] *In III Sent.*, d. 7, q. 2, a. 1, ad 3.
[33] See nn. 16 and 29 above. Also *In V Phys.*, lect. 3; *De Pot.*, q. 7, a. 8, ad 5. The phrase 'is or is in *a* (or *b*)' is meant to cover real relations whose foundations are either substantial forms (as the relations of specific identity) or accidental forms.
[34] See n. 16 above. Also *In V Phys.*, lect. 3; *De Pot.*, q. 7, a. 9, ad 7.

commentary he calls the foundation the root of the relation: 'But there are certain relatives in which there is a real relation existing in each extreme as in equality and similarity. For in each [extreme] there is quantity or quality which is the root of this relation; and similarly in many other relations.'[35] The root of the relation is already in me because its accidental being is identical with that of its foundation, that is my size. My becoming really related to you consists in my acquiring the second necessary constituent of a real relation, the respect. And as shown in Section Four, because the reality of the respect consists solely in being-toward, and not being-in, by (T7) my acquiring it does not change me in any way. In sum, the accidental being of the foundation is identical with the accidental being of the relation.

4. The Respect of a Real Relation

With regard to the ontological status of the other constituent, one might hold that this respect, the *esse-ad*, is another entity or thing, perhaps not an absolute thing but a relative thing (*res relativa*), really distinct from the *esse-in*. As we shall see, Richard of Mediavilla adopts such a position. Sentences of the form '*aRb*' are true if and only if (i) *a* and *b* are really distinct extra-mental things, (ii) *a* exists with its foundation, and (iii) there exists a real relation in *a*, the accidental being of which is identical with the accidental being of the foundation in *a*, and the respect of which is an entity or thing really distinct from its foundation. This position is consistent with Thomas's comments on Aristotle's passage in the *Physics*. I am in no way changed when I become really related to you by equality, for by (T7) something changes only if there is a change *in* it. And I am not changed by acquiring this respect, the *esse-ad*, to you, since its whole reality is to be toward another, not to be in anything.

But it is precisely this characteristic of not having *esse-in* that makes this solution so problematical. For Thomas, extra-mental reality is divided into the ten categories of substance and accidents. If this *esse-ad* is an extra-mental reality, it must be either a substance or an accident. Certainly not a substance, but neither

---

[35] *In V Phys.*, lect. 3. See also *De Pot.*, q. 7, a. 9, ad 7.

an accident. For it lacks the being of an accident, *esse-in*. It seems there is no room in Thomas's Aristotelian ontology for such a 'free-floating' thing as this *esse-ad*.

An alternative position is to agree that the accidental being of the real relation and that of its foundation are really identical, but deny that the respect, the *esse-ad*, is any additional entity or thing. What, then, is it?

Thomas says that in each thing 'a double perfection is found: one by which it subsists in itself and another by which it is ordered to other things'.[36] These two aspects are also found in the foundation of a real relation. In the case at hand, quantity is an intrinsic perfection of me by virtue of which I am some height. But it is by virtue of that same accident that I am able to be equal to others. This is what Thomas means when he says, 'since I have such quantity, it pertains to me that I be equal [in size] to all those who have the same quantity'.

So too does knowledge have this double aspect. It is an accident in the mind, and is thus an intrinsic perfection of the knower, as the quality of hardness is in a rock. But knowledge also has the aspect of being ordered toward the knowable which the hardness of the rock does not have. To give another instance, heat is, on the one hand, an accidental form intrinsic to and perfecting its subject. But another aspect of its reality is that it is able to heat what is brought into contact with it. Like knowledge, it has a relative aspect to its reality.

Thomas refers to these two aspects in various ways, the first, for example, as *informatio*, and the second as an operation or 'extension' of one thing to another.[37] It is these two aspects of the one accidental form or foundation that are referred to when it is

---

[36] *In III Sent.*, d. 27, q. 1, a. 4, corp. Also *Summa Theol.* I, q. 22, a. 1, corp. For a different version of this basic position, see Francisco Suarez, 'De relatione reali in communi', sect. 2, in *Disputationes Metaphysicae* 47, in *Opera Omnia* (Paris, 1856–78), vol. 26, pp. 785–94. Suarez rejects an opinion in which the *esse-ad* is a thing really distinct from the *esse-in* (pp. 791–2). Between a real relation and its foundation he finds a distinction of reason with a foundation in reality.

[37] See *De Veritate*, q. 27, a. 3, ad 25. Thomas speaks of these two aspects of the one reality in varying contexts. One source for this distinction is Aristotle's doctrine that form is the principle of operation; for the scholastics, *agere sequitur esse*. At times Thomas speaks of two perfections of the one reality: *Summa Theol.* I, q. 42, a. 1, ad 1; q. 73, a. 1, corp.; III, q. 29, a. 2, corp.; or of two acts: *Summa Theol.* I, q. 48, a. 1, ad 4; q. 48, a. 5, corp.; I–II, q. 49, a. 3, ad 1; regarding two aspects of knowledge, see *De Veritate*, q. 2, a. 14, corp.; *Quodl.* VII, q. 1, a. 4, corp.

said that the accidental being of the foundation is identical with the accidental being of the relation. So, in the case at hand, the *esse-in quantitatis*, i.e. my height in its aspect as an intrinsic perfection, is identical with the *esse-in relationis*, i.e. my height in its aspect as a foundation for possible relations of equality to determinate terms.

But the *esse-in relationis* alone does not constitute a real relation. It is only when you change height and become equal to me that I become equal to you and really related to you by equality. At the moment you change and become the same height as I, I am not adequately described by saying that I, by virtue of my height, am able to be equal to others of that same height. For now my height is actually serving as a foundation for my being really related to a determinate term. Hence, Thomas says: '. . . if someone [else] has that quantity for the first time, that common root of equality [in me] is determined to him'. By (T6), then, the final condition for a real relation has been fulfilled. For not only do I have the accidental being of the relation, i.e. my height, but I have a respect toward you solely by virtue of our both being of the same height. No further entity need be posited.

For clarity through contrast, compare briefly Thomas's position with the strongly realist position of Scotus and with the conceptualist position of Peter Aureoli. For Scotus, statements of the form '*a*R*b*' are true if and only if (i) *a* and *b* are really distinct extra-mental things, (ii) there is a real foundation in *a* for R, and (iii) there exists an extra-mental 'relative thing' R with its own accidental reality really distinct from that of its foundation.[38] If no such extra-mental relative thing, no real relation. Aureoli agrees with the first two conditions, but substitutes: (iii) there exists in some mind a concept connecting *a* and *b*.[39] If no such concept, no real relation.

Thomas's theory is more parsimonious than either of these, for though it requires the first two conditions, his third is only that *a* and *b* exist in a certain way. In the case at hand, *a* and *b* both exist with the same height. One need not posit any further entity, whether a relative thing or concept.

[38] See ch. 5.
[39] As will become clear in ch. 8, Peter Aureoli significantly changes what is traditionally meant by foundation. But here, for purposes of exposition, I pass over a discussion of Peter's innovations.

While avoiding strong realism, then, Thomas does not reduce real relations to beings of reason, as in Aureoli's theory. Thomas specifically denies such a conceptualist theory of real relations. He presents two considerations to which Aureoli, some forty years later, will respond.

[i] For in no category is anything posited except a thing existing outside the soul, for being of reason is distinguished from being as divided into the ten categories.... If, however, a relation did not exist extra-mentally, 'toward-something' would not be posited as one type of category. And besides, [ii] the perfection and good which are in extra-mental things follow not only upon something inhering in things absolutely, but also upon the order of one thing toward another, as also the good of an army consists in the order of the parts of the army, for to this order the Philosopher compares the order of the universe. There-fore it is necessary that in those [extra-mental] things there be a certain order; but this order is a certain relation. So it is necessary that in those [extra-mental] things there be certain relations, according to which one [thing] is ordered to another.[40]

The idea of an extra-mental order of the universe pervaded the thought of Thomas and his colleagues; as Aristotle had taught them, 'all things are ordered together'.[41] Then, as today, a metaphysician fails in his task if he gives only an inventory of all the types of things in the universe. He must also say how they are related to each another, for this, while not another 'thing' in the universe, is an intelligible aspect of the universe.

Our understanding of medieval philosophy would be enhanced by a study of the fortunes of Thomas's ontology of relations in the years following his death. Before passing on to the final Sections Five and Six, I would like to make one small contribution regarding Giles of Rome (*c.*1243–1316) who studied at the University of Paris and was probably a student of Aquinas during the latter's second regency there, 1269–72.[42] Aquinas' influence on Giles was certainly strong, but in this century the myth that

---

[40] *De Pot.*, q. 7, a. 9, corp. See also *In I Sent.*, d. 26, q. 2, a. 1, corp.

[41] See n. 36 above. Aristotle, *Metaph.* XII, c. 10 (1075^{a}16).

[42] On Giles's life, see P. Mandonnet, 'La Carrière scolaire de Gilles de Rome (1276–1291)', *Revue des sciences philosophiques et théologiques* 4 (1910), pp. 480–99; P. W. Nash, 'Giles of Rome', *New Catholic Encyclopedia* (New York, 1967), vol. 6, pp. 484–5. For a list of the printed works of Giles (Doctor Verbosus), see G. Bruni, 'Saggio bibliografico sulle opere stampate di Egidio Romano', *Analecta Augustiniana* 24 (1961), pp. 331–55.

Giles was a faithful follower of his teacher has been dispelled.[43] Where he departs from or retains Thomas's views is revealed only by reading their works.

It happens that Giles does adopt Thomas's teaching on categorical relations. He makes his own Aquinas' distinction between real relations and relations of reason: a relation R of a to b is real if and only if a and b are really distinct extra-mental things, and there is a real extra-mental foundation in a for R.[44] A relation R of a to b is of reason if and only if (i) a and/or b is not real, or (ii) a and b are not really distinct, or (iii) there is no extra-mental foundation in a for R.[45] In discussing relations of reason, he recites Aquinas' examples of our relation to future generations, the relation of self-identity, and that between the knowable and the knower.[46] Finally, Giles's proof that there are real relations existing outside the mind is a version of Thomas's argument from the order of the universe.[47]

Furthermore, Giles adopts Thomas's theses (T1–6):

In every thing there is a double consideration: being and quiddity [T1]. Now those things other than relation [i.e. absolute accidents] that are in substance, both according to their being and according to the *ratio* of the quiddity are something and posit something in that in which they are, and they are not extrinsically affixed [T2–4]. For wisdom both by its being and by the *ratio* of its quiddity bespeaks something in the wise one. But a relation, although according to its being it is not present to nor extrinsically affixed (because it is in [its subject] as the rest of the

---

[43] On his relation to Thomas, see E. Hocedez, 'Gilles de Rome et saint Thomas', *Mélanges Mandonnet* 1 (1930), pp. 385–409; P. W. Nash, 'Giles of Rome: Auditor and Critic of St. Thomas', *The Modern Schoolman* 28 (1950), pp. 1–20.

[44] *Primus Sententiarum Aegidii* (Venice, 1521), d. 26, q. 1: 'Requiritur etiam ultra reale fundamentum ad hoc, quod relatio sit realis, realis distinctio relatorum . . .' (fol. 141ᵛ M). *In I Sent.*, d. 27, q. 1: 'Ideo notandum quod ad hoc, quod relatio sit realis . . . duo requirit: primo quod ponat aliquid reale in quo existit, secundo quod dicat realem differentiam relatorum' (fol. 144ᵛ O). See also *In I Sent.*, d. 20, q. 2 (fol. 115ʳ AB); d. 33, q. 1 (fol. 170ᵛ N).

[45] *In I Sent.*, d. 30, q. 3: 'Sed quod aliqua habeant realem ordinem tria requiruntur. Primo quod utrumque habeat rationem entis, quia nihil ad aliquid vel alicuius ad nihil non potest esse realis dependentia. Secundo requiritur quod utrumque esse habeat distinctum ab altero, quia indistinctorum realiter non potest esse realis ordo. Nam et ordo realis realem distinctionem postulat. Tertio requiritur quod unum realiter ordinetur ad aliud. Et quodcumque istorum deficiat non est relatio secundum rem, sed secundum rationem' (fol. 157ᵛ PQ).

[46] Ibid. (fols. 157ᵛ Q–158ʳ A).

[47] See n. 40 above. Giles of Rome, *In I Sent.*, d. 30, q. 2 (157ʳ DE).

accidents are in), still by the *ratio* of its quiddity it seems to be extrinsically affixed; for the whole *ratio* of a relation is taken from its being toward another and not from its being in another [T5–6].[48]

In addition, with Thomas Giles holds that the accidental being of a relation, its *esse-in*, is not other than that of its foundation. A relation and its foundation, however, are not simply identical.

If [a relation] is considered with regard to its being, it is not distinguished from its foundation. For the being of similarity or its *esse-in* is not other than the *esse-in* of that whiteness in which it is founded. But if it is considered according to the *ratio* of its quiddity, the relation does differ from its foundation, because its foundation is something absolute, but the *ratio* of a relation is taken from its condition of being toward another. So if a form, according to the being which it has, makes a composition in its subject, [but] according to the *ratio* of its quiddity it is put in a category, it follows that a relation is in a different category from its foundation. For similarity is in a different category from whiteness.[49]

Giles, like Thomas, comments on the passage of Aristotle in *Physics*, book five, chapter two, in which Aristotle seems to deny all change in the category of relation. As Giles and Thomas interpret this passage, it is possible, contrary to the strongly realist position, that *a* could cease (or begin) to be really related to *b* without any change in *a*, but only in *b*. That is, Giles like Thomas affirms

---

[48] *In I Sent.*, d. 26, q. 1: '. . . in omni re est considerare duo: esse et quidditatem. Ea autem quae sunt in substantia alia a relatione et secundum esse suum et secundum rationem quidditatis habent quod sint aliquid et ponunt aliquid in eo in quo sunt, et non sunt extrinsecus affixa. Nam sapientia et secundum esse suum et secundum rationem quidditatis dicit aliquid in sapiente. Relatio autem licet secundum esse suum non sit assistens nec extrinsecus affixa quia inest sicut cetera accidentia insunt, tamen ratione suae quidditatis videtur extrinsecus affixa. Nam tota ratio relationis sumitur ex eo quod est ad aliquid, non ex eo quod est in alio' (fol. 141ʳ G).

[49] *Egidii Romani in Libros de Physico Auditu Aristotelis Commentaria* (Venice, 1502), bk. 5: 'Dicendum quod relativum dupliciter potest considerari, scilicet, quantum ad esse et quantum ad rationem suae quidditatis. Si consideretur quantum ad esse, sic non distinguitur a suo fundamento. Esse enim similitudinis vel in-esse eius non est aliud quam in-esse ipsius albedinis in qua fundatur. Sed si consideretur secundum rationem suae quidditatis, sic relatio differt a suo fundamento, quia fundamentum suum est quid absolutum, ratio vero relationis sumitur in ad aliud se habere. Cum ergo forma secundum esse quod habet faciat compositionem in subiecto, secundum rationem suae quidditatis reponatur in praedicamento, sequitur quod relatio sit in alio praedicamento quam suum fundamentum. Similitudo enim est in alio praedicamento quam albedo' (fol. 105ʳa). Also *B. Aegidii Columnae Romani . . . Quodlibeta . . .* (Louvain, 1646; repr. Frankfurt am Main, 1966), *Quodlibet* V, q. 13 (fols. 305a–306a).

(T8)   *a* comes to be or ceases to be really related to *b* through
       some change of the foundation that is or is in *a* and/or of
       the foundation that is or is in *b*.[50]

Hence, *a* can become really related to *b* with a change not of *a*, but
only of *b*.

From an examination of the relevant texts, then, I conclude that
Giles does in fact adopt Thomas's teaching on the ontological
status of categorical relations.

5. Real Distinction between a Real Relation and its Foundation

Although Thomas himself did not ask whether a real categorical
relation is really distinct from its foundation, we can ask this
question in the light of my interpretation of his theory.

Obviously the answer depends on what is meant by 'really
distinct'. One criterion for a real distinction is separability:

(A)   *a* is really distinct from *b* if and only if it is logically possible
       that *a* exist without *b*.

According to (A), what of the distinction between a real relation in
creatures and its foundation? On the one hand, there is some
distinction between the reality of an accident as intrinsic perfection and the reality of that accident as foundation for possible
relations. That is, there is some distinction between the two
aspects of the one accidental form: between the *esse-in* of the
accident as absolute and the *esse-in* of the relation, i.e. between
the *esse-in qualitatis* and the *esse-in relationis*.

But by (A) there is no real distinction, since it is contradictory,
for example, that a white thing exist and not be a foundation for
possible relations of similarity. That is, it is not logically possible
that '*a* is white' is true and '*a* is able to be similar to another white

---

[50] *Quodlibet* V, q. 13: 'Defectus ergo similitudinis in utroque potest contingere ex solo
defectu qualitatis in alio. Et sicut defectus similitudinis in utroque potest contingere ex
solo defectu qualitatis in alio, sic acquisitio similitudinis in utroque potest contingere ex
sola mutatione facta in alio. Et inde est quod ad ad-aliquid dicatur 'esse motus per
accidens' quia potest aliquid relationem acquirere ex sola mutatione facta in alio' (fol.
306a). See also Giles's *Super Authorem Libri de Causis, Alfarabium* (Venice, 1550), fol. 90ʳ
PQ.

thing' is false. This latter cannot be false, for it is possible that another white thing *b* exists; and then *a* would be similar to *b*.

On the other hand, by (A) there is a real distinction between the foundation and the real relation with its respect, the *esse-ad*, to some particular thing. For it is logically possible that '*a* is white' is true and that '*a* is really similar to *b*' is false, for it is contingent whether *b* comes to exist and to be white.

It is only in the latter case that there is a real relation in *a*. For

(T6)   The respect toward another *and* the accidental being of a relation are each necessary and jointly sufficient for a real relation.

So by (A) there is a real distinction between a real relation and its foundation.

Another criterion for a real distinction can be taken from Thomas's *intellectus essentiae* argument in chapter four of *On Being and Essence*. Much has been written on the nature of this argument, its role in that chapter, and the type of distinction it establishes or purports to establish between being and essence.[51]

Everything that does not belong to the concept (*non est de intellectu*) of an essence or quiddity comes to it from outside and enters into composition with the essence, because no essence can be understood without its parts. Now, every essence or quiddity can be understood without knowing anything about its being. I can know, for instance, what a man or a phoenix is and still be ignorant whether it has being in reality. From this it is clear that being is other than (*est aliud ab*) essence or quiddity, unless perhaps there is a reality whose quiddity is its being.[52]

For our purposes the key idea is that if the essence or quiddity of *a* is not included in the essence or quiddity of *b*, there is some non-identity between *a* and *b*. A criterion for a real distinction or metaphysical composition can be offered by interpreting 'not belong to' in the following way: if *a* and *b* are both real, then

(B)   If the *ratio* of *a* neither is the same as, nor is part of, nor follows as a necessary consequence from, the *ratio* of *b*, then *a* is really distinct from *b*.

[51] See S. MacDonald, 'The *Esse/Essentia* Argument in Aquinas's *De ente et essentia*', *Journal of the History of Philosophy* 22 (1984), pp. 157–72; J. Wippel, 'Aquinas's Route to the Real Distinction: A Note on *De ente et essentia*', *The Thomist* 43 (1979), pp. 279–95; J. Owens, 'Quiddity and Real Distinction in St. Thomas Aquinas', *Mediaeval Studies* 27 (1965), pp. 1–22. For other references, see n. 2 of Owens's article.

[52] *On Being and Essence*, trans. A. Maurer, 2nd rev. edn. (Toronto, 1968), p. 55.

Conversely,

(C)   If the *ratio* of *a* either is the same as, or is a part of, or follows as a necessary consequence from, the *ratio* of *b*, then *a* is not really distinct from *b*.

According to (B) and (C), is there a real distinction between a real relation and its foundation? Again, there is need to distinguish, and the results are the same as with criterion (A). For by (C), on the one hand, there is no real distinction between the reality of an accident as an intrinsic perfection, e.g. *esse-in qualitatis*, and the reality of the accident as a foundation for possible relations, i.e. *esse-in relationis*. For from '*a* is white' it follows as a necessary consequence 'if another white thing *b* came to exist, *a* would be similar to *b*'.

But by (B) there is a real distinction between the foundation and the real relation with a respect, the *esse-ad*, to some particular thing. For *a*'s being really related to *b* is not the same as, nor part of, nor does it follow as a necessary consequence from, *a*'s being white. That is, '*a* is really similar to *b*' does not follow from '*a* is white' for it is contingent whether *b* comes to exist and be white. Both by (A) and by (B), then, there is a real distinction between a real relation and its foundation.

6. A Specific Issue: The Relations between God and Creatures

In the Introduction I mentioned that it is beyond the scope of this study to discuss how the scholastics' various theories of relation affected their handling of specific philosophical and theological questions. Nevertheless, I give one example to illustrate how an understanding of a person's theory of relation sheds light on his discussion of a key issue.

Thomas held the common but by no means universal doctrine that creatures are really related to God and God is related to them only by a relation of reason. I believe this technical formulation is ultimately based on a religious intuition that all creatures are absolutely dependent on a transcendent creator. The scholastics formulated this intuition in terms of Aristotle's category of relation: each creature has a real relation of dependence on God, while He is in no way dependent on them.

The medievals' arguments for denying that at creation God acquires a real relation to creatures depend in part upon their prior philosophy of the ontological status of relation. Those who held the strongly realist position, as Duns Scotus and the early Henry of Harclay, had arguments ready at hand: if *a* becomes really related to *b*, then *a* is changed in some way. But God is essentially immutable. Therefore, at creation God cannot become really related to creatures. Or: if *a* becomes really related to *b*, then *a* becomes composed. But God is essentially simple, etc.

Charles Hartshorne among others takes the argument from immutability to be the main support for the medieval denial of real relations in God to creatures: because of their commitment to God's immutability, the scholastics deny any real relation to creatures in God.[53] Hartshorne attacks this as religiously scandalous and philosophically unsound. He hopes to liberate theism from the Greek metaphysics of immutability.

Whatever the merits of Hartshorne's own views, his interpretation of the medievals is deficient. He ignores the diversity of scholastic theories on the ontological status of real relations. Thomas, for one, does not use the argument from immutability.[54] He could not, given his theory of the ontological status of real relations. As we have seen, he holds that a thing can become really related to another without any change. Specifically, he held

(T8) *a* comes to be or ceases to be really related to *b* through some change of the foundation that is or is in *a* and/or of the foundation that is or is in *b*

and

(T9) If the foundation that is or is in *a* changes, then there is a change of *a*; but if only the foundation that is or is in *b*

---

[53] C. Hartshorne, *The Divine Relativity* (New Haven and London, 1948), pp. 6–9. Also see J. Felt, 'Invitation to a Philosophic Revolution', *The New Scholasticism* 45 (1971), pp. 87–109, esp. pp. 96, 104.

[54] I do not take the one small argument from immutability in *Summa contra Gentiles* II, c. 12 as a serious counter-example, for (i) it is incoherent with Thomas's theory of relation found in his other works, (ii) it is a short reply to a single objection, not a systematic treatment of the ontological status of relation, and (iii) in this work Thomas writes for 'missionaries in Spain and North Africa [who] needed a great number of arguments, even dialectical arguments, to show the errors in gentile philosophy' (J. Weisheipl, *Friar Thomas D'Aquino: His Life, Thought and Works* (Washington, DC, 1983), p. 133).

changes, there is no change of *a*, for there is no change *in a*.

Still, he upheld the traditional view that at creation God does not become really related to creatures. His reasons show him transforming yet another doctrine of Aristotle, that of the category of relation, in the light of his metaphysics of the act of existence.[55]

Thomas modelled the God–creature relations on the third class of relations in Aristotle's *V Metaphysics* list, i.e. on non-mutual relations. The prime examples are the relations between knower and known: the knower-to-known relation is real, the known-to-knower relation is only of reason. So also for Thomas, the creature-to-God relation is real, the God-to-creature relation is only of reason. To understand his position on the theological question of the God–creature relations, we must examine his philosophy on non-mutual relations.

It might be thought that the reason for non-mutuality would be that at the moment of, say, knowledge, there is a real change in the knower, while there is no corresponding change in the thing known, for knowledge is an immanent activity and does not terminate in and so change the thing known. This occurrent act of knowledge would function as the foundation of a real relation in the knower to the thing known. But since there would be no corresponding change in the thing known, so there is no foundation in it for a real co-relation to the knower.[56]

However this cannot be the case given, once again, Thomas's commitment to

(T8)   *a* comes to be or ceases to be really related to *b* through some change of the foundation that is or is in *a* and/or of the foundation that is or is in *b*.

Hence, if *a* is the thing known, it would be sufficient for *a* to be really related to *b* that there be some change in the foundation of *b*, while *a* remains unchanged.

---

[55] In what follows, I examine what I consider the most radical and fully developed reason Thomas gives for the God–creature relations. In *De Pot.*, q. 7, a. 10, corp., he gives two other arguments, each based on a different premiss: (i) if *a* is perfected by *b*, then *a* depends on *b*, and so *a* is really related to *b*; and (ii) if *a* is moved by *b* to move *c*, then *a* is ordered to move *c*, and so *a* is really related to *c*. Each is taken to be a sufficient condition for a real relation. Thomas shows that these conditions cannot be met in God.

[56] Thomas seems to argue this way in *In V Metaph.*, lect. 17, nn. 1026–7.

Thomas's basis for non-mutual relations is more radical. The fullest statement I have found is in *De Potentia*, book seven, article ten. A brief examination of his doctrine of mutual relations helps to understand non-mutual relations. It is not enough to claim relations R and R′ are mutual if and only if aRb and $bR'a$, and both R and R′ are real relations. For then Tolstoy's being the author of the book and the book's weighing less than Tolstoy will count as mutual relations.[57] Something more must be said about the relations and their foundations. Thomas claims that if a and b are distinct extra-mental things, and the relations between a and b are real and mutual, then a and b have the same reason for the relation (*eadem ratio ordinis*).[58] I interpret this condition (that a have the 'same reason for the relation' R to b that b has for its co-relation R′ to a) to mean that the foundations in a and in b must be of the same type. So, if a and b are distinct extra-mental things, then

(T10)   The relations R and R′ are real and mutual if and only if there are real extra-mental foundations of the same type in a for the relation R to b and in b for the relation R′ to a.

Hence those relations obtaining between Tolstoy and the book are not mutual since the foundations are not of the same type, i.e. writing (an action) and weight (a quantitative accident).

The intuition is that two things cannot be mutually really related if the two foundations are incommensurable, i.e. radically different. For example, take relations of Aristotle's first class. The reason why the real relations of similarity between two white things are mutual is that they each have a foundation of the same type, i.e. colour. And the reason why the real relations of equality or inequality between two things are mutual is that they each have a foundation of the same type, i.e. a quantitative accident of the same type, such as height, weight, etc. Thomas argues that the personal relations in the Trinity, like paternity and filiation, are real and mutual. Their foundations are of the same type, indeed in this unique case they are numerically the same, i.e. the divine nature which they share.[59]

---

[57] I am grateful to a reader for the *Journal of the History of Philosophy* for this example.
[58] *De Pot.*, q. 7, a. 10, corp. See also *De Pot.*, q. 7, a. 10, ad 1, ad 7.
[59] *Summa Theol.* I, q. 28, a. 1, corp.; *In I Sent.*, d. 30, q. 1, a. 3, ad 3; d. 33, q. 1, a. 1, ad 2.

Thomas claims all relations are mutual that are members of Aristotle's first and second class,[60] while non-mutual relations are to be found among Aristotle's third class. We have already seen that relations of the first class fulfil his criterion for mutual real relations, but what of relations of the second and third classes?

Departing from Aristotle, Thomas claims that both these classes of relations are based on action and passion or on active and passive potencies.[61] In all such relations, the foundation is some type of motion, either action or passion, or at least powers for such motion. This move on Thomas's part makes sense since relations of the third class, as those of the knower to the known, are based on the action of knowing. And, as we shall see, Thomas has a keen motive for maintaining that relations of the third class are based on actions.

He applies to both classes the criterion for mutual relations: if *a* and *b* are distinct extra-mental things, then

(T10)   The relations R and R′ are real and mutual if and only if there are real extra-mental foundations of the same type in *a* for the relation R to *b* and in *b* for the relation R′ to *a*.

According to this criterion, he claims, relations of the second class are mutual. For example, the same type of foundation is found in one, the action of heating, as in the other, the passion of being heated. But relations of the third class fail this criterion for mutual real relations.[62] While there may be an action of a certain type serving as a foundation in *a* for a real relation to *b*, there may not be a corresponding action or passion of the same type in *b*. In this case, the relations are non-mutual, *a* being really related to *b*, but not vice versa.

In short, Thomas explains non-mutual relations in terms of the condition in (T10) being unfulfilled. That is,

(T11)   If *a* is really related by R to *b*, but there is no foundation in *b* of the same type as *a*'s foundation for R to *b*, then there is no real co-relation R′ in *b*, and R and R′ are non-mutual.

[60] *De Pot.*, q. 7, a. 10, corp.   [61] Ibid.
[62] Ibid. *Summa Theol.* I, q. 13, a. 7, corp.; *In I Sent.*, d. 26, q. 2, a. 1, corp. Also see *In V Metaph.*, lect. 17. nn. 1026–9; *In V Phys.*, lect. 3.

In the case of the relation between knower and known, the knower knows some thing through a spiritual or non-material action.[63] The spiritual action is the foundation of the real relation of knowledge in the knower toward the known. But there is no foundation of the same type in the thing known, i.e. there is no corresponding spiritual passion.

In fact, there are certain things [a] to which other things [b] are ordered but not vice versa, because they [a] are completely extrinsic to that type of actions or [type] of powers that such an order accompanies. This is clear since knowledge is referred to the thing known because the knower through an intelligible act has an order to the thing known which is outside the soul. But that thing which is outside the soul is not at all touched by such an act, since the act of intellect is not transient, changing exterior matter. And so that thing which is outside the soul is altogether outside the genus of the intelligible.[64]

Thomas holds that the object exists in the natural or physical order, while the knower's act is of the intelligible or intentional order.[65] The physical order can be distinguished from the intentional, mathematical, moral, psychic, and spiritual orders. And these orders are incommensurable, i.e. they lack a common basis for comparison. So here the intentional act of knowledge is of a different order from the natural order of the object, and so they are incommensurable, not 'of the same type', according to (T11). Hence, by (T11), there is no real co-relation in the known to the knower. In brief, with (T11) Thomas puts the underlying intuition that things of radically different types are incommensurable and cannot be mutually compared in terms of his theory (T10) that mutual real relations require foundations of the same type.

Why, at last, does Thomas maintain that the relations between God and creatures are non-mutual? He reasons that God is 'altogether outside the genus of created being by which the creature is really referred to God'.[66] So, Thomas concludes, God and creatures are non-mutually related. The reasoning here is that if *b* is 'outside the order of' the action of *a* which serves as the

---

[63] *De Pot.*, q. 7, a. 10, corp.; *In I Sent.*, d. 30, q. 1, a. 3, ad 3.
[64] *De Pot.*, q. 7, a. 10, corp.; *In I Sent.*, d. 30, q. 1, a. 3, ad 3.
[65] See n. 64. Also *Summa Theol.* I, q. 13, a. 7, corp.
[66] *De Pot.*, q. 7, a. 10, corp. See also *De Pot.*, q. 7, a. 8, ad 3; *Summa Theol.* I, q. 13, a. 7, corp.

foundation of *a*'s real relation to *b*, then there cannot be in *b* a foundation of the same type required for mutual real relations. Hence, by (T11) the relations are non-mutual.[67]

A point-by-point explication of the parallel between the knower–known relations and the creature–God relations is helpful. First, the knower is really related to the object known, but the object known is only related by reason to the knower. So also the creature is really related to God, but God is only related to the creature by reason. The creature (the measured) is related to God as the knower (the measured) is related to the known object.[68]

Second, there is a real relation of knowledge in the knower, as there is a real relation of dependence in the creature. But as there is no corresponding real relation of being known in the object, so there is no corresponding real relation of lordship in God. This relation of lordship is a relation of reason. This much was common doctrine among many scholastics.

But why this difference? According to Thomas, the two relata do not have foundations of the same type. In the knower there is a non-material action of knowing which serves as the foundation of the real relation. But there is no corresponding foundation of the same type in the object known. The object is of a different order, the material order.

So with creatures and God. What is the foundation of the creature's real relation of dependence on God? It is created being, or as Thomas says, *esse creatum*. 'God however does not act through a mediating action which is understood as proceeding from God and terminating in the creature. But His action is His substance, and whatever is in it is altogether outside the genus of created being (*extra genus esse creati*) through which the creature is referred to God.'[69]

The foundation is an action, but as transformed by Thomas. It is the finite, created act of existence which serves as the foundation for the creature's real relation of dependence on God. More precisely, the foundation is the creature's act of existence as limited by essence.[70] Hence a limited, finite act of existence

---

[67] For other versions of this argument, see *In I Sent.*, d. 30, q. 1, a. 3, ad 3; *Summa Theol.* I, q. 28, a. 1, ad 3.   [68] See n. 62 above.

[69] See n. 66 above and *De Pot.*, q. 7, a. 9, ad 4.

[70] For more on the role of essence, see F. D. Wilhelmsen, 'Creation as a Relation in Saint Thomas Aquinas', *The Modern Schoolman* 56 (1979), pp. 107–33.

serves, appropriately, as the foundation for the relation of dependence which is creation. 'For [passive] creation is not a change, but that dependence of created being (*esse creati*) on its source from which it is set forth. And so it [creation] is of the category of relation.'[71]

But there is no corresponding foundation of the same type in God. Thomas does not spell out the reason for this in his argument in *De Potentia.* But I think it is clear. God is not *esse creatum*; He is *ipsum esse subsistens.* He is *esse per essentiam*, not *esse participatum.* God and creatures are of radically different orders.[72] In sum, the God–creature relations are non-mutual because they lack foundations of the same type, as required by the criterion (T10) for mutual real relations.

As noted by others, in dealing with the Christian mystery of creation, Thomas transforms the original Aristotelian notion of potency/act, with its home in natural change, by his doctrine that the act of existence is received in a limiting principle, the essence. Thomas's basic intuition of creaturely dependence on a transcendent creator God is understood in terms of *ipsum esse subsistens* and *esse participatum.*[73] Many have also noted that the scholastics treat the God–creature relations in the context of a very elaborate Aristotelian theory of relations—mutual and non-mutual, with foundations of various very specific types, as quantity, quality, and actions and passions. However it has not been noticed that Thomas transforms the Aristotelian theory of relation in the light of his basic metaphysics of *esse.* Specifically, he expands the Aristotelian notion of action-as-foundation from its original meaning as a determination of an already existing substance to the creature's created act of existence which serves as the foundation of the real relation of dependence on God. Contrary to Hartshorne, it is not the Greek metaphysics of immutability that

---

[71] *Summa contra Gentiles* II, c. 18; *Compendium Theol.* I, 99. See also *In V Metaph.*, lect. 17, n. 1004 where he explains the basis for the third category of relations in terms of ontological dependence.

[72] *Summa Theol.* I, q. 104, a. 1, corp. Also *Summa Theol.* I, q. 6, a. 2, ad 3.

[73] The central role of participation in the metaphysics of Thomas Aquinas is one of the key contributions of Thomistic studies in this century. In addition to the ground-breaking work of C. Fabro and L. B. Geiger, particularly the latter's *La Participation dans la philosophie de S. Thomas d'Aquin*, 2nd edn. (Paris, 1953), see W. N. Clarke, 'The Limitation of Act by Potency: Aristotelianism or Neoplatonism', *The New Scholasticism* 26 (1952), pp. 167–94.

motivates Thomas to deny that God becomes really related to creatures at creation. It is rather his sense of the transcendence and otherness of God.

3

Relation as Mode of Being

HENRY OF GHENT

HENRY OF GHENT (d. 1293), secular master of theology at Paris from *c.*1275 to *c.*1292, contributed in important ways to the development of scholastic thought in the last quarter of the thirteenth century.[1] He played a role in the condemnation of 1277, being appointed by Étienne Tempier, Bishop of Paris, to a commission that drew up two hundred and nineteen condemned propositions. His own writings reveal a conservative thinker concerned to uphold the primacy of the Augustinian tradition against the inroads of Averroism and Aristotelianism.[2] But he was an original thinker with the boldness to create a metaphysical system of his own. Among others, John Duns Scotus developed his thinking in response to Henry's positions.

As is to be expected, Henry's discussion of the ontological

---

[1] For Henry of Ghent's life, see F. Ehrle, 'Beiträge zu den Biographien berühmter Scholastiker: I. Heinrich von Ghent', in *Archiv für Litteratur- und Kirchengeschichte des Mittelalters*, vol. 1 (Rome, 1885), pp. 365–401. See also, for Henry's life and works, *Henrici de Gandavo Quodlibet I*, in *Henrici de Gandavo Opera Omnia*, ed. R. Macken, vol. v (Louvain and Leiden, 1979), pp. vii–xxiv; R. Macken, 'Hendrik van Gent (Henricus de Gandavo): Wijsgeer en theoloog', *Nationaal Biografisch Woordenboek*, vol. 8 (Brussels, 1979), cols. 377–95; *Henri de Gand (d. 1293), maître en théologie à l'Université de Paris, archidiacre de l'évêché de Tournai: Dates et documents*, in *Henrici de Gandavo Opera Omnia*, ed. R. Macken, vol. iv (forthcoming).

[2] His two main works of undoubted authenticity are *Summa* (= *Quaestiones Ordinariae*), 2 vols. (Paris, 1520; repr. St Bonaventure, NY, 1953), and *Quodlibeta Magistri Henrici Goethals a Gandavo Doctoris Solemnis*, 2 vols. with continuous pagination (Paris, 1518; repr. Louvain, 1961). A commentary on the *Physics* of Aristotle has been attributed to Henry by L. Bellemare, *Les 'Quaestiones super VIII libros Physicorum', attribuées à Henri de Gand (Ms. Erfurt, Amplon., F.349, ff. 120ʳa–184ʳb): Étude sur l'authenticité de l'œuvre; Étude et texte des Quaestiones super VIII libros Physicorum, attribuées à Henri de Gand*, Université de Louvain, Institut Supérieur de Philosophie, dissertation, 3 vols. (Louvain, 1961). R. Macken lists the commentary provisionally among the doubtful works of Henry; see his *Bibliotheca Manuscripta Henrici de Gandavo*, ii, in *Henrici de Gandavo Opera Omnia*, vol. ii (Louvain and Leiden, 1979), pp. 1100–12, esp. 1112.

status of relations affected the medieval debate. With respect to those who preceded him, particularly Thomas Aquinas and Giles of Rome, the discussion takes an 'essentialist' turn, influenced by Henry's doctrine of essential being. Looking forward, a new terminology along with a complexity and fullness of detail hitherto unknown marks succeeding discussions of the problem.

1. Preliminary Remarks on the Metaphysics of Henry of Ghent

As is well known, Plato and Augustine for both moral and epistemological reasons were suspicious of the senses and placed abundant faith in the autonomous activity of the intellect. Henry of Ghent shared their suspicion and faith: he was no more convinced than they that the changing, confusing data of the senses can provide a sure basis for the fixed, unchanging knowledge of metaphysics.[3] *Nemo dat quod non habet*: because of their mutability, the sensible object, the sensible *species*, and our souls are utterly incapable, of themselves, of yielding immutable knowledge. It is in the realm of the intellect that one finds a stable starting-point for metaphysics.

In the writings of Ibn Sīnā Henry found this starting-point: the notion of being. In his epistemology, Ibn Sīnā taught that the first concept we have is that of being. By 'first' he seems to ascribe both a temporal and logical priority to the notion of being. He makes the controversial psychological point that 'thing and being and to be necessary are such that they immediately are impressed on the

---

[3] *Summa*, a. 1, q. 2 (i, fol. 5 E). For Henry's metaphysics, see J. Paulus in his still extremely helpful work, *Henri de Gand: Essai sur les tendances de sa métaphysique* (Paris, 1938); J. Gómez Caffarena, *Ser participado y ser subsistente en la metafísica de Enrique de Gante* (Analecta Gregoriana, 93; Rome, 1958). For his epistemology, esp. the problem of divine illumination, see J. V. Brown, 'Duns Scotus on the Possibility of Knowing Genuine Truth: The Reply to Henry of Ghent in the "Lectura Prima" and in the "Ordinatio"', *Recherches de théologie ancienne et médiévale* (henceforth cited as *RTAM*) 51 (1984), pp. 136–82; id., 'The Meaning of *Notitia* in Henry of Ghent', in *Sprache und Erkenntnis im Mittelalter*, ed. J. P. Beckmann *et al.* (Miscellanea Mediaevalia, 13/2; Berlin and New York, 1981), pp. 992–8; id., 'Divine Illumination in Henry of Ghent', *RTAM* 41 (1974), pp. 177–99; id., 'Abstraction and the Object of the Human Intellect according to Henry of Ghent', *Vivarium* 11 (1973), pp. 80–104; R. Macken, 'La Théorie de l'illumination divine dans la philosophie d'Henri de Gand', *RTAM* 39 (1972), pp. 82–112.

soul by a first impression that is not acquired from others better known than these'.[4]

But he makes more than a merely psychological point. For he uses the notion of being as the point of departure for his metaphysics. The notion of being has logical priority to the other notions we possess, and because of this priority it can be used as his metaphysical starting-point from which he unfolds the whole articulated system of his metaphysics. All other notions are in some sense 'contained in' the initial notion of being. The metaphysician progressively explicates these notions, unfolding his metaphysics through ever more specific determinations of this first notion of being. In this process, Ibn Sīnā moves from the notion of being to the notions of necessity and possibility, then to the divisions of possible (or created) being, i.e. substance and its accidents—in short, the categories.

Following Ibn Sīnā, Henry as metaphysician extracts from the notion of being the two modal notions, the notions of each of the categories, and finally arrives by further determinations at the true essence of the particular thing known. In what follows I briefly trace Henry's move from the notion of being to those of the categories (Sections Two and Three), and within this context present his theory of relations (Section Four).[5] In Sections Two and Three I present only outlines of his metaphysics, those necessary for understanding his theory of relations.

---

[4] Avicenna, *Philosophia Prima*, tract. 1, c. 5: 'Dicemus igitur quod res et ens et necesse talia sunt quod statim imprimuntur in anima prima impressione, quae non acquiritur ex aliis notioribus se, sicut credulitas quae habet prima principia, ex quibus ipsa provenit per se, et est alia ab eis, sed propter ea' (ed. Van Riet, pp. 31–2).

[5] Henry's teaching on relations is basically constant throughout his long career. Early: *Quodl.* III, q. 4 and q. 10, Easter 1278 (or Easter 1279); *Summa*, a. 32, q. 5, *c.*1279; a. 35, q. 8, *c.*1280; *Quodl.* V, q. 2 and q. 6, Christmas 1280 or Easter 1281; *Quodl.* VII, qq. 1–2, Christmas 1282. Middle: *Summa*, a. 55, q. 6 and a. 59, q. 2, *c.*1285–6; *Quodl.* IX, q. 3, Easter, 1286. Late: *Quodl.* XV, q. 5, Christmas 1291 (or Easter 1292); *Summa*, a. 62, q. 4; a. 63, q. 3; a. 66, q. 1, *c.*1291. The dating of these works is problematic; see R. Macken, *Quodlibet I*, vol. v, pp. xvi–xviii. The most helpful chronology we have is that of J. Gómez Caffarena, 'Cronología de la "Suma" de Enrique de Gante por relación a sus "Quod-libetos"', *Gregorianum* 38 (1957), pp. 116–33. Following Macken, I list the dates of the pertinent works according to Gómez Caffarena, adding in parentheses the alternative dates suggested by Paulus.

2. From the Notion of Being to the Categories

For Henry, then, the point of departure for a metaphysician is the notion of being. This first and most common concept of being is predicated of all that is not pure nothing. By 'pure nothing' Henry means what neither is nor can be, either as existing within or outside the intellect.[6] Henry further distinguishes: 'But [being taken in the widest sense] is distinguished by a similar distinction into [i] that which is apt only to exist either in a concept of the intellect or in that intellect, and into [ii] that which, with this [first mode of existing] either is or is apt to be in extra-mental reality.'[7] Entities existing with merely cognitive being, as a goat-stag, do or can exist only in some intellect, and what reality they have is derived from the intellect that thinks them. On the other hand, entities existing with real being can not only be thought of and so exist in merely cognitive being; they also do or can exist outside the mind.[8] Henry calls 'thing' (*res*) in this sense whatever is a nature or an absolute essence.[9] 'Real thing' in this sense includes what actually exists, whether necessarily or contingently, and all

[6] *Quodl.* VII, q. 2: 'Sciendum quod omnium communissimum omnia continens in quodam ambitu analogo, est res sive aliquid sic consideratum ut nihil sit ei oppositum nisi purum nihil, quod nec est nec natum est esse, neque in re extra intellectum neque etiam in conceptu alicuius intellectus, quia nihil est natum movere intellectum nisi habens rationem alicuius realitatis' (i, fol. 258 B).

[7] Ibid.: 'Sed distinguitur distinctione analogica in id quod est aut natum est esse tantum in conceptu intellectus sive in ipso intellectu, et in id quod cum hoc aut est aut natum est esse in re extra intellectum. Res primo modo est res secundum opinionem tantum, et dicitur a reor, -reris quod idem est quod opinor, -naris, quantum res est secundum opinionem quoad modum quo ab intellectu concipitur. . . . Aliquid autem sive res quae nata est esse vel quae est aliquid extra intellectum dicitur res a ratitudine . . .' (i, 258 B). See also *Quodl.* V, q. 2 (i, fol. 154 D); V, q. 6 (i, 161 K); *Summa*, a. 21, q. 2 (i, fol. 124 K).

[8] Henry calls entities of the first type 'things' (*res*) from the Latin verb *reor*, to suppose, to imagine, or to believe. He calls entities of the second type 'things' from *ratitudo*, derived from the participial adjective *ratus* (also from *reor*) meaning fixed, established, settled. See the references in the previous note. Henry's use of *ratitudo* is similar to Ibn Sīnā's use of *certitudo* which Ibn Sīnā attributes to quiddities. See Ibn Sīnā's *Metaph.*, tract. 1, c. 5: '. . . unaquaeque enim res habet certitudinem qua est id quod est, sicut triangulus habet certitudinem qua est triangulus et albedo habet certitudinem qua est albedo. Et hoc est quod fortasse appellamus esse proprium, nec intendimus per illud nisi intentionem esse affirmativi, quia verbum *ens* significat etiam multas intentiones, ex quibus est certitudo qua est unaquaeque res, et est sicut esse proprium rei' (ed. S. Van Riet, pp. 34–5: 55–61).

[9] *Quodl.* V, q. 6: 'Res hic appellatur non figmentum et ens secundum animam tantum, quod dicitur a reor reris . . . sed quicquid est natura et essentia aliqua absoluta habens rationem exemplarem in deo nata existere in existentia operatione divina . . .' (i, fol. 161 K).

possibles. In what follows I am concerned with '*res*' or 'real being' in this sense.

Henry distinguishes the real being outlined above into that which exists necessarily and that which exists contingently.[10] Only God exists necessarily while all creatures exist contingently, i.e. are able to actually exist or not exist.

In most texts of Henry, the creature's intrinsic possibility is founded ultimately on the divine ideas.[11] God knows His own essence not only in itself, but also as capable of being imitated by others. These relations of imitability are the divine ideas. They are the various ways that God knows His essence as capable of being imitated. They do not add anything to the divine essence, for they are only relations of reason produced eternally by the divine intellect. As such, they do not destroy the divine simplicity.[12] But there is no relative without a co-relative. The terms of these relations of reason are the essences of creatures. Henry does not identify them with the divine essence nor with the divine ideas.[13] He claims that they are in some way real, they have some reality of their own as essences. In short, they possess 'essential being', which, while dependent on God's knowledge, is other than God.

What is meant by 'essential being' (*esse essentiae*)? Henry draws

---

[10] I take the distinction between necessary and contingent being to be implied in the following passage from *Quodl.* VII, q. 2: 'Sed dividitur divisione analogica in id quod est aliquid quod est ipsum esse, et in id quod est aliquid cui convenit aut natum est convenire esse. Primum est ens increatum. Secundum continet rem omnis creaturae' (i, fol. 258 B).

[11] For difficulties in interpreting Henry's doctrine of the ground of possibility, see J. Wippel, 'The Reality of Nonexisting Possibles according to Thomas Aquinas, Henry of Ghent, and Godfrey of Fontaines', *The Review of Metaphysics* 34 (1981), pp. 729–58, esp. 748–51.

[12] *Quodl.* IX, q. 2: 'Obiectum primarium non est nisi obiectum informans ad actum intelligendi, et non est nisi ipsa divina essentia quae per se intelligitur a Deo, et nihil aliud ab ipso secundum determinationem Philosophi ibidem. Obiectum vero secundarium est aliud a se. . . . Sic autem sua essentia, qua cognoscit se, cognoscit et alia a se, non dico, sua essentia ut est simpliciter essentia, secundum quam rationem sua essentia se solum cognoscit et non alia, nisi ut sunt in ipso id quod ipse, sed ut ipsa essentia est ratio et habet rationem respectus quo respicit alia a se, non ut quae sunt per existentiam aliquid extra in se ipsis, sed ut quae sunt per essentiam aliquid in divina cognitione, videlicet in eo quod divina essentia est ratio et forma exemplaris illorum. . . . Illa autem ratio in divina essentia, secundum quam sua essentia est ratio qua cognoscit alia a se, nihil aliud est quam imitabilitas qua ab aliis imitetur, quam vocamus ideam' (*Henrici de Gandavo Quodlibet IX*, in *Henrici de Gandavo Opera Omnia*, ed. R. Macken, vol. xiii (Louvain and Leiden, 1983), pp. 27–8).

[13] *Quodl.* IX, q. 2 (ed. Macken, vol. xiii, pp. 25–46). See also Wippel, 'Nonexisting Possibles', p. 747; Gómez Caffarena, *Ser participado*, pp. 30–5.

from a particular interpretation of certain texts of Ibn Sīnā. It seems that Ibn Sīnā taught that the essences of things could exist either in extra-mental reality or in the intellect. But an essence could be considered in three different ways: (i) in terms of its existence in the intellect actually understanding it, (ii) in terms of its existence in singular extra-mental things, or (iii) in itself and unrelated to anything else.[14] Henry interpreted Ibn Sīnā as holding that essences not only can be considered in the third way, i.e. 'absolutely', but exist absolutely.

For the being of nature in things outside [the soul] has one [mode of existing]; but a being of reason has another [mode], and essential being has a third [mode]. For animal taken with its accidents in singular things is a natural thing; but taken with its accidents in the soul it is a thing of reason; and taken by itself it is a thing of essence, from which it is said that its being [of essence] is prior to its being of nature or of reason, as the simple is prior to the composite.[15]

This essential being consists in that by which a thing is what it is in its essence or nature. It excludes other modes of being, as actual being and cognitional being, and all conditions that follow upon such modes of being, as singularity and universality.[16] There is, then, a world of fixed 'absolute essences' existing in essential

[14] Avicenna, *Liber de Philosophia Prima sive Scientia Divina* V–X, ed. S. Van Riet in *Avicenna Latinus* (Louvain and Leiden, 1980), tract. 5, cc. 1–2, pp. 227–45; *Logica* I in *Avicennae Perhypatetici Philosophi ac Medicorum Facile Primi Opera . . . Logyca . . .* (Venice, 1508): 'Essentiae vero rerum aut sunt in ipsis rebus aut sunt in intellectu; unde habent tres respectus. Unus respectus essentiae est secundum quod ipsa est non relata ad aliquod tertium esse, nec ad id quod sequitur eam secundum quod ipsa est sic. Alius respectus est secundum quod est in his singularibus. Et alius secundum quod est in intellectu' (fol. 2ʳb).

[15] *Quodl.* III, q. 9: 'Est igitur intelligendum quod circa quidditatem et naturam rei cuiuscumque triplicem contingit habere intellectum verum et unum falsum. Triplicem quidem habet intellectum verum sicut et tres modos habet in esse. Unum enim habet esse naturae extra in rebus, alterum vero habet esse rationis, tertium vero habet esse essentiae. Animal enim acceptum cum accidentibus suis in singularibus est res naturalis; acceptum vero cum accidentibus suis in anima est res rationis; acceptum vero secundum se est res essentiae de qua dicitur quod esse eius est prius quam esse eius naturae vel rationis, sicut simplex est prius composito' (i, fol. 61 O). See *Summa*, a. 43, q. 2 (ii, fol. 9 E); *Quodl.* I, q. 9 (ed. Macken, vol. i, p. 53: 64–8).

[16] *Quodl.* III, q. 2: 'Unum quod dicitur esse essentiae quod nihil aliud est quam rem secundum se acceptam esse id quod est in sua natura, de quo dicitur quod definitio est oratio indicans quid est esse . . .' (i, fol. 49 E). Also *Quodl.* III, q. 9: 'Sicut enim esse naturae rei appellatur certitudo eius cum conditionibus quas habet ab efficiente extra in particularibus, et esse rationis appellatur certitudo eius cum conditionibus quas habet ab intellectu in eius conceptu in relatione et comparatione ad aliquid aliud, sic esse essentiae rei appellatur certitudo eius concepta absolute, absque omni conditione quam nata est habere in esse naturae vel rationis' (i, fol. 61ᵛ O).

being founded upon, though distinct from, the divine essence and divine ideas. Creatures exist 'essentially', whether or not they come to exist actually in time.[17]

At creation, God chooses to actualize some of these essences, and so some creatures begin to exist in actual being, what Henry calls 'existential being' (*esse existentiae*). All creatures that actually exist extra-mentally (and so all categorical being) have this ontological status of existential being. With characteristic use of parallel, Henry sums up his teaching: God through the divine ideas is the formal cause of the essence of creatures by virtue of which causality eternal essential being is ascribed to them. God, through His free creation, is the efficient cause of creatures by virtue of which causality non-eternal existential being is ascribed to them.[18]

In every creature existing in existential being, there is a composition of its essence and existence (*esse existentiae*), these two ontological constituents being distinguished 'intentionally'.[19] It was through Henry's attacks on Giles of Rome's doctrine of a real distinction between essence and existence that Henry developed his own doctrine of an intentional distinction. A distinction of this type, less than a real distinction and more than a mere distinction of reason, was introduced by many scholastics for a variety of reasons.[20] In one formulation of this distinction Henry says

[17] On the peculiar ontological status of these essences, see Wippel, 'Nonexisting Possibles', pp. 740–51.

[18] *Quodl.* III, q. 9: 'Et, ut dicit Avicenna cap. octavo, hoc esse proprie dicitur definitivum esse et est Dei intentione. Quod intelligo quia tale esse non convenit alicui nisi cuius ratio exemplaris est in inellectu divino, per quam natum est fieri in rebus extra, ita quod sicut ex relatione et respectu ad ipsam ut ad causam efficientem habet quod sit ens in effectu, sic ex relatione quadem et respectu ad ipsam ut ad formam extra rem, habet quod sit ens aliquod per essentiam, iuxta illud quod dicit Avicenna in octavo *Metaphy.*' (i, fol. 61ʳ O). Also *Quodl.* IX, q. 1 (ed. Macken, vol. xiii, pp. 7–8); *Quodl.* V, q. 4 (i, 158 O–159 Q); *Summa*, a. 21, q. 2 (i, fol. 124ᵛ I).

[19] See Gómez Caffarena, *Ser participado*, pp. 93–156.

[20] Henry makes extensive use of this distinction in his metaphysics, psychology, and natural philosophy; see R. Macken, 'Les Diverses Applications de la distinction intentionnelle chez Henri de Gand', in *Sprache und Erkenntnis im Mittelalter*, ed. J. P. Beckmann *et al.* (Miscellanea Mediaevalia, 13/2; Berlin and New York, 1981), pp. 769–76. For Henry's controversy with Giles of Rome, see E. Hocedez, 'Gilles de Rome et Henri de Gand sur la distinction réelle (1276–1287)', *Gregorianum* 8 (1927), pp. 358–84. Also see Macken, 'La Volonté humaine: Faculté plus élevée que l'intelligence selon Henri de Gand', *RTAM* 42 (1975), pp. 5–51; 'Le Statut de la matière première dans la philosophie d'Henri de Gand', *RTAM* 46 (1979), pp. 130–82; 'La Temporalité radicale de la créature selon Henri de Gand', *RTAM* 38 (1971), pp. 211–72, esp. 227–30; Gómez Caffarena, *Ser participado*, pp. 65–92.

For with those that are really identical in the same [thing], sometimes diverse concepts are formed such that neither of them in its concept includes the other, as there are concepts of diverse differences which are present together in the same [thing], such as in man there are rational, sensible, [and] vegetable in so far as they are differences. And similarly the concepts of a genus and a difference that constitute a simple species, as are animal and rational.[21]

Accordingly, Henry's own criterion for an intentional distinction is

> If *a* and *b* are really the same, and neither the concept of *a* includes that of *b*, nor vice versa, then *a* and *b* are intentionally distinct.

Here I take 'include' to mean 'to be the same as, or to be part of, or to follow as a necessary consequence from'.[22]

The concept of existential existence is not included in that of humanity, for example. All that is included in this latter concept is rationality and animality. Humanity is a 'real thing', an absolute nature, eternally existing in essential being. That humanity be actualized by God's creative power in Socrates and Plato is accidental to or 'not included in' the essence of humanity. Hence, there is an intentional distinction in, say, Plato, between what he is, i.e. a man, and how he exists, i.e. in existential being. This distinction between essence and existence, between what something is and how it exists, is found in all categorical being and is one of the keys to understanding Henry's theory of the categories.

---

[21] For the sake of clarity, I have restricted my remarks to Henry's 'major' intentional distinction. *Quodl.* V, q. 6: 'Sed in eis quae intentione differunt sunt gradus secundum differentiam maiorem et minorem. De eis enim quae sunt idem re in eodem, aliquando sic formantur conceptus diversi, ut neutrum eorum in suo conceptu alterum includat, ut sunt conceptus diversarum differentiarum quae concurrent in eodem, sicut sunt in homine rationale, sensibile, vegetabile, inquantum differentiae sunt. Et similiter conceptus generis et differentiae quae constituunt simplicem speciem, sicut sunt animal et rationale. Et in istis duobus modis est maxime differentia intentionum. Sunt et alii quatuor modi in quibus minor est differentia, quia conceptus unius intentionis includit alterum, sed non e converso, ut conceptus speciei conceptum generis et differentiae, non autem e converso' (i, fol. 161^{r-v}L). On the intentional distinction between essence and existence, see *Summa*, a. 28, q. 4 (i, fols. 167 S–168 Z).

[22] For much of what more could be said on Henry's intentional distinction, see Paulus, *Henri de Gand*, pp. 220–37; Gómez Caffarena, *Ser participado*, pp. 88–92; J. Wippel, *The Metaphysical Thought of Godfrey of Fontaines* (Washington, DC, 1981), pp. 80–5.

3. The Categories

In each category there is a distinction between the *res* and the *ratio* of that category.[23] By '*res*' or 'thing' Henry means a real thing, i.e. a nature or absolute essence. Hence to inquire about the *res* of a category is to inquire about the essence of the entities in that category. The *ratio* refers to the mode of existing peculiar to entities of the category.

> the thing of a category is other than the *ratio* of a category . . . as the *ratio* of a substance is to subsist or to stand under; a thing of the category of substance is anything to which this *ratio* pertains. The *ratio* of quantity is to measure a thing according to parts. A thing of quantity is anything in which *per se* such a *ratio* is found. . . . The *ratio* proper to quality is to inform a subject [by qualifying it]. . . . A thing of quality is anything to which such a *ratio* pertains.[24]

To understand any one category, then, one must understand the type of things or essences that are included in that category and also the way or mode of existing peculiar to those things.

All categorical realities have the *ratio* or mode of existing of participated being.[25] He divides this general mode of categorical being into two other modes of being.

[23] *Summa*, a. 32, q. 5: '. . . aliud est res praedicamenti, aliud vero ratio praedicamenti. Res praedicamenti est quidquid per essentiam et naturam suam est contentum in ordine alicuius praedicamenti. Ratio praedicamenti est proprius modus essendi eorum quae continentur in praedicamento. Ex quibus duobus, scilicet, ex re praedicamenti et ratione essendi eius quae est ratio praedicamenti, constituitur ipsum praedicamentum et diversificatur unum praedicamentum ab alio. Non enim ex hoc quod aliquid sit res et natura aliqua, sive substantiae sive accidentis quantumcumque in universali et abstracto intelligatur, habet rationem generis praedicamenti, neque similiter ex hoc quod est esse non in subiecto vel esse in subiecto, quoniam esse ex se nullo modo potest habere rationem generis . . . et multo minus ratione illarum determinationum in subiecto vel non in subiecto, cum non rem sed modum rei et rationem essendi dicunt. Sed natura generis praedicamenti ex utroque simul, scilicet, ex re et ratione praedicamenti constituitur' (i, fol. 196 B). See also *Quodl.* V, q. 2 (i, fol. 154 E); VII, q. 2 (i, fol. 257ʳ A).

[24] *Summa*, a. 32, q. 2: 'Sciendum quod aliud est res praedicamenti, aliud ratio praedicamenti . . . ut ratio substantiae est subsistere sive substare: res praedicamenti substantiae est omne illud cui convenit ista ratio. Ratio quantitatis est secundum partes rem mensurare. Res quantitatis est omne id in quo per se ratio talis invenitur. . . . Ratio propria qualitatis est subiectum informare. . . . Res qualitatis est omne cui talis ratio convenit' (i, fol. 189 I).

[25] *Quodl.* V, q. 2: 'Esse vero secundum quod participatum est dicatur ratio praedicamenti qua praedicamentum est. Ita quod ratio participationis esse est ratio quae facit rem ipsam esse in praedicamento simpliciter' (i, fol. 154 E). See also *Quodl.* XV, q. 5 (ii, fol. 577 G); *Summa*, a. 32, q. 5 (i. fols. 196 C–197 C); and Gómez Caffarena, *Ser participado*, pp. 65–156.

First, therefore, participated being, in so far as it is the *ratio* of whatever general category, is divided into two special *rationes* which distinguish the category of substance from the categories of the accidents. For being is participated by a thing either by subsisting or by inhering in what subsists. In the first mode there is the category of substance which is a predicament because it names a thing to which being-by-subsisting pertains. In the second mode is generally the category of accident because it names a thing to which being-in-another-by-inhering pertains.[26]

There are certain 'real things', i.e. certain essences or absolute natures existing in essential being, which if they exist in existential being subsist in themselves. There are other such real things which if they exist in existential being do so in another way, namely by inhering in another. For example, the essence of whiteness is such that if it comes to exist in existential being, it will not subsist on its own, but will inhere in another.

There are further divisions.

But the category of accident is distinguished according to two modes of participating in being by inhering in another. For being pertains to something by inhering in another either [i] by itself and absolutely or [ii] with respect to another. In the first mode are two categories of accidents, namely quantity and quality. In the second mode are the other seven categories of relation spoken of commonly, which therefore are reduced to one category [i.e. that of relation] as presented in the question mentioned before.[27]

---

[26] *Quodl.* V, q. 2: 'Primo ergo esse participatum inquantum est ratio cuiuslibet praedicamenti generalis dividitur penes duas rationes speciales quae distinguunt praedicamentum substantiae a praedicamentis accidentium. Esse enim participatur a re aut subsistendo aut subsistenti inhaerendo. Primo modo est praedicamentum substantiae quae est praedicamentum quia nominat rem cui convenit esse subsistendo. Secundo modo est generaliter praedicamentum accidentis quia nominat rem cui convenit esse alteri inhaerendo' (i, fol. 154 F). Also *Quodl.* V, q. 6 (i, fol. 161 O), *Quodl.* XV, q. 5 (ii, fol. 577 G); *Summa*, a. 32, q. 5 (i, fol. 197 C). A year or two later, in 1282, instead of dividing the categories into two parts, he divides them into three parts, substance, absolute accidents, and relations, on the basis of three modes of existing, i.e. *esse in se, esse in alio*, and *esse ad aliud*; see *Quodl.* VII, q. 2 (i, fol. 258 B).
[27] *Quodl.* V, q. 2: 'Praedicamentum vero accidentis distinguitur secundum duos modos participandi esse alteri inhaerendo. Esse enim convenit alicui alteri inhaerendo aut secundum se et absolute aut in respectu ad aliud. Primo modo sunt duo praedicamenta accidentium, scil., quantitas et qualitas. Secundo modo sunt alia septem praedicamenta relationis communiter dictae, quae ideo ad unum praedicamentum habent reduci, ut expositum est in praenominata quaestione' (i, fol. 154 G). For further references, see n. 26 above.

As Henry elaborates his theory of the categories,[28] he spells out the specific *ratio* or mode of being proper to each of the categories. Those natures to which it pertains to inhere in another absolutely can do so in one of two ways: either by qualifying their subjects or by measuring them. The former are the absolute accidents in the category of quality, while the latter are in the category of quantity.[29]

The reason quantities and qualities that exist by inherence are said to exist absolutely is not because they could exist in existential being separated from a subject. That latter mode of existence is proper only to substances.[30] Rather they exist absolutely because such accidents are 'real things' in Henry's sense of absolute natures or essences. In this, quantities and qualities have something in common with substances. Only they are absolute natures, essences, 'real things'. This follows since only they are the terms of the divine ideas, the various ways that God conceives of Himself as able to be imitated. Only such 'real things' can imitate God. It is, then, his ontology of absolute natures and their eternal generation by the divine ideas that is behind Henry's repeated assertions that the only created things (*res*) that exist, either in essential or existential being, are substances, qualities, and quantities: '. . . in the whole universe of creatures there are only three genera of things, namely substance, quality, [and] quantity, which . . . agree among themselves in this, that they signify a thing which is a nature and some essence to which being pertains'.[31]

One of the most striking features of Henry's doctrine of the categories is the sharp division he makes between the first three absolute categories and the last seven 'relative' categories. He found support in an influential text of Boethius cited often in

---

[28] For the *locus classicus* for Henry's theory of the categories, see *Summa*, a. 32, q. 5 (i, fols. 196 A–203 I). In 'Cronología', p. 129, Gómez Caffarena draws attention to the large number of citations made to this question by Henry himself in other places.

[29] For more on the categories of quantity and quality, see *Summa*, a. 32, q. 5 (i, fols. 197 K–198 K).

[30] This is true even though many scholastics allowed for one exception, when the accidents of the bread and wine after transubstantiation do not inhere in a subject.

[31] *Quodl.* V, q. 6: '. . . in tota universitate creaturae non sunt nisi tria genera rerum videlicet substantia, qualitas, quantitas, quae . . . in hoc inter se conveniunt, quod significant rem quae est natura et essentia aliqua cui convenit esse, et differunt a re increata quod illa est natura et essentia quae est ipsum esse' (i, fol. 161 O). See also *Quodl.* VII, q. 2 (i, fol. 259 D); *Summa*, a. 32, q. 5 (i, fol. 198 L).

discussions of relation. Henry refers to it frequently.[32] Boethius writes:

Have I now made clear the difference between the kinds of predication? Because one set [of predicates] points, as it were, to the thing, the other set to the circumstances of the thing; and because those things which are predicated in the first way point to a thing as being something, but the others do not point to it as being something, but rather in some way attach something external to it.[33]

In Henry's terminology, each of the ten categories has a *ratio* or mode of being proper to it. But only the first three absolute categories have things or *res* proper to them. The last seven derive their reality (*res*) from the first three.

In support of this Henry argues: 'Of those three modes of being, however, the first two [i.e. existing by subsisting and existing in another absolutely] are so diverse that they are altogether incompatible, nor can they come about in the same thing. For in no way can being-in-another pertain to that thing to which being-in-itself pertains.'[34] So what is a substance must be other than what is a quality or quantity. Similarly,[35] he argues that the mode of existing of a quality, i.e. inhering in a subject by affecting or qualifying it, is incompatible with the mode of existing of a quantity, i.e. inhering in a subject by measuring it. When dealing with absolute categories, one can conclude from a diversity of modes of existing to a diversity of things. In short, if *a* and *b* are entities of different absolute categories, not only are

---

[32] *Summa*, a. 32, q. 5 (i, fols. 198 L–M, 199 O).

[33] Boethius, *De Trinitate*, c. 4: 'Iamne patet quae sit differentia praedicationum? Quod aliae quidem quasi rem monstrant aliae vero quasi circumstantias rei; quodque illa quae ita praedicantur, ut esse aliquid rem ostendant, illa vero ut non esse, sed potius extrinsecus aliquid quodam modo affigant' (*The Theological Tractates*, ed. and trans. H. F. Stewart, E. K. Rand, and S. J. Tester (Cambridge, Mass., 1978), pp. 24–5).

[34] *Quodl.* VII, q. 2: 'Istorum autem trium modorum essendi duo primi ita sunt diversi quod omnino repugnantes, nec possunt fieri circa eandem rem. Ei enim rei cui convenit esse in se nullo modo potest convenire esse in alio' (i, fol. 258 B).

[35] Ibid.: 'Esse autem in alio per inhaerentiam distinguitur in duo secundum duos modos inhaerendi, scilicet, sub ratione afficientis subiectum quod proprium est praedicamento qualitatis, vel in ratione mensurantis quod proprium est praedicamento quantitatis. Et sic res cui convenit esse inhaerendo pertinet ad duo praedicamenta quorum rationes diversae sunt et repugnantes ut circa eandem rem esse non possint. Inesse enim mensurando nullo modo convenire potest rei qualitatis, neque rei quantitatis inesse afficiendo' (i, fol. 258 C). See also *Quodl.* V, q. 2 (i, fol. 155 L).

their *rationes* or modes of existence different, they are also different things or *res*.

4. The Category of Relation

4.1. The Ontological Status of a Real Relation

This last point does not hold in any of the last seven categories. In particular, it does not hold for the category of relation. Neither the mode proper to a substance (to be in itself) nor the mode proper to quantity and quality (to be in another absolutely) is incompatible with the mode proper to a relation (to be toward another). For one and the same thing can exist both absolutely and relatively at the same time. 'For being-toward-another according to the category of relation is easily able to pertain to that thing to which pertains being-in-itself according to the *ratio* of the category of an absolute accident.'[36] For example, one thing, whiteness, can exist in another as an absolute accident and also with a respect toward another. This is one of the reasons Henry claims that a real relation and its foundation are really identical, i.e. identical as things or *res*. But this foundation can exist in two ways or modes, absolutely and relatively.

Again, the quality of whiteness is a real thing inhering in Socrates. If Plato also becomes white, Socrates becomes really related to Plato by similarity. This real relation is a real accident of Socrates, but it is no thing added to him. Rather, that same quality of whiteness now has an additional mode of existing. For in addition to the mode of existing by inherence in Socrates as an absolute accident, the whiteness now has the mode of existing with respect toward another. There is one thing with two *rationes* or modes of existing.

Further, this relation of similarity is a real accident, composed of a *ratio* and a thing as all other categories. The *ratio* is the mode of being proper to the category of relation, to be toward another. But the category of relation (as also the remaining six other categories) does not have a *res* or thing proper to it: '. . . a relation

---

[36] *Quodl.* VII, q. 2: 'Cui enim rei convenit esse in se secundum rationem praedicamenti accidentis absoluti bene potest convenire esse ad aliud secundum praedicamentum relationis' (i, fol. 258 B). See also *Quodl.* V, q. 6 (i, fol. 161 O).

has [its] total accidentality by reason of its reality which it does not have of its own, but "contracts" it from the thing of another predicament of accident upon which it is founded'.[37] As a thing, it is identical with its foundation, though its mode of existing is other than that of the absolute thing that serves as its foundation. Put in Henry's technical terms, if *a* is an entity of an absolute category that serves as a foundation for a real relation, there is only one thing *a* existing in two modes, *esse-in absolute* and *esse ad aliud.*

Because of this we often said elsewhere that a relation 'contracts' its reality from its foundation, and of itself is only a bare condition that is only a certain mode holding a thing toward another, and so not a thing in so far as it is of itself, but only a mode of a thing (unless it could be called 'thing' by extending [the meaning of] 'thing' even to a mode of a thing).[38]

This doctrine on the ontological status of real relations is constant throughout Henry's long career. In his *Summa* fifty-five, question six (*c.*1285), he summarizes his position on relations, again in terms of *res* and *ratio.*

this name 'relation' in one way signifies a respect as it is a pure intention and the *ratio* of the category [of relation]. And so a relation is not a thing, neither a substance nor an accident, nor is it real. Rather it is a pure mode [of existing] having reference to another (unless . . . one calls a 'thing' a mode of a thing, or one calls a mode 'real' because it follows upon a thing). In another way it ['relation'] signifies a respect as it is a thing of an absolute category on which it [i.e. the relation] is founded.

---

[37] *Quodl.* V, q. 2: 'Nunc autem quamquam praedicamentum accidentis duo dicit sicut et alia, scilicet, rem subiectam et determinatum modum essendi, totam tamen accidentalitatem habet relatio ratione suae realitatis quam non habet propriam, sed contrahit eam a re alterius praedicamenti accidentis supra quam fundatur . . .' (i, fol. 154 I). See also *Quodl.* V, q. 6 (i, fols. 161 O–162 O). The last six categories are all founded on the absolute accident of quantity, although in different ways; see *Quodl.* VII, q. 2 (i, fol. 258ᵛ C). For more on the bases or foundations for the last six categories, see *Quodl.* XV, q. 3 (ii, fol. 577 H). Henry extensively treats each of these categories in *Summa*, a. 32, q. 5 (i, fols. 199 P–201 T).

[38] *Quodl.* IX, q. 3: 'Propter quod saepius alibi diximus quod relatio realitatem suam contrahit a suo fundamento, et quod ex se non est nisi habitudo nuda, quae non est nisi modus quidam rem habendi ad aliud, et ita non res quantum est ex se, sed solummodo modus rei, nisi extendendo rem ut etiam modus rei dicatur res, secundum quod alibi exposuimus . . .' (ed. Macken, vol. xiii, p. 56: 85–9; p. 59: 61–8). See also *Quodl.* V, q. 2 (i, fol. 154 I); *Quodl.* VII, q. 2 (i, fol. 257ᵛ A); *Summa*, a. 32, q. 5 (i, fol. 198 L); *Summa*, a. 43, q. 2 (ii, fol. 9 K).

This is what all names of the species of relation signify, as 'paternity' and 'filiation' and the like.[39]

In his final years, *c*.1291, Henry continues to insist that as a *res*, the relation is identical with its foundation. 'But that reality is not proper to the category of relation, nor does a relation have it by the *ratio* of its category, but [it has such reality] only from the other categories on which the whole category of relation is founded and from which it arises and is caused.'[40]

He consistently calls this reality of a real relation a thing (*res*), and he explicitly asserts in *c*.1285 that this thing is something absolute which serves as the foundation of the relation.[41] Furthermore, he argues against the strongly realist position that holds that in creatures one thing is the foundation and another thing is the relation which is an accident inhering in the subject as other types of absolute accidents.[42]

4.2. Intentional Distinction between a Real Relation and its Foundation

One of the distinguishing marks of Henry's theory of relations is his teaching that there is an intentional distinction between a real relation and its foundation. Is the criterion for an intentional distinction fulfilled in this case? The criterion for an intentional distinction is

> If *a* and *b* are really the same, and neither the concept of *a* includes that of *b*, nor vice versa, then *a* and *b* are intentionally distinct.

---

[39] *Summa*, a. 55, q. 6: '. . . hoc nomen relatio uno modo significat respectum ut est intentio pura et ratio praedicamenti. Et sic relatio non est res, neque substantia neque accidens nec est realis, sed modus ad aliud se habendi purus (nisi secundum modum praetactum, appellando rem modum rei vel appellando modum realem quia sequitur rem). Alio modo significat respectum ut est res praedicamenti absoluti super quem fundatur, sicut et significant omnia nomina specierum relationis, ut paternitas, filiatio et huiusmodi. Et sic in divinis significat rem quae est substantia et est substantia sed sub ratione respectus significata' (ii, fol. 112 V). See also ibid. (ii, fols. 110 O–111 O).

[40] *Summa*, a. 62, q. 4: 'Sed realitas illa non est propria praedicamento relationis, nec habet eam relatio a ratione sui praedicamenti, sed solummodo ab aliis praedicamentis super quae fundatur totum praedicamentum relationis et a quibus oritur et causatur . . .' (ii, fol. 193 F). See also ibid. (ii, fols. 192 E–193 F); *Summa*, a. 63, q. 3 (ii, fol. 198 M–O).

[41] See n. 39 above.

[42] *Summa*. a. 55, q. 6 (ii, fol. 112 S).

Again, I take 'include' to mean 'be the same as, or be part of, or follow as a necessary consequence from'.

First, a real relation and its foundation are really the same because they are the same thing or *res* in Henry's sense of absolute nature or essence. Further, it can be conceded that the concept of a quality like whiteness does not include the concept of similarity. But might the concept of similarity include that of the quality that serves as its foundation?

Henry responds[43] that the concept of similarity does include that of quality, but only of quality as inhering in numerically diverse subjects and so serving as the foundations for the relations of similarity. But this is not the concept of quality spoken of in the criterion. For there, by 'the concept of *b*' is meant the essence considered in itself, i.e. as indifferent to any mode of existence, such as inherence in numerically diverse subjects. This mode of existence is accidental to or not included in the concept of quality. So, Henry claims, while the concept of similarity does include that of quality *qua* inhering in the diverse subjects, it does not include that of quality *simpliciter*. For Henry, then, the final condition is fulfilled for a real relation being intentionally distinct from its foundation.

4.3. Real Relation: Thing or Mode?

As we have seen,[44] Henry mentions the possibility of extending the meaning of the term 'thing' to include the mode of a thing. In itself the issue may seem trivial. But it is indicative of the beginning of a controversy over whether one should allow into one's ontology relative things (*res relativae*). From Scotus onwards, there is much talk of relative things, but we have not yet encountered this terminology in Thomas Aquinas or Giles of Rome, nor is it found in Henry of Ghent. But in article fifty-five of his *Summa* (*c.*1285), Henry does talk at length of a doubt which centres on this issue.

---

[43] *Quodl.* V, q. 6: '. . . similitudo accidentalis non fundatur super qualitatem ut qualitas est, scilicet ratione essentiae suae ut secundum se essentia quaedam est, sed solum ut concreta est subiecto, scilicet ratione suae inhaerentiae. . . . Similitudo ergo sic supra esse qualitatis fundatur, ut sit omnino. extra conceptum esse qualitatis secundum rationem essentiae suae, ut qualitas est simpliciter. Talia autem, ut dictum est supra, necesse est saltem secundum intentionem differre inter se' (i, fol. 162 S).

[44] See n. 39 above.

Henry's position is that a real relation is to be called a thing only because it is founded on a thing, an absolute thing which is its foundation.[45] The specifically relational character is a *ratio*, a mode of being toward another. But others argue that both aspects of a real relation are things.[46] Both aspects—that it is founded on an absolute thing and that it looks to its term—equally arise from or are caused by reality (*ex natura rei*). Hence, it is argued, both can equally be called a thing. The one aspect, being identical with the foundation, is a thing in an absolute category, while the other is a thing in the category of relation. Here a non-Henrician ontology is assumed according to which all extra-mental reality has equal claim to the honorific title 'thing'.

Henry replies that 'it is only a dispute over a name, calling by the wider name "thing" what others call "a mode of a thing"'.[47] He certainly discourages this practice, but if it is done, he says, 'it seems to me that it is better to say with precision that there are many and diverse "things of relation" than that there are many and diverse things, taking "thing" simply'.[48]

Henry's own view, however, is that if the respect or mode of being is called a thing, it is only because it is founded on some real thing. A relation is real by reason of its being founded on something real, and for this reason the subject is really related to the term. A real relation is called a thing having an order to its term, but it is not called a thing because of its order to its term.[49] For that it has a real order to its term does not make it a thing, but rather vice versa. Because a real relation is a thing (by reason of its foundation in something real), so the real relation is a thing having an order to its term and really related to it.[50]

---

[45] *Summa*, a. 55, q. 6: 'Sed dubium est utrum cum hoc quod sunt reales relationes, possunt dici res. Et est verum proculdubio quod inquantum includunt in se suum fundamentum, sicut reales dicuntur quia fundantur in re, sic et res sunt quia rem sui fundamenti in se includunt' (ii, fol. 111 P).

[46] Ibid.

[47] Ibid.: 'Sed tunc non est disputatio nisi de nomine, appellando extenso nomine rem quod alii appellant modum rei' (ii, fol. 111 Q).

[48] Ibid.: 'Propter quod si omnino dicendum sit quod relationes sint diversae et plures res iam dicto modo, videtur mihi quod melius sit dicere cum determinatione quod sunt plures et diversae res relationis quam quod sint plures et diversae res re simpliciter accepta . . .' (ii, fol. 111 R).

[49] Ibid.: 'Quod etsi respectus qui sequitur ex natura rei possit dici res vera aliquo modo, hoc non convenit ei ratione illa et comparatione qua est ad aliud sive ex eo quod est respectus aut relatio' (ii, fols. 110–111 O).

[50] Ibid.: 'Attamen si sic respectus possint dici res, hoc non est nisi quia ex natura rei

5. Conclusion

Henry of Ghent's doctrine on relation looks back to previous discussions and also looks forward to the debates of the fourteenth century.

Along with Thomas Aquinas and Giles of Rome, he distinguishes two aspects in a real relation. For his predecessors these are *esse* and *ratio*; for Henry they are *res* and *ratio*. In both theories, the first term of the pair is prior to, more fundamental than, the second. But for Thomas's *esse*, Henry substitutes *res*, the absolute nature or essence. The basic Platonic-Augustinian metaphysics of essence reasserts itself in Henry's thought and results in a theory of the ontological status of relations quite different from that of Thomas and Giles. The motto of Henry of Ghent, the conservative Doctor Solemnis,[51] could well be *Semper Idem*. If, following Plato and Augustine, something is real to the extent it is immutable, then the essences of creatures are, apart from God, the most real; they are *res par excellence*. Further, Henry often explains realities other than those *res* as various modes of being.[52] Like so much else, then, Henry accounts for the specifically relational character of the world in terms of a mode of being.

Henry also looks forward. In the fourteenth century a new terminology enters the debate, that of *res absolutae* and *res relativae*. This is signalled in Henry's discussion (*c*.1285) of the doubt whether modes can be called things. This doubt is most likely part of the larger debate Henry was having in the mid-1280s with Giles of Rome over the distinction between being and essence.

fundantur in vera re. Quia enim realiter et ex natura ipsius rei fundantur in re secundum dictum modum ut dicantur res ex ordine ad fundamentum, ideo etiam realiter respiciunt obiectum et dicuntur res in ordine ad obiectum, non autem ex ordine ad obiectum. Non enim respicere obiectum realiter dat eis quod sunt res etiam in comparatione ad obiectum, immo e converso. Quia enim sunt res ex ordine ad fundamentum, etiam sunt res in ordine ad obiectum et etiam realiter respiciunt obiectum' (ii, fol. 111 Q).

---

[51] One meaning of *solemnis* is 'established'.

[52] For example, contrasting the mode of being proper to rocks, plants, and animals, i.e. *esse existentiae*, Henry speaks of a mode of being proper to persons, *esse actualis substentiae*, *esse actualis existentiae*, or *esse personalis existentiae*. See G. Wilson, 'Henry of Ghent and René Descartes on the Unity of Man', *Franziskanische Studien* 64 (1982), pp. 97–110.

For in these years it was precisely Giles's tendency to reify the Thomistic distinction that Henry attacked, substituting his own intentional distinction. Hence, to call both aspects of a relation 'things' would be an instance of Giles's reifying tendency and also would blur the all-important Henrician priority of essence over any mode of existing.[53]

[53] Although I have characterized Henry's thought as essentialism, R. Macken insists this needs to be nuanced by noticing the place Henry accords existence. See Macken, 'Les Diverses Applications', pp. 774–6; id., 'La Volonté humaine'.

4

Relation as Thing

RICHARD OF MEDIAVILLA

SINCE most know little of Richard of Mediavilla (*c*.1245/9–1302/7), a few remarks on his life and intellectual orientation are necessary.[1] While a Bachelor of Theology at Paris in 1283, he was appointed to a commission to investigate the writings of Peter John Olivi; the following year he incepted as Master of Theology. He was named Franciscan minister provincial of France in 1295. He was called Doctor Clarissimus for his clear and orderly presentation and had an interest in physical science, often using arguments drawn from experience.[2] Although solidly of the old school of Augustine and Bonaventure, he at times departs, adopting opinions of Thomas Aquinas. For example, Richard holds that intellectual knowledge comes through the abstractive activity of the agent intellect with no need of special divine illumination.[3] But against Thomas, he accords some small degree of actuality to matter, so that God could preserve it without a form.[4] Richard's independence is also seen in his theory of relations.

---

[1] For his life and works, see E. Hocedez, *Richard de Middleton: Sa vie, ses œuvres, sa doctrine* (Louvain, 1925); R. Zavalloni, *Richard de Médiavilla et la controverse sur la pluralité des formes* (Philosophes médiévaux, 2; Louvain, 1951); F. A. Cunningham, 'Richard of Middleton, O.F.M. on *Esse* and Essence', *Franciscan Studies* 30 (1970), pp. 49–76, esp. pp. 49–56.

[2] P. Duhem, *Études sur Léonard de Vinci: Ceux qu'il a lus et ceux qui l'ont lu*, 3 vols. (Paris, 1909), vol. 2, p. 371.

[3] P. P. Rucker, *Der Ursprung unserer Begriffe nach Richard von Mediavilla: Ein Beitrag zur Erkenntnislehre des Doctor Solidus* (Beiträge zur Geschichte der Philosophie und Theologie des Mittelalters, 31/1; Münster, 1934).

[4] *Clarissimi Theologi Magistri Ricardi de Mediavilla super Quatuor Libros Sententiarum Petri Lombardi Quaestiones Subtilissimae*, 4 vols. (Brescia, 1591); at the end of vol. 4 is his *Quodlibeta Doctoris Eximii Ricardi de Mediavilla Ordinis Minorum*. For matter having some actuality, see *In II Sent.*, d. 3, a. 2, q. 1, ad 2m (ii, fol. 54a).

1. Richard's Theory of Categorical Real Relations

Richard's teaching on real relations is found in his *Sentences* commentary, finished probably around 1282/3, and in his first *Quodlibet*, perhaps Easter 1285.[5] In his commentary, Richard argues for the traditional position that the God–creature relations are non-mutual. He gives a clear statement of Thomas's argument from different orders.[6] But that his theory of relation is not simply Thomist quickly becomes evident.

when it is said that a real relation can come to another without its changing, etc., I say it is true without change according to something absolute, not however without change according to a relative thing, because that relative thing which afterwards is in that [subject] was not in it before. Or it can be said that the reason why some real relation cannot come to God anew is not only because He would be changed, but also because He is outside the order of creatures, and so there cannot be in Him a real relation to a creature.[7]

He still maintains the response of Thomas based on different orders. But he also holds that if *a* becomes really related to *b* only because of a change in *b*'s foundation, then *a* is changed, for now a 'relative thing' exists in *a*. That is, he rejects Thomas's

(T9)   If the foundation that is or is in *a* changes, then there is a change of *a*; but if only the foundation that is or is in *b* changes, there is no change of *a*, for there is no change *in a*.

Instead Richard holds

(T9′)   If the foundation that is or is in *a* changes, then there is a change of *a*; and if only the foundation that is or is in *b* changes, there is a change of *a*, for *a* acquires or loses a relative thing.

---

[5] For dating of the pertinent works, see P. Glorieux, *La Littérature quodlibétique de 1260 à 1320* (Kain, 1925), vol. 1, p. 267.

[6] *In I Sent.*, d. 30, a. 1, q. 4, corp. (i, fol. 269ab).

[7] Ibid.: 'Ad sextum cum dicitur quod relatio realis potest advenire alteri sine sui mutatione, etc., dico quod verum est sine mutatione secundum aliquid absolutum, non tamen sine mutatione secundum rem relativam, quia ante non erat in ipso illa res relativa quae postea in ipso est. Vel potest dici quod ratio quare non potest advenire Deo aliqua realis relatio de novo non est tantum quia mutaretur, sed etiam quia est extra ordinem creaturarum, quapropter non potest in ipso esse realis relatio ad creaturam' (i, fol. 269b).

Richard also does what Henry of Ghent specifically warned not to do: he calls a real relation a 'thing'. It is a relative thing that changes its subject. This is a significant difference from the doctrines of his predecessors, and the terminology of relative thing becomes part of the fourteenth-century debate. What motivated Richard to talk of relations as 'relative things'?

First, talk of 'things' was in the air at Paris during the mid-1280s. Giles of Rome's reified version of the real distinction between essence and existence was sharply attacked by both Henry of Ghent and Godfrey of Fontaines.[8] Richard's formulation of his own solution is that existence does not add any absolute thing to essence, but only a relationship to God as the giver of being. Essence and existence really differ as an absolute and a real relation really differ and make a real composition.[9]

But apart from this controversy, Richard had other motives for talking of relations as relative things. In book one of his *Sentences* commentary, distinction twenty-six, after again affirming (T9′) he adds that if *a* becomes newly really related only because of a change in the foundation in *b*, it can be said in another way that *a* itself is *not* changed. But 'because of this it does not follow that [a relation] does not bespeak some thing in comparison to the term, although in comparison to the subject it only differs in reason from its foundation'.[10] This formulation becomes somewhat intelligible if seen within the context of the doctrine of the Trinity and the constraints Richard sees this placing on an adequate theory of relation.

In question nine of the first *Quodlibet* a few years later, he asks explicitly whether a real relation is really the same as its

---

[8] J. Wippel, 'The Relationship between Essence and Existence in Late-Thirteenth-Century Thought: Giles of Rome, Henry of Ghent, Godfrey of Fontaines, and James of Viterbo', in *Philosophies of Existence Ancient and Modern*, ed. P. Morewedge (New York, 1982), pp. 131–64.

[9] For Richard's doctrine, see *Quodl.* I, q. 8 (iv, fols. 12a–14a); *In II Sent.*, d. 3, a. 1, q. 1 (ii, fols. 48b–51a). See also Cunningham, '*Esse* and Essence', pp. 56–76; P. Mandonnet, 'Les Premières Disputes sur la distinction réelle entre l'essence et l'existence 1276–1287', *Revue thomiste* 18 (1910), pp. 741–65, esp. 759–61.

[10] *In I Sent.*, d. 26, a. 3, q. 1, ad 4m: '. . . dico quod quamvis relatio adveniat alicui creaturae et recedat ab ea sine illius creaturae mutatione penes aliquid absolutum, non tamen sine mutatione quae est penes respectum. . . . Vel potest dici ad argumentum quod quamvis relatio adveniat alicui creaturae et recedat ab ea quandoque sine eius mutatione, non propter hoc sequitur quod non dicat aliquam rem per comparationem ad terminum, quamvis per comparationem ad subiectum non differt a suo fundamento nisi secundum rationem' (i, fols. 239b–240a).

foundation.[11] He argues that it is not, for if they were really the same, this would endanger the doctrine of the Trinity. Following tradition, Richard teaches that each divine person is constituted in some way by a relation. Each divine person only 'adds' to the divine essence a relation to the other persons. Further, it was accepted doctrine that while the persons are really identical with the divine essence, they are really distinct from one another. This real distinction of persons was held to be necessary to maintain the reality of the Trinity. Richard argues that if each of the divine relations were not something besides the divine essence, there would not be a real distinctio of persons in the Godhead.[12]

With the Trinity as model, Richard makes two comments about real relations in creatures.[13] A real relation 'in comparison to its subject' does not add anything to its foundation (as each of the divine persons is identical with the divine essence). But a relation 'as it looks to its term' is a thing other than its foundation. The ontological commitments attendant on this formulation are not clear. But it is evident that Richard had a strong theological motive to insist on the reality of relation: 'as it looks to its term' it must be a true thing.

Another motive for calling a relation a thing is found in authority. According to many philosophers, Aristotle's categories are 'the ten first genera of things'.[14] A few years earlier, in 1283, Henry of Ghent had interpreted this dictum to accord with his own ontology in which only three types of things exist, i.e. substances, quantities, and qualities, entities of all other cat-

---

[11] *Quodl.* I, q. 9: 'Utrum relatio realiter idem sit cum suo fundamento' (iv, fol. 14a); 'Ad istam quaestionem respondeo quod relatio non est realiter idem cum suo fundamento' (iv, fol. 14b).

[12] *Quodl.* I, q. 9: 'Certum est enim quod in divinis est Trinitas personarum et unitas substantiae. Certum est etiam quod persona ultra essentiam (ut ita loquar) non dicit nisi relationem. Ergo Trinitas in divinis attenditur penes ipsas relationes personarum constitutivas. Tunc arguo sic: si relatio non dicat ultra suum fundamentum nisi rem rationis, tunc in divinis non esset realis distinctio personarum, quod falsum est' (iv, fol. 14b).

[13] Ibid.: 'Si autem ipsa relatio in divinis dicit rem veram quae per comparationem ad illud in quo est transit, et per comparationem ad illum ad quem est manet (cum vera relatio maneat in divinis, secundum Boetium in libro *De Trinitate*), sequitur etiam quod relatio in creaturis dicit rem aliam a suo fundamento, inquantum respicit terminum, quamvis in comparatione ad subiectum nullam rem addat ultra suum fundamentum.' See also *In I Sent.*, d. 33, a. 2, q. 1, ad 4m (i, fol. 288b).

[14] Ps.-Boethius, *In Categ. Arist.* I (PL 64, 159–63). For example: 'Quoniam rerum prima decem genera sunt, necesse fuit decem quoque esse simplices voces quae de subiectis rebus dicerentur' (PL 64, 162 D).

egories being various modes of these things.[15] Richard does not share Henry's general ontology nor his theory of the categories. He interprets the dictum more literally:

The ten predicaments are the ten first genera of things according to the opinion of many philosophers. But according to the Philosopher, *On the Categories*, relation is one of those ten genera distinct from the others. So relation, in so far as it bespeaks something distinct from the other predicaments, bespeaks some thing. But a relation bespeaks some thing distinct from the other predicaments only for this reason, that it adds to its foundation, because sometimes it has a quality for foundation, sometimes a quantity, sometimes a substance. Therefore a relation bespeaks some thing besides its foundation.[16]

This reifying language is a prominent feature of Richard's discussion of relation.

But what type of thing is a real relation? In book two, distinction thirty-seven, he says that 'thing' can be taken in three ways: '. . . "thing" can be accepted commonly and so it takes in all that which can be thought, and so it is named ["*res*"] from *reor, -reris*. In another way [it is accepted] properly, and so it is converted with being. In a third way, [it is accepted] most properly, and thus it is said only of being *per se* which is substance.'[17] This is not helpful. All that is clear from Richard's remarks is that a relation is a thing in the very broad second category (all extra-mental reality?). If so, we want to know what type of extra-mental thing a real relation is.

Richard explains that there are some

who consider just one extreme of a relation, and they do not find that the relation posits anything other than those absolute things that are in it [the extreme]. Then again turning their attention only to the other

---

[15] Henry of Ghent, *Quodl.* VII, q. 2 (i, fol. 259D).

[16] *Quodl.* I, q. 9: 'Contra: decem praedicamenta sunt decem prima genera rerum secundum plurium philosophorum sententiam. Sed secundum Philosophum, *In Praedicamentis*, relatio est unum de illis decem generibus distinctum contra alia. Ergo relatio, inquantum dicit aliquid distinctum contra alia praedicamenta, dicit rem aliquam. Sed relatio non dicit quid distinctum contra alia praedicamenta nisi ratione huius, quod addit supra suum fundamentum, quia aliquando habet qualitatem pro fundamento, aliquando quantitatem, aliquando substantiam. Ergo relatio ultra suum fundamentum dicit rem aliquam' (iv, fol. 14b).

[17] *In II Sent.*, d. 37, a. 4, q. 2, *circa litteram*: '. . . res potest accipi communiter et sic comprehendit omne illud quod cadit in cognitione, et sic dicitur a reor, -reris. Alio modo proprie, et sic convertitur cum ente. Tertio modo magis proprie, et sic tantum modo dicitur de ente per se, quod est substantia' (ii, fol. 458a).

extreme they do not find that a relation posits something other than
those absolute things that are in that [extreme]. And so it seems to them
that a relation between some two extremes posits no thing other than an
absolute thing. And these are deceived, for wishing to seek the nature
and cause of a relation they seek the nature and cause of an absolute
being. For if considering only some one [thing] they were to find there
that a relation posits something other than the foundation, then the
relation would not be a relation but some absolute accident. For this is
the nature of a relation: to depend simultaneously on two. And so if it is
not found that a relation posits anything other than its foundation when
considering only one [extreme], still if they consider two [extremes]
simultaneously they would find that a relation does posit something
other than the foundation, namely some condition of those two
[extremes] between them.[18]

This is the first hint of a more modern, less Aristotelian
concept of relation: instead of two numerically distinct relational
accidents inhering in the terms, he talks of *one* relation of both
terms. The specifically relational feature, involving more than
one term, briefly takes precedence over the usual substance
–accident ontology.

This novel way of conceiving a relation is seen also in another
argument that a real relation is not identical with its foundation. It
is a typically Ricardian argument from experience.[19] An object

---

[18] *Quodl.* I, q. 9: 'Quarto removendum est aliquid quod inducit vel inducere potest
aliquos ad opinandum quod relatio sit realiter idem cum suo fundamento. Quare enim
quidam aspiciunt ad unum extremum relationis per se et non inveniunt relationem aliquid
ponere ultra ea quae absoluta sunt in eo. Item respicientes ad aliud extremum per se non
inveniunt relationem ponere aliquid ultra ea quae absoluta sunt in illo. Ideo videtur eis
quod relatio inter aliqua duo extrema nullam rem ponat ultra rem absolutam. Et isti
decipiuntur, quia volentes quaerere naturam et causam relationis, quaerunt naturam et
causam entis absoluti. Si enim aspicientes aliquid unum per se invenirent ibi relationem
aliquid ponere ultra fundamentum, iam relatio non esset relatio, sed aliquod accidens
absolutum. Haec est enim natura relationis: ex duobus simul dependere. Unde quamvis
aspiciens ad unum per se non inveniat relationem aliquid ponere ultra fundamentum,
tamen si ad duo simul aspiciant, invenient relationem aliquid ponere ultra fundamentum,
scilicet, habitudinem aliquam illorum duorum inter se' (iv, fol. 15a).

[19] Ibid.: 'Tertio declaro hoc per experientiam. Experimur enim per visum quod
eaedam res in numero sub uno ordine aliam passionem realem efficiunt in visu quam sub
alio ordine. Et similiter idem soni sub uno ordine aliam passionem in auditu efficiunt
quam sub alio ordine. Sed illud quod nulla res est non est causa, nec cum [*sic*] causa
variationis realis effectus. Ergo cum illae res maneant eaedam, et propter solius ordinis
imitationem [*lege* mutationem] fiat realis variatio in effectu, sequitur quod ordo dicat rem
aliam a rebus ordinatis. Sed ordo est relatio quaedam, ergo relatio dicit rem aliam a suo
fundamento' (iv, fols. 14b–15a).

seen from one perspective causes an image in the eye which is different from that caused by the same object seen from a different perspective. Now only that which is a thing can be the cause of a variation in real effect. Here he is presumably taking 'thing' in the broad second sense above, i.e. that which enjoys some sort of extra-mental existence. But if the object remains the same, and only the perspectival relation between the object and the viewer changes, this relation is the cause of the variation in real effect. This relation, then, has some extra-mental reality and is a thing other than the things related. What is more important than the stated conclusion is his underlying conception of a real relation. Instead of two relational accidents inhering in two subjects, he talks throughout the example of one relation existing between the object and the eye.[20]

Still, these are only isolated instances. In the conclusion to the argument from experience, Richard reverts to talking of a relation as other than its foundation, emphasizing again the substance–accident ontology. His primary approach to relations remains rooted solidly in a substance–accident ontology. He argues at length in distinction nineteen that as foundations are multiplied, so are real relations.[21] Two numerically distinct quantities inhering in two creatures serve as foundations for two numerically distinct equalities. If there are two brothers, there are two relations of fraternity; if two friends, there are two friendships. Despite lapses, the Doctor Solidus remained squarely within the tradition.

However, the modification of the traditional view of relation as accident is reflected in some of Richard's remarks on the categories. His discussion is typical of the prominent role played by interpretations of the categories in the late thirteenth- and early fourteenth-century debate on relations.[22] He divides actual being into what is apt to exist 'standing by itself' and what

---

[20] He also talks of one relation obtaining among a number of quantitative parts, ibid. See also *In I Sent.*, d. 3, q. 2: '. . . quanto extrema relationis minus habent de entitate, tanto relatio inter illa est minus ens' (i, fol. 59a).

[21] *In I Sent.*, d. 19, a. 1, q. 3, corp., ad 1m, ad 2m (i, fol. 183b). See also *In II Sent.*, d. 1, a. 2, q. 4, ad 4m (ii, fol. 13b).

[22] See e.g. Peter John Olivi's discussion, *Quaestiones in Secundum Librum Sententiarum*, q. 28, ed. B. Jansen, in Bibliotheca Franciscana Scholastica Media Aevi, 4: vol. 1 (Quaracchi, 1922), pp. 482 ff.

is not.[23] Substances belong to the first type of being, while accidents belong to the second. The latter are divided into beings which inhere, i.e. the absolute accidents of quantity and quality, and those which cannot inhere, i.e. relations. Regarding the latter Richard says,

For the being of a relation, with respect to that which it bespeaks besides the foundation, is not being in something, but toward something. Wherefore the Philosopher, in the book on the predicaments, does not say that they are relatives whose being is to be in another, but whose being is to be toward another, for which reason he calls relatives 'toward-something'.[24]

Richard acknowledges that some find peculiar the idea of a non-inhering accident, for some call 'accident' only that which inheres.[25] But he extends the term to all that which is not substance. So although an accident cannot exist 'standing by itself', it need not inhere in a subject.

Richard departs from Thomas and Giles, then, not only in substituting (T9′) for (T9). When dealing with accidental change, he also denies

(T7)   Something changes only if there is a change *in* it if by 'in' is meant inherence. He substitutes

(T7′)   Something can be accidentally changed by acquiring or losing either (i) an accident which inheres, i.e. an absolute thing, or (ii) an accident which does not inhere, i.e. a relative thing.

---

[23] *Quodl.* I, q. 9: 'Et cum tu arguis ultra, ergo accidens esset sine subiecto, dico quod prima divisio entis creati est in ens in potentia et in ens in actu. Prima autem divisio entis creati in actu est in ens quod est natum per se stare et in ens quod non est natum per se stare. Ens autem quod est natum per se stare substantia est. . . . Ens . . . quod non est natum esse pars entis per se stantis nec est ens natum per se stare naturaliter dividitur in ens quod inhaeret, et hoc est accidens absolutum, et in ens quod non est natum inhaerere, et haec est relatio, quantum ad id, quod dicit ultra fundamentum' (iv, fol. 15a–b).

[24] Ibid.: 'Esse enim relationis, quantum ad illud quod dicit ultra fundamentum, non est esse in aliquo, sed ad aliquid. Quapropter Philosophus, in libro praedicamentorum, non dicit quod relativa sunt quorum esse est esse in aliquo, sed quorum esse est ad illud se habere, quapropter relativa nominat "ad-aliquid"' (iv, fol. 15b).

[25] Ibid.: 'Quare tamen nomine accidentis multi intelligunt tantummodo ens inhaerens, ideo ad removendam omnem controversiam dici potest quod si extendamus nomen "accidentis" ad omne illud quod non est substantia nec pars substantiae, quod quamvis tale dependeat ita ut non sit natum existere per se, tamen non oportet quod omne tale natum sit alicui inhaerere' (iv, fol. 15b). See also *In I Sent.*, d. 30, q. 2, corp. (i, fols. 266b–267a); *In II Sent.*, d. 3, a. 1, q. 1, ad 2m (ii, fol. 50a).

2. Conclusion

It is significant that Richard does not begin his discussion by distinguishing, like his predecessors, two aspects of a real relation. There is no talk of a relation's accidental being as identical with the being of its foundation (Thomas Aquinas and Giles of Rome) or of it being the same 'thing' as its foundation (Henry of Ghent), though in both cases differing in *ratio*. For Richard, a real relation is certainly based on a foundation. But the relation is conceived of as slightly cut off or separated from its foundation; it does not inhere. This is formulated in two ways: (i) it is a *res relativa* really distinct from its foundation, or (ii) it is a condition obtaining between two terms. In the fourteenth century, John Duns Scotus will develop (i) into a strongly realist theory of relation, and Peter Aureoli will develop (ii) into a conceptualist theory of relation.

5

Relation as Thing

JOHN DUNS SCOTUS

In book two, distinction one, of his *Ordinatio*, John Duns Scotus (*c.*1265–1308) asks whether the relation of any creature to God is identical with its foundation, namely the creature itself.[1] He immediately reduces this to an even more fundamental metaphysical issue: whether in general a relation is identical with its foundation.[2] In answering these questions, Scotus develops a highly articulated theory of relations, incorporating traditional elements with a number of innovations.

A brief overview of Scotus' position is helpful before plunging into the subtleties of his arguments. He upholds the common Aristotelian view that a real categorical relation is an accident inhering in one of the relata and being 'toward' another: 'A real relation is not a being *per se* [i.e. a substance], nor an interval between two extremes, nor in two as in one subject, but [is] in one [extreme] and toward another.'[3] He also holds that while creatures are really related to God, He is not really related to them.[4]

---

[1] *Ordinatio* II, d. 1, q. 5, n. 188 (ed. Vatican, vol. vii, p. 94); *Lectura* II, d. 1, q. 5, n. 163 (ed. Vatican, vol. xviii, p. 53). For references to Duns Scotus' *Ordinatio* and *Lectura*, I use the Vatican critical edition, *Ioannis Duns Scoti Ordinis Fratrum Minorum Opera Omnia* (Vatican City, 1950–). For the rest, I use the Wadding edition, *Ioannis Duns Scoti . . . Opera Omnia*, 12 vols. (Lyons, 1639).

[2] *Ordin.* II, d. 1, q. 5, nn. 192–240 (vii, pp. 96–120); *Lectura* II, d. 1, q. 5, nn. 167–221 (xviii, pp. 54–75).

[3] *Quaestiones super Libros Metaphysicorum Aristotelis* v, q. 11, n. 6: 'Relatio realis non est ens per se, nec intervallum inter duo extrema, nec in duobus ut in uno subiecto, sed in uno et ad aliud' (iv, p. 635). See also *Opus Oxoniensis* IV, d. 12, q. 2, n. 14 (viii, p. 733).

[4] *Ordin.* I, d. 30. q. 2, nn. 49–51 (vi, p. 192). Scotus' main argument that there is no real relation in God to creatures is as follows: (i) No reality in God requires necessarily the existence of something other than God. (ii) A real relation in *a* requires for its being a term *b* of that relation, which is other than *a*. (iii) Therefore, there is in God no real relation to what is other than God. Premiss (ii) is a common axiom in theories of relations; (i) is proved by a *reductio* using divine simplicity and necessity. See also *Lectura* I, d. 30, q. 2, nn. 55–6 (xvii, pp. 414–15).

He presents a strongly realist theory of relations. His orientation toward realism is seen in the six references to '*res*' ('thing') or variants ('reality' and 'really') in the three severally necessary and jointly sufficient conditions for a real relation:

... according to common opinion a real relation requires only these three [conditions]: first, a real foundation that, of course, is in a thing and in extra-mental reality; second, also that the extremes [be] real and really distinct; third, also that that [relation] in extra-mental reality be in the extremes without, of course, any consideration of the intellect or without the operation of a power extrinsic [to the extremes].[5]

In arguing for his theory, he exploits a number of key elements in his philosophy. He uses his doctrine of the formal distinction on the part of the thing in analysing a creature's relation to God and the personal relations in the Godhead which constitute the divine persons. He uses his separability criterion for real distinction in determining the ontological status of categorical relations. As a result of this latter determination, Scotus does what Henry of Ghent warned not to do: he calls relations 'things' (*res*). More significantly, he accords these relative things (*res relativae*) an accidental existence of their own really distinct from that of their foundations. In this, he departs from three of his predecessors, Thomas Aquinas, Giles of Rome, and Henry of Ghent. He does this consciously, as evidenced in his examination and rejection of the theory of Henry of Ghent.

He also distinguishes sharply between two types of relations, categorical and transcendental.[6] The first are those that fall under the category of relation and, as we have seen, are divided into (i) relations of a numerical nature, but including also qualitative similarity and specific identity, (ii) causal relations, and (iii) relations between 'the measured and the measure', such as those between the knower and the knowable. Transcendental relations, as their name implies, transcend the categories and characterize

---

[5] *Quodl.* q. 6, n. 33: '. . . secundum communem sententiam relatio realis non requirat nisi ista tria: primum, fundamentum reale quod scilicet sit in re et ex natura rei. Secundum, et extrema realia, et realiter distincta. Tertium, et quod ipsa ex natura rei insit extremis absque scilicet omni consideratione intellectus vel absque operatione potentiae extrinsecae' (xii, p. 166). Also ibid., n. 1 (xii, p. 142); *Ordin.* I, d. 31, q. un., n. 6 (vi, p. 204); *Lectura* I, d. 31, q. un., n. 6 (xvii, pp. 424–5).

[6] For a history of transcendental relations, see A. Krempel, *La Doctrine de la relation chez saint Thomas* (Paris, 1952), pp. 645–70.

all being irrespective of division into the ten categories.[7] They are not founded on some determinate thing of another category, as equality is founded on quantity. In this sense, the dependence relation of a creature to God is transcendental.

Scotus' doctrine of relation is found in his *Ordinatio*, in a few questions of his *Quodlibet*, in his *Lectura*, and in his *Quaestiones super Libros Metaphysicorum Aristotelis*.[8] Between the earlier *Lectura* and the more detailed treatment in the *Ordinatio*, I have not detected a break or any significant development. With the precisions found in his *Quodlibet* and commentary on the *Metaphysics*, Scotus presents a consistent account of the ontological status of relations, both categorical and transcendental.

I use the *Ordinatio* and the *Quodlibet* as my principal sources for a number of reasons. First, the *Ordinatio* is the text that Scotus himself 'ordered' or prepared for publication toward the end of his life. Second, in the *Ordinatio* (particularly book two, distinction one, questions four and five) Scotus treats relations most extensively and systematically, discussing specifically whether a real relation is really the same as or distinct from its foundation. Third, in the *Quodlibet* (also a late work: probably either Advent 1306 or Lent 1307) Scotus debates particular points in extreme detail, providing valuable clarifications. For example, in the third question he takes great pains to distinguish various meanings of 'thing' and to contrast these with 'mode'. This helps to distinguish more clearly his position from the modal theory of Henry of Ghent.

Scotus teaches that real categorical relations are really distinct from their foundations, while transcendental relations are for-

---

[7] *Ordin.* II, d. 1, q. 5, n. 277 (vii, pp. 137–8). Also *Lectura* II, d. 1, q. 5, n. 261 (xviii, p. 89); *Ordin.*, ibid., n. 231 (vii, p. 116); *Lectura*, ibid., n. 215 (xviii, p. 72). See A. B. Wolter, *The Transcendentals and their Function in the Metaphysics of Duns Scotus* (Washington, 1946).

[8] For the principal sources of Scotus' teaching on relations, see: *Ordin.* II, d. 1, qq. 4–5 (Vatican viii, pp. 91–146); *Ordin.* I, d. 30, qq. 1–2 (Vatican vi, pp. 169–202); *Lectura* II, d. 1, qq. 4–5 (Vatican xviii, pp. 51–93); *Lectura* I, d. 30, qq. 1–2 (Vatican xvii, pp. 397–421); *Quodlibetal Questions* 3, 4, 6, 12 (Wadding xii); *Quaestiones super Libros Metaphysicorum Aristotelis* V, qq. 6 and 11 (Wadding iv, pp. 607–15, 633–43). Also see *In Librum Praedicamentorum Quaestiones*, qq. 25–9 (Wadding i, pp. 156–66). All page references are to the respective editions and volumes. For secondary literature, see O. Holzer, 'Zur Beziehungslehre des Doctor Subtilis Johannes Duns Scotus', *Franziskanische Studien* 33 (1951), pp. 22–49; J. P. Beckmann, *Die Relationen der Identität und Gleichheit nach J. Duns Scotus* (Bonn, 1967); G. Martin, *Wilhelm von Ockham: Untersuchungen zur Ontologie der Ordnungen* (Berlin, 1949), pp. 120–37.

mally distinct yet really identical with their foundations. I first present his views on categorical relations, followed by those on transcendental relations. I then offer his arguments against real relations being mind-dependent, and finally I consider his critique of Henry of Ghent.

1. Categorical Relations

1.1. The Separation Argument

Scotus' main argument for the thesis that categorical relations are really distinct from their foundations is the so-called separation argument. I formulate it as follows:[9]

- (A) (i) If *a* is identical with *b*, then it is contradictory that *a* exist but not *b*.
  - (ii) In many cases of a relation R and its foundation F, it is not contradictory that F exist but not R.
  - (iii) Therefore, in many cases of a relation R and its foundation F, R is not identical with F.

The minor is proved by a number of examples:

. . . for if there is this white [thing] and not that white [thing], this white [thing, i.e. the former] is without [the relation of] similarity; and if the other white [thing] comes to be, there is [the relation of] similarity in this white [thing, i.e. the former]. Therefore it is possible that there not be similarity and there be similarity in this white [thing, i.e. the former].[10]

The major is implied by the separability criterion for real distinction: there is a real distinction between two entities if it is possible to separate one from the other in such a way that at least one can exist without the other. Before the time of Scotus, the term 'real distinction' had a broader meaning, as seen in Section five of Chapter Two. After Scotus, however, it seems that a commonly held meaning for 'real distinction' involved some form of the separability criterion.

---

[9] *Ordin.* II, d. 1, q. 5, n. 200 (vii, pp. 101–2); *Lectura* II, d. 1, q. 5, n. 184 (xviii, p. 61).
[10] *Ordin.*, ibid., n. 205 (vii, pp. 103–4). In my translation, I have followed the variant reading of Q in the apparatus, p. 104.

For Scotus, there is an asymmetry between absolute accidents, such as whiteness, and relative accidents, such as relations. Not only can a substance exist without an absolute accident, but the converse is true. As will be explained, in the case of transubstantiation absolute accidents do exist separated from substance. But although the foundation of a real relation can exist without the relation (as stated in the minor), the relation, Scotus holds, cannot exist without its foundation. It is part of Scotus' (and most other scholastics') theory that a real foundation is a necessary condition for a real relation. Hence, for Scotus, it is contradictory that a real relation exist without its foundation. The major, then, does not commit him to the possibility of relations existing without their foundations. As we shall see, this asymmetry is crucial to Scotus' reply to an old objection, that a position such as his involves an infinite regress of relations.

Scotus argues for the major[11] claiming that it seems contrary to the principle of contradiction that one and the same both really exist and not really exist at the same time. If contradictories are said of beings, one can immediately conclude to some diversity. In the case at hand, the foundation really exists and the relation does not really exist. Hence, they are not really the same.

Scotus is strongly committed to the major, for he claims that without it there is no way of proving a real distinction between beings.[12] Further, if the major is denied, one abandons the principle of contradiction and so cannot disprove a proposition or eliminate a problem by showing it involves a contradiction.[13] Finally, from authority, he argues that Aristotle used the major to prove that matter is other than form.[14]

Part of the plausibility of this argument comes from its formal simplicity and its few assumptions. In addition, the separability criterion for real distinction was widely accepted at Scotus' time, and he emphasizes its close connection with the principle of contradiction. The minor seems undeniable. But the argument's deceptive simplicity masks ontological and semantic assumptions deep in Scotus' philosophy which soon became the focus of repeated criticism.

---

[11] *Ordin.* II, d. 1, q. 5, n. 201 (vii, p. 102); *Lectura*, ibid., n. 185 (xviii, p. 61).
[12] *Ordin.*, ibid., n. 202.
[13] *Ordin.*, ibid., n. 203 (vii, p. 103); *Lectura*, ibid., n. 187 (xviii, p. 62).
[14] *Ordin.*, ibid., n. 204; *Lectura*, ibid., n. 186 (xviii, p. 61).

I believe Henry of Ghent would agree with Scotus here—but only if Henry were studying the problem of relations from the standpoint of the physicist. For Henry, one and the same thing can be studied by two distinct sciences, physics and meta-physics.[15] The former, starting with the senses, attains only an imperfect and partial understanding of reality. The latter is the product of the autonomous activity of the intellect. It begins with the notions of being, thing, and necessity, and proceeds by further determinations arriving at the true essences of the things to be known.

Furthermore, different methods yield different conclusions. Considered by the physicist, a human being is constituted by a soul and a body, two really distinct and separable physical principles. But considered by the metaphysician, a human being is constituted by the metaphysical principles animality and rationality, which are intentionally distinct.[16]

So also here. If one is doing physics, Henry can concur with Scotus in (A). Henry himself uses the separability criterion for a real distinction and in fact illustrates the criterion by the separ-ability of a real relation of similarity from its foundation, as Scotus does in the minor of his argument.[17] But if one is concerned with the true ontological status of a real relation, this is a matter for the metaphysician who alone discovers the true essences of things. But by 'thing', Henry the metaphysician means an absolute nature or essence. And only absolute things, i.e. substances, quantities, and qualities, are such things. A real (*realis*) distinction obtains only between such things (*res*). But, as Henry insists, a real relation is not a thing. Therefore, there cannot be a real

---

[15] Henry of Ghent, *Quodl.* IV, q. 4: 'Quod quid est autem est eius [*scilicet* rei] definitiva ratio, continens principia rei essentialia expressa per definitionem; quae dupliciter habent assignari secundum duplicem considerationem rei in se subsistentis, intellectu scilicet physico et metaphysico' (i, fol. 91 B).

[16] Ibid.: 'Idem enim re quod intelligit physicus cum dicit hominem esse corpus et animam, intelligit metaphysicus cum dicit quod est animal rationale . . .' (i, fol. 91 D).

[17] Henry of Ghent, *Summa*, a. 27, q. 1: 'Quaedam vero differunt re et hoc vel absoluta ex parte utriusque vel relata saltem ex parte alterius. Absoluta, ut quae sunt aliquid et aliud in natura, sicut materia et forma, et ista Deus posset separare. Re non absoluta sed relata differunt aliqua dupliciter: aut enim relatio fundatur in natura et essentia rei aut super aliquod accidens in re. Et talis relatio secundo modo potest separari ab absoluto, sicut accidens potest super quod fundatur, ut similitudo per quam habet Sortes respectum ad Platonem ex sua albedine si fiat niger' (i, fol. 161 M).

distinction between a thing, e.g. the foundation, and what is not a thing, i.e. the real relation.[18]

Scotus does not have an ontology in which only absolute natures or essences have the elevated status of being things. Real relations are things, albeit relative things. Not sharing Henry's ontology, Scotus extends the scope of his separability criterion for a real distinction beyond absolute things to relations or relative things.

Scotus 'confirms' his separation argument with four other arguments, two with theological premisses and two without. Each is a *reductio ad absurdum* of the thesis—call it (I), i.e. the identity thesis—that a real relation is really identical with its foundation.

1.2. Denial of the Incarnation[19]

The Christian doctrine that God became a human being is understood to involve the union of the Word, the second person of the Trinity, with Christ's human nature. Christ's human nature has a real relation of union with the Word. Suppose (I) that a real relation is really identical with its foundation. If so,

(B) (i) Christ's relation of union to the Word is really identical with its foundation, i.e. His human nature.
   (ii) But then, even if the Word had never assumed the human nature of Christ, that human nature would be as really united to the Word as it is now.
   (iii) So the incarnation, i.e. the assumption of the human nature by the Word, would be for nothing.

---

[18] Henry of Ghent, *Quodl.* V, q. 6: 'Res hic appellatur non figmentum et ens secundum animam tantum, quod dicitur a reor, -reris, neque respectus aliquis, licet quoquo modo res appellari possit maxime in deo . . . sed quicquid est natura et essentia aliqua absoluta habens rationem exemplarem in deo nata existere in existentia operatione divina. . . . Unde re differunt quaecumque diversas naturas et essentias important secundum rem, sive fuerint simplicia, ut materia et forma, sive composita, ut homo et asinus. Re vero sunt eadem quaecumque eandem rem sive simplicem sive compositam important, nec unum eorum aliquid rei super alterum ponit, ut sunt universaliter definitio et definitum, et partes definitionis inter se et cum definito, et similiter res absoluta et respectus fundatus super ipsam. Nullus enim respectus aliquid rei ponit praeter rem eius super quod fundatur' (i, fol. 161 K). For a discussion of the real distinction in Henry of Ghent and the opposition between the physical and metaphysical criteria, see J. Paulus, *Henri*, pp. 1–19, 208 ff.

[19] *Ordin.* II, d. 1, q. 5, n. 207 (vii, pp. 104–5); *Lectura* II, d. 1, q. 5, n. 190 (xviii, pp. 62–3).

Scotus even argues conversely: if in the future the Word put down the human nature, the human nature would still be as really united with the Word as now when the Word has not put down the human nature.

Scotus supports premiss (ii) claiming that if (I), then the 'total reality' of the assumption of the human nature by the Word would be the same before as after the Incarnation, the 'total reality' being the Word, the human nature, and its relation of union with the Word. This is so, since on (Ai) and (I) it is contradictory for Christ's human nature ever to exist without the relation of union with the Word.

1.3. Denial of the Separation of Accidents from the Subject in Transubstantiation[20]

At Mass, when the priest says the words of consecration, the bread and wine become the body and blood of Christ. This is explained theologically by the doctrine of transubstantiation. The substance of bread is no longer present, i.e. the matter and substantial form of bread cease to exist and are replaced by the real presence of Christ. But the accidents or 'Eucharistic species' of the bread remain, i.e. the qualities of shape, colour, taste, etc. This explanation entails a change in the accepted Aristotelian schema in which accidents can exist only in substances. In transubstantiation, God miraculously preserves the accidents separated from the substance. For some scholastics, it was the accident of quantity that was miraculously preserved in separated existence, and this accident supported the other accidents.

With this background, one can understand Scotus' following argument:

(C) (i) Before transubstantiation, the accident of quantity inheres in its subject (the bread), while afterwards this accident does not inhere in this subject.

 (ii) But the same accident of quantity remains both before and afterwards.

 (iii) Suppose (I), i.e. that a real relation is really identical with its foundation.

---

[20] *Ordin.*, ibid., n. 208 (vii, p. 105); *Lectura*, ibid., n. 191 (xviii, p. 63).

(iv) Then the accident of quantity is identical with its relation of inherence in the bread.

(v) Therefore, the quantity is really united to or informs the bread throughout transubstantiation (ii, iv)

which is inconsistent with (i).

Both theological arguments had such force that Ockham, who strenuously tried to excise all relative things from his ontology, was forced to concede that in all cases of transubstantiation there exist such relative things really distinct from their foundations.[21]

1.4. Denial of All Composition[22]

(D) (i) *a* and *b* form a composition *ab*.

(ii) If (I), then the union of *a* and *b* is nothing more than those absolute things *a* and *b*.

(iii) If *a* and *b* are separated, the total reality which the composition *ab* had remains. (ii)

(iv) While separated, then, *a* and *b* remain united. (iii)

(v) But when the parts of a composition are separated, there is no real composition, but only an aggregate.

(vi) Hence, a composition is not a composition. (iv, v)

This argument is very old; Aristotle uses it in a quite different context.[23] Still, the shared conclusion is that an essential unity of elements must involve some reality over and above just the elements.

Henry of Ghent holds that a real relation and its foundation are really identical (though intentionally distinct). He would object to (ii) using his distinction between thing and mode. At the union of *a* and *b*, no further thing (*res*) or absolute nature is involved, but there are two modes or relations in addition to the absolute things *a* and *b*: *a*'s relation R of union with *b*, and *b*'s relation R′ of union with *a*. Hence, (ii) is false. And if in (iii) 'total reality' refers not only to *res* but to modes, (iii) is also false. For when *a* and *b* are

---

[21] See sect. 4 of ch. 7.

[22] *Ordin.* II, d. 1, q. 5, n. 209 (vii, p. 105); *Lectura* II, d. 1, q. 5, n. 192 (xviii, p. 63). See also *In Metaph.* V, q. 11, n. 3 (iv, p. 633).

[23] Aristotle, *Metaph.* VII, c. 17 (1041ᵇ11–33). Aristotle argues that to account for an essential unity one must posit, besides the constituents, something else which is not another element. It is a cause or principle (*arche*), the substance (*ousia*) of the thing.

separated, the two relations or modes of being, R and R', do not remain.

1.5. Denial of Secondary Causality[24]

In the earlier *Lectura* version of this argument, Scotus uses the example of fire (*b*) and wood (*c*), the effect being, presumably, burning (*a*).

(E) (i) *a* can be caused by secondary causes *b* and *c* only if there is the required relation of spatial proximity between *b* and *c*.

   (ii) If (I), then the relation of spatial proximity between *b* and *c* is nothing more than the absolute things *b* and *c*.

   (iii) Whether *b* and *c* are spatially proximate or not, the same things exist. (ii)

   (iv) Only by positing some other reality can what was once not causally possible become causally possible.

   (v) Without the required spatial proximity, *b* and *c* cannot cause *a*. (i)

   (vi) With the required spatial proximity, *b* and *c* cannot cause *a*. (iii–v)

   (vii) Therefore, *b* and *c* cannot cause *a* in any case (v, vi)

which is equivalent to a denial of secondary causality.[25] As with the previous argument, Henry of Ghent could object to (ii) on the same grounds: the relation of spatial proximity is more than the absolute things; it is a mode of being.

A clue to a key assumption of Scotus in both arguments (D) and (E) is found in premiss (iv) of (E). Scotus writes:

There is never a passage from contradictory to contradictory apart from change. For if there were no change in anything, there would be no more reason why one contradictory be now true than the other, nor [any] more [reason] why the other be false than the former. And thus both are simultaneously false or both are simultaneously true.[26]

[24] *Ordin.* II, d. 1, q. 5, n. 210 (vii, pp. 105–6); *Lectura* II, d. 1, q. 5, n. 193 (xviii, pp. 63–4). See also *In Metaph.* V, q. 11, n. 3 (iv, p. 633).

[25] I have omitted Scotus' references to *proportio*, which are not found in the *Lectura* version, since I am not sure what they mean. For our purposes, the force of the argument is not affected.

[26] *Ordin.* I, d. 30, q. 2, n. 41 (vi, pp. 186–7); *Lectura* I, d. 30, q. 2, n. 48 (xvii, p. 412). See Aristotle, *Physics* v, c. 1 (225ª12–20).

In (D) the passage is from '*a* and *b* are composed' to '*a* and *b* are not composed', and in (E) from '*b* and *c* cannot cause *a*' to '*b* and *c* can cause *a*'. The passage in both cases must be accounted for by some change in the world. But Scotus assumes that the change must be in what things are existing in the world. Henry of Ghent could reply that there is a change in the way *a* and *b* exist in (D), and in the way *b* and *c* exist in (E). No further thing need be posited in existence to account for the change in truth-value. The problem over what must be posited to account for the truth of statements containing relative terms is, of course, at the heart of the dispute. The differences between Scotus' realist position and Henry of Ghent's modalist position will be explored further in Section Four when considering Scotus' criticism of Henry's position.

2. Transcendental Relations

After the condemnations of 1270 and 1277, there was a general reaction against Greek necessitarianism in all its forms. As a result, many thinkers were concerned to understand as precisely as possible the nature of the contingent relation of dependence that each creature has to God. John Duns Scotus was no exception. In *Ordinatio*, book two, distinction one, question five, he asks whether the relation of a creature to God is the same as its foundation, i.e. the creature. He takes great pains to avoid two extremes: to exalt the creature to the level of absolute existence independent of God, or to degrade it by devaluing the limited independent existence it does enjoy.

In the course of arguing against these two extremes, he prepares for his own position. On the one hand, a creature cannot be totally identical with its relation to God. If so, then all creatures would be formally relative. But Scotus holds that there are creatures, i.e. substances, that are formally absolute and not relative.[27] And, as we shall see, for Scotus it is not possible that one and the same thing be both formally relative and absolute.[28]

---

[27] *Ordin.* II, d. 1, q. 5, nn. 189, 276, 246–50 (vii, pp. 94, 136–7, 122–3); *Lectura* II, d. 1, q. 5, nn. 164, 259, 226–31 (xviii, pp. 53, 88, 77–8). The editors of Scotus' *Opera Omnia* attribute to William of Ware the opinion against which Scotus argues here; see *Ordin.*, ibid., nn. 241–2 (vii, pp. 120–1); *Lectura*, ibid., nn. 223–4 (xviii, pp. 75–6).

[28] See n. 40 below.

On the other hand, a creature and its relation to God cannot be really distinct, for then they would be separable, and it is absurd that a stone exist without being really related by dependence to God.[29] Scotus steers a middle course, holding that a creature and its relation to God are really identical, yet formally distinct.[30]

It is here that Scotus presents the second part of his theory of relation, having to do with transcendental as opposed to categorical relations. Categorical relations are really distinct from their foundations. Transcendental relations are (i) really identical with yet (ii) formally distinct from their foundations. I treat in turn these two aspects of his theory of transcendental relations.

2.1. A Creature and its Relation of Dependence are Really Identical

One argument Scotus gives that a creature and its relation of dependence are really identical is the following:[31]

(F) (i) If b properly inheres in a, and a cannot exist without b, then b is really the same as a.

(ii) A relation to God properly inheres in a stone, and the stone cannot exist without it.

(iii) Therefore, that relation is really the same as the stone.

The minor can be admitted.[32] He defends the major by using the notions of priority, posteriority, and simultaneity. The general thesis is that non-mutual implication between two elements A and B implies that one is prior to the other, while the latter is

---

[29] *Ordin.* II, d. 1, q. 5, n. 257 and *textus interpolatus* (vii, pp. 126–7). The editors of Scotus' *Opera Omnia* attribute to Peter of Tarantasia (Innocent V) and Romanus of Rome the opinion against which Scotus argues here; see *Ordin.*, ibid., nn. 253–6 (vii, pp. 125–6); *Lectura*, ibid., nn. 232–6 (xviii, pp. 78–9).

[30] *Ordin.*, ibid., n. 260 (vii, p. 128); *Lectura* II, d. 1, q. 5, n. 238 (xviii, p. 80). Regarding further precisions on the formal distinction, according to Scotus (*Reportatio Parisiensia* I, d. 33, q. 2, nn. 12–13 (xi, 186–7)) x is not adequately identical with y when one exceeds the other or vice versa, either according to predication or perfection. It would appear that the foundation, being absolute, exceeds the relation in perfection, while the concept of a relation to God, being predicated of more things than the concept of any one individual creature, exceeds the foundation in predication.

[31] *Ordin.*, ibid., nn. 261–2 (vii, p. 129); *Lectura*, ibid., nn. 240–2 (xviii, pp. 81–2). For another argument, see *Ordin.*, ibid., nn. 266–71 (vii, pp. 132–4); *Lectura*, ibid., nn. 250–4 (xviii, pp. 84–6).

[32] *Ordin.*, ibid., n. 263 (vii, p. 130); *Lectura*, ibid., n. 243 (xviii, p. 82).

posterior to the former. For example, Scotus sometimes distinguishes in the Godhead between various attributes or 'acts' of God that do not imply a temporal order, but do imply a logical order. God's knowing that a certain creature could be created does not entail that He decides to create it, but God's decision to create it does entail a knowledge of this possibility. In his doctrine of predestination and God's foreknowledge, Scotus distinguishes four such logically discrete moments in the Godhead. A. B. Wolter explains the notion of priority of nature in this way:

> If any two distinguishable elements are so related in virtue of what they are that the very notion or existence of one, call it B, entails the notion or existence of the other, call it A, but not vice versa, then A is prior by nature to B even if neither is temporally prior to the other. If A entails B and B entails A, however, the two are said to be simultaneous by nature.[33]

Using these notions, Scotus constructs a supporting argument to prove the major in (F):[34]

(G) (i) If a cannot exist without b, then either (a) b is naturally prior to a, or (b) b is naturally simultaneous with a, or (c) b and a are really identical.

(ii) But if b properly inheres in a, then not (ia) nor (ib).

(iii) So if b properly inheres in a, and a cannot exist without b, then (ic) b is really the same as a

which is the major (i) of (F).

He argues for the minor (ii) in (G):

> but what properly inheres in something, as a relation in [its] foundation (that is, it inheres in such a way that if it were other, it would be posterior by nature to that [in which it inheres]), is not prior by nature or simultaneous by nature with that in which it inheres.[35]

If b properly inheres in a, then b is naturally posterior to a; and if b is naturally posterior to a, then it is not naturally prior or simultaneous to a (which is (ii) of (G)).

Scotus does not hold that b is posterior to a because b's existence depends on a's, while a's does not depend on b's. For a,

[33] Wolter's glossary in *God and Creatures: The Quodlibetal Questions*, trans. F. Alluntis and A. B. Wolter (Princeton, 1975), p. 529.

[34] *Ordin.* II, d. 1, q. 5, n. 262 (vii, p. 129); *Lectura* II, d. 1, q. 5, n. 242 (xviii, pp. 81–2).

[35] *Ordin.*, ibid.

the creature, cannot exist without its relation *b* to God. They are *really* simultaneous, i.e. in extra-mental reality one cannot exist without the other. The relation of dependence on God is an inseparable accident of the creature.[36] But this does not exclude a relation of priority and posteriority by nature.

To understand this, notice that Scotus uses the general principle of priority and posteriority in widely varying contexts. By it, he discerns an order of priority and posteriority in the purely conceptual order, as between the second intentions 'genus' and 'species'. He also discerns an order of priority and posteriority in the extra-mental world. Besides temporal priority and posteriority, there is an order of natures. He discovers such an order between (i) things (*res*) and (ii) realities or formalities. The distinction between (i) and (ii) is that while in both (i) and (ii) both elements are separable in thought, only the elements in (i) are also separable in reality, as a quality from its subject. Regarding (ii), A. B. Wolter has written, 'The beauty of the formal distinction, if one accepts it, is that it assumes not only that the perfections referred to are objective, i.e. are characteristic of the extramental subject, but that they are interrelated in various objective ways.'[37]

Hence, for Scotus, within one real thing there are not only a number of distinct formalities or realities, but also a certain order of priority and posteriority obtaining among them. This order is discovered by examining the relations of implication among their formal notions. Hence, there is a priority/posteriority relation based on the essential meanings of two really inseparable entities.

So it is in the case at hand—the order of priority and posteriority between a relation and its foundation. It is a specific case of the general inherence relation which holds between any accident and its substance or any property (*proprium*) and its subject. The inherence relation is a special case of priority/posteriority. In general, the subject is prior to that which inheres. The formal notion of the subject does not logically imply the formal notion of what inheres in it. But not vice versa. As Aquinas had said, the definition of the accidents is incomplete 'because

---

[36] *Ordin.*, ibid., nn. 258–9, 278–80 (vii, pp. 127–8, 138–9); *Lectura*, ibid., nn. 237, 262 (xviii, pp. 79–80, 89); Augustine, *De Trinitate* V, c. 4, n. 5 (P L 42, 913). See also Henry of Ghent, *Summa*, a. 27, q. 1, ad 5 (i, fol. 161 M).
[37] I thank A. B. Wolter, who in personal correspondence was very helpful in commenting on this section dealing with the orders of priority and posteriority.

they cannot be defined without including a subject in their definition'.[38] The nature of an accident is to exist in a substance as in a subject.

Thus, in the case at hand, the formal notion of a foundation does not imply the formal notion of a relation, as 'white' does not imply 'similarity'. But the formal notion of a relation does imply that of a foundation. Hence, the relation is posterior by nature to its foundation.

In summary, the major premiss in (F), namely

(Fi)   If *b* properly inheres in *a*, and *a* cannot exist without *b*, then *b* is really the same as *a*

is defended by (G), relying on the notions of priority and posteriority of natures. As we shall see, (Fi) is also the central premiss in Scotus' defence against the charge of an infinite regress. His reply stands or falls with (Fi). It becomes one focus of William of Ockham's charge that Scotus' position does indeed lead to an infinite regress.

2.2. A Creature and its Relation to God are Formally Distinct

In arguing for his thesis that a creature, e.g. a stone, and its relation to God are formally distinct, Scotus uses his criterion for formal distinction:

> *x* and *y* are formally non-identical or distinct if and only if (a) *x* and *y* are or are in what is really one thing (*res*); and (b) if *x* and *y* are capable of definition, the definition of *x* does not include *y* and the definition of *y* does not include *x*; or if *x* and *y* are not capable of definition, then if they were capable of definition, the definition of *x* would not include *y* and the definition of *y* would not include *x*.[39]

He argues that the *ratio* of something absolute does not include the *ratio* of what is relative nor vice versa.

---

[38] Thomas Aquinas, *On Being and Essence*, c. 6, trans. A. Maurer, 2nd rev. edn. (Toronto, 1968), p. 66.

[39] *Ordin*. I, d. 8, p. 1, q. 4, n. 193 (iv, pp. 261–2). For this formulation of Scotus' formal distinction, see M. Adams, 'Ockham on Identity and Distinction', *Franciscan Studies* 36 (1976), p. 35.

But the *ratio* of absolute is something that is 'to itself' (*ad se*), but the formal *ratio* of relation is a condition 'toward another' (*ad aliud*). But the formal entity [i.e. the extra-mental formality] of what is 'to itself' and what is 'toward another' is not [formally] the same.[40]

Hence, what is absolute, e.g. a substance like a stone, is formally distinct from what is relative, its relation of dependence on God.[41]

This solution has the advantage of avoiding the problems attendant on each of the other rival positions. Since the creature and its relation are really identical, it is not possible that a stone exist without its relation to God. On the other hand, they are not totally identical, so Scotus avoids making creatures essentially relative, thus obliterating their character as absolute.

He accomplishes this by positing in one thing two formalities which can be distinct bearers of incompatible properties, i.e. absolute and relative properties. This is one function of Scotus' formal distinction. In a similar manner, for example, he posits a formal distinction in the Godhead between each divine person and the divine essence. In this way, he hopes to be able to predicate incompatible properties of the one Godhead: the persons are incommunicable and formally

---

[40] *Ordin.* II, d. 1, q. 5, *textus interpolatus* (vii, p. 122). This text is an addition by Scotus himself, and most likely is later than the *Ordinatio*. Also see ibid., nn. 229, 244 (vii, pp. 114–15, 121–2); *Lectura* II, d. 1, q. 5, n. 211 (xviii, p. 70); *Quodl.* q. 3, n. 15 (in n. 81 below), along with *Quodl.* q. 4, n. 16 and q. 6, n. 29 (xii, pp. 102 and 164). In *Quodl.* q. 13 he asks 'whether the acts of knowing and appetition are essentially absolute or essentially relative'. His arguments that they are essentially absolute frequently take the form: If *a* is an essentially absolute entity, then it is not an essentially relative entity; but the acts of intellection and appetition are essentially absolute, being qualities in the soul, therefore they are not essentially relative. See nn. 1, 3–5 (xii, pp. 301–3). In n. 24, he concludes: 'Videtur autem probatum in primo articulo quod [actus cognoscendi] essentialiter includat absolutum et praecipue in prima ratione; igitur videtur quod actus talis non sit essentialiter relativus, sicut per se includens relationem' (xii, p. 337). For Henry of Ghent, see *Quodl.* VII, q. 2: 'Cui enim rei convenit esse in se secundum rationem praedicamenti accidentis absoluti bene potest convenire esse ad aliud secundum praedicamentum relationis' (i, fol. 258 B). See also *Quodl.* V, q. 6 (i, fol. 161 O). This question was increasingly debated in the early fourteenth century. For example, John Quidort in the first question of his first quodlibet (*c.*1304–5) asks whether one and the same thing can have the *ratio* of an absolute and also that of a relative accident. Quidort calls a relation a mode and in general follows Henry of Ghent. See 'The First Quodlibet of Jean Quidort', ed. A. J. Heiman, in *Nine Mediaeval Thinkers*, ed. J. R. O'Donnell (Toronto, 1955), pp. 271–4.

[41] *Ordin.* II, d. 1, q. 5, n. 272 (vii, p. 135); *Lectura* II, d. 1, q. 5, n. 256 (xviii, pp. 86–7). For absolute and relative as disjunctive transcendentals contradictorily opposed, see Wolter, *Transcendentals*, pp. 145, 155–7.

finite, while the divine essence is communicable and formally infinite.

But how are a creature and its relation to God really identical? How are the creature and its dependence relation united? Scotus explains that when one creature contains another by identity, this is because of the perfection of the one containing.[42] For example, because of its perfection, the intellective soul is said by some to contain and be really identical with the vegetative soul. Or because of its perfection, being is said to contain and be really identical with its *passiones*, such as truth, goodness, and unity, though it is formally distinct from them.

This latter remark helps illuminate the real identity of a creature and its relation of dependence on God. Goodness, truth, and unity are proper attributes or *propria* of being. Proper attributes or *propria* are those characteristics of something which are necessarily connected with it, but are not part of its essential definition.[43] That the angles of a triangle are equal in degrees to two right angles is a proper attribute of a Euclidean triangle. Risibility was thought to be a proper attribute of a human being, as also male and female taken disjunctively with respect to animal. The intellect and will were in a way proper attributes of the human soul. The soul, because of its perfection, contains them, and they are formally distinct but really identical with it.[44]

Although Scotus does not explicitly state it, he implies that a creature's relation of dependence on God is like a proper attribute of the creature.[45] Like a proper attribute, this relation does not enter into the essential definition of a creature, e.g. into the essential definition of a stone. Still, the relation is inseparable from it. As being and its *passiones*, and the soul and the intellect and will, so a creature, because of its perfection, contains within it

---

[42] *Ordin.*, ibid., nn. 273–5 (vii, pp. 135–6); *Lectura*, ibid., nn. 257–8 (xviii, pp. 87–8). See also Holzer, 'Zur Beziehungslehre', pp. 43–9.

[43] See Wolter's glossary in *God and Creatures*, p. 494.

[44] *Opus Oxoniensis* II, d. 16, q. un., nn. 17–18: 'Alia sunt contenta in aliquo unitive quasi posteriora, quia quasi passiones continentis, nec sunt res aliae ab ipso continente. Isto modo ens continet multas passiones, quae non sunt res aliae ab ipso ente ... distinguuntur tamen ab invicem formaliter et quidditative, et etiam ab ente. . . . Sic ergo possumus accipere de intellectu et voluntate, quae non sunt partes essentiales animae, sed sunt unitive contenta in anima quasi passiones ejus, propter quas anima est operativa, non quod sint essentia ejus formaliter, sed sunt formaliter distinctae, idem tamen identice et unitive . . .' (vi, pp. 772–3).

[45] See n. 42 above.

its relation to God, and so is really identical with it, though still formally distinct from it.

Furthermore, Scotus insists that the creature's relation does not add any perfection to the creature. He is here concerned to preserve the absolute character of the creature even if it is really identical with its relation of dependence on God: '. . . the foundation is not only the relation (which it contains through identity), but is as absolute as if the relation had been added to it or it had no relation altogether'.[46]

Finally, one sees why Scotus uses the notion of an inseparable accident. On the one hand, he has to avoid totally identifying a creature with its relation, for this makes the creature essentially relative. On the other hand, it is absurd that a creature exist without this relation. So Scotus employs the notion of an inseparable accident, in Aristotelian terms, a proper attribute. It is neither totally identified with the creature, nor separable from it.

3. Against Relations Being Mind-Dependent

Scotus offers four arguments against the view that real relations are mind-dependent and have no extra-mental reality.[47] He argues that this position destroys the unity of the universe:

according to Aristotle, XII *Metaphysics*, the unity of the universe is in the order of the parts to each other and to the first [mover], as the unity of an army is in the order of the parts of the army among themselves and to the leader; and from this, against those denying a relation to be a thing outside the act of the intellect, there can be spoken the saying of the Philosopher, XII *Metaphysics*, that those who so speak, 'make the substance of the universe [to be] disjointed'.[48]

Among others, Ibn Sīnā and Thomas Aquinas had countered with the same basic argument.[49]

[46] *Ordin.* II, d. 1, q. 5, n. 274–5 (vii, p. 136); *Lectura* II, d. 1, q. 5, n. 258 (xviii, p. 88).

[47] *Ordin.*, ibid., nn. 223–7 (vii, pp. 111–13); *Lectura*, ibid., nn. 204–9 (xviii, pp. 67–9). All four arguments are sketched in *In Metaph.* V, q. 11, n. 3 (iv, p. 633).

[48] *Ordin.*, ibid., n. 224 (vii, pp. 111–12); *Lectura*, ibid., n. 205 (xviii, p. 68).

[49] Avicenna, *Philosophia Prima* tract. 3, c. 10: 'Ex hominibus autem quidam fuerunt qui tenuerunt quod certitudo relativorum non est nisi in anima cum intelliguntur res. Et alii dixerunt . . . scimus etiam quod ipsum caelum est super terram et terra est inferius eo, sive apprehendatur sive non, (ed. Van Riet, p. 178). Thomas Aquinas, *De Potentia*, q. 7, a. 9, corp.

Another old argument, found in Simplicius, has to do with mathematics.[50] Many mathematical statements contain relative predicates. But if all relations were mind-dependent, our mathematical knowledge would be radically subjective. As Scotus says in the *Lectura*, all mathematical knowledge would be destroyed. Rather, mathematical proofs demonstrate that real (extramental) subjects possess real (extra-mental) properties, i.e. real mathematical relations.[51]

Scotus' other two arguments are variations of (D) and (E) above, having to do with composition and secondary causality. He argues[52] that all composition requires as a necessary condition a relation of union of the componible parts. But nothing real depends on what is only a being of reason. So if all relations are mind-dependent, and so only beings of reason, there will be no real composition. Like (D), this argument has its roots in Aristotle, who argues that something more than the elements is needed to account for an essential unity.[53]

Scotus' final argument[54] is that the relation of spatial proximity of *b* to *c* is needed for an effect *a*. But, as he argued before, this relation must be something extra-mental, for only by positing some other extra-mental reality can what was once not causally possible become causally possible (Eiv). But if a relation were only a being of reason, it would not be an extra-mental reality. Hence, the relation of spatial proximity is no extra-mental reality, and so secondary causality is impossible.

These arguments help clarify why the subjectivist position on relations was the minority opinion throughout the later Middle Ages. Historically, one finds this position in the Stoics and the Mutakallimūn, and so outside Aristotelianism, Platonism, and Neoplatonism. It would be extremely difficult for a scholastic, given the pervasive Aristotelianism, to deny all extra-mental reality to relations. The scholastics interpreted Aristotle as explicitly teaching that relation is one of the ten categories of extra-mental being. But more fundamentally, his philosophy and

---

[50] Simplicius, *In Aristotelis Categorias Commentarium*, c. 7 (ed. C. Kalbfleisch, p. 169: 13–15); for the medieval Latin translation by William of Moerbeke, see Simplicius, *In Praedicamenta Aristotelis*, c. 7 (ed. A. Pattin and W. Stuyven p. 229: 30–2).

[51] *Ordin.* II, d. 1, q. 5, n. 227 (vii, pp. 112–13); *Lectura* II, d. 1, q. 5, n. 208 (xviii, p. 69).

[52] *Ordin.*, ibid., n. 225 (vii, p. 112); *Lectura*, ibid., n. 206 (xviii, p. 68).

[53] See n. 23 above.

[54] *Ordin.* II, d. 1, q. 5, n. 226 (vii, p. 112); *Lectura* II, d. 1, q. 5, n. 207 (xviii, p. 69).

that of the scholastics is pervaded by the idea of an extra-mental order, whether this be the cosmos of the Greeks or the universe of the medievals. This is reflected in the central place accorded the argument from the unity of the universe for the mind-independent status of real relations. Hence, for most of the scholastics the principal problem was not whether relations had extra-mental reality, but rather what specific type of extra-mental reality was to be accorded them.

4. Scotus' Criticism of Henry of Ghent

In the *Ordinatio*, Scotus does not present Henry of Ghent's theory of relations within the context of Henry's theory of the categories, nor does he relate this to Henry's general ontology of *esse essentiae*. Rather, Scotus presents arguments of varying quality as representative of Henry's position, and he often neglects a number of fine distinctions Henry draws. He simply represents his opponent as holding that a real relation is really identical with its foundation, without the important qualifications that Henry holds them to be intentionally distinct and that a relation is a mode. In Scotus' replies, however, these distinctions do finally surface and provide an opportunity for comparing the competing doctrines. I consider three arguments in turn.

First, against the thesis that a real relation is really other than its foundation, Henry of Ghent had used the old Stoic argument that something is not changed by becoming or ceasing to be really related. Hence, a real relation is no thing. And like others, he used in support the texts from Aristotle's *Physics* which deny that there is any change in the category of relation.[55]

Scotus responds by taking a position similar to that of Richard of Mediavilla. As we have seen, Thomas Aquinas and Giles of Rome agree that

(T8)   *a* comes to be or ceases to be really related to *b* through some change of the foundation that is or is in *a* and/or of the foundation that is or is in *b*

and

(T9)   If the foundation that is or is in *a* changes, then there is a

---

[55] *Ordin.*, ibid., n. 195 (vii, p. 98); *Lectura*, ibid., n. 172 (xviii, p. 57); Henry of Ghent, *Quodl.* VII, qq. 1–2 (i, fol. 255 N).

> change of *a*; but if only the foundation that is or is in *b* changes, there is no change of *a*, for there is no change *in a.*

Scotus, however, disagrees:

> I say that ... with regard to a relation there is change, for it is not intelligible that a new form come to something unless it be changed by that form. And so that to which the new form of relation comes is not changed with respect to itself but with respect to the other [extreme]; and as a form is a being and perfects, so something must be changed by it. And so that to which a relation comes is changed in being 'toward another', such that it is now 'toward another' differently than before; and this is to be changed by a relation.[56]

Scotus believes that in (T9), if only *b*'s foundation changes, *a is* changed, for it gains or loses a real relation, a form that perfects it. He will speak of this form as a relative thing as opposed to an absolute thing like a quantity or a quality.

This is similar to the position of Richard of Mediavilla in his *Sentences* commentary, for both he and Scotus hold that something can undergo change by acquiring or losing a relative thing. But there is a difference between the two positions.

Recall that Richard of Mediavilla denies that real relations inhere. And Richard denies Aquinas'

(T7)   Something changes only if there is a change *in* it

if by 'in' is meant inherence. He substitutes

(T7′)   Something can be accidentally changed by acquiring or losing either (i) an accident which inheres, i.e. an absolute thing, or (ii) an accident which does not inhere, i.e. a relative thing.

This leads him to reject thesis (T9) of Aquinas, and instead hold

(T9′)   If the foundation that is or is in *a* changes, then there is a change of *a*; and if only the foundation that is or is in *b* changes, there is a change of *a*, for *a* acquires or loses a relative thing.

---

[56] *Lectura* II, d. 1, q. 5, n. 214 (xviii, p. 71). See also *Ordin.*, ibid., nn. 234–6 (vii, pp. 117–18); *In Metaph.* V, q. 6, nn. 1–2 (iv, p. 607).

Scotus, on the other hand, holds that real relations inhere,[57] and adopts (T7). Without Richard's complication of non-inhering accidents, Scotus simply holds against Richard's (T7′)

(T7″) Something can be accidentally changed by acquiring or losing an inherent accident whether it be an absolute or relative thing.

And finally, because of (T7″) and not (T7′), Scotus holds with Richard (T9′).

To understand the second argument I am presenting, recall that Henry of Ghent had maintained that if a real relation were really distinct from its foundation, an infinite regress would result.[58] According to Scotus' formulation,

it is argued that if it [i.e. a real relation] were a thing other than the foundation, then there would be an infinite regress in relations. For if that relation [R] is a thing other than the foundation, by the same reason also that otherness (which is a certain relation [R′]) will be a thing other than [its] foundation, and also that otherness [R″] from its foundation, and so to infinity, which is unbefitting.[59]

Like some of his predecessors, Scotus replies by stopping the regress at the first relation R. Others, as Aquinas and Ibn Sīnā, had tried to stop the infinite regress by arguing that a real relation relates by its nature without the need to posit further relational accidents.[60] Neither, however, presents a clear and well-articulated argument for this position; Scotus does provide such an argument. It turns on identifying relation R with its relation R′ of otherness to R's foundation F. Therefore, R is related to F through itself, and no third separate entity need or can be posited to start an infinite regress.

Scotus' argument is as follows:[61]

(H) (i) It is not possible without contradiction that R exists without its foundation F.

---

[57] See n. 81 below. See also *Ordin.*, ibid., n. 237: 'Ad tertium de inesse, concedo quod relatio habet proprium inesse . . .' (vii, p. 118); ibid., n. 222 (vii, p. 110); *Lectura*, ibid., n. 219 (xviii, p. 74).

[58] Henry of Ghent, *Summa*, a. 32, q. 5, corp. (i, fol. 199 O).

[59] *Ordin.* II, d. 1, q. 5, n. 198 (vii, p. 100); *Lectura* II, d. 1, q. 5, n. 182 (xviii, p. 60).

[60] Avicenna, *Philosophia Prima* (ed. Van Riet, pp. 179 f.); Thomas Aquinas, *In I Sent.*, d. 26, q. 2, a. 1, corp.: 'Quarto modo quando ponitur relatio relationis: ipsa enim relatio per seipsam refertur, non per aliam relationem. Unde in creaturis paternitas non conjungitur subiecto per aliquam relationem mediam.'

[61] *Ordin.* II, d. 1, q. 5, n. 239 (vii, p. 119).

(ii) If R and F exist, then a relation of otherness R' to F
exists in R.

(iii) So it is not possible without contradiction that R exists
without R'.

(iv) Therefore, R and R' are really identical.

Conceding (ii), one could question (i) and also inquire into the
assumption behind the inference from (iii) to (iv).

It might be objected against (i) that as it is not contradictory that
an absolute accident exists without a substance, as occurs in
transubstantiation, so it is not contradictory that a relative accident exists without its foundation. But in the third question of his
Quodlibet, Scotus contends that there is an asymmetry between
absolute and relative accidents: (a) if a foundation can exist
without the relation founded on it, the relation is really identical
with its relation of inherence, but really distinct from its foundation, and (b) an absolute accident is really distinct from both its
substance and its relation of inherence.

Both (a) and (b) are established by using the separability
criterion for real distinction.[62] Regarding (b), an absolute accident can and does exist in separation from its substance, as in
transubstantiation.[63] Since it can exist without inhering in a
substance, and so without its relationship of inherence, it is really
distinct from this relationship. Regarding (a), however, Scotus
contends this is not so with relations:

For it is always the case that where something pertains to something else
in such a way that it would be a complete contradiction for the latter to
exist without the former, this former is really identical with the latter.

---

[62] *Quodl.* q. 3, nn. 15–16: 'Sed quaeras de accidentalitate similitudinis, si ipsa est alia a
similitudine. Dico quod non, quia similitudo est sua accidentalitas ad fundamentum et
seipsa accidit fundamento, sicut seipsa est ad oppositum. Universaliter enim quod
convenit alicui sic, quod omnimoda contradictio sit illud esse sine hoc, hoc est idem
realiter illi; et per oppositum, ubi non est omnimoda contradictio, non oportet esse
omnino. Nunc autem contradictio est similitudinem esse et non esse ad fundamentum et
etiam non esse ad terminum. Ideo accidentalitas sua ad fundamentum est idem sibi, sicut
ipsamet est similitudo vel habitudo ad oppositum. Status est ergo, quia accidentalitas
similitudinis non est alia res a similitudine, sed similitudo est quaedam res alia ab albedine,
quia habitudo et etiam accidentalitas albedinis potest poni quaedam res alia ab albedine,
quia albedo est quaedam res absoluta, et accidens absolutum potest esse sine contradictione sine subiecto' (xii, pp. 81–2).

[63] See Scotus' discussion of separable accidents in transubstantiation, *Opus Oxon.* IV,
d. 12, q. 2 (viii, pp. 728–38, esp. 733–8). Although it is not necessary that absolute
accidents inhere actually, it is necessary that they aptitudinally inhere; see *Opus Oxon.* IV,
d. 12, q. 1, n. 5 (viii, p. 711).

And by contrast, where there is no such contradiction, there is no need for it to exist at all. Now there is a contradiction, however, that there be similarity which is unrelated either to its foundation or to its term. Therefore, its accidentality with reference to the foundation is identical with itself just as its similarity or relationship to its opposite is.[64]

First, it is contradictory for a relation to exist without its foundation, a foundation being one of the necessary conditions for a real relation.[65] A relation's existence depends upon there being two really distinct relata and a real basis or foundation for the relation. If the foundation for the relation does not exist, the relation cannot exist.

Second, he is using a formulation of the principle that we have seen in Section Two, Subsection One:

(Fi)   If *b* properly inheres in *a*, and *a* cannot exist without *b*, then *b* is really the same as *a*.

Here, since the relation of inherence R' 'pertains to' R, and R cannot exist without R', R' is really identical with R.

It might be objected that the shift from 'properly inheres' in (Fi) to 'pertains' (*convenit*) affects the argument. One can see the reason for the shift, for it is surely odd to speak of a relation R' of inherence properly inhering in another relation R. An accident inheres in a substance, but what sense is there in talking of a relation of inherence inhering in another relation? But what, then, is meant by 'pertains'? And (Fi) was supported by argument (G) which works in the argument formulated with 'properly inhering'. It cannot be assumed that it also will support a formulation of (Fi) in terms of 'pertaining'.

Scotus might reply by telling us what he meant by 'pertains'. Lacking that, I would reply that as long as 'pertains', like 'properly inheres', implies that the relation of inherence R' is posterior in nature to R, then the formulation of (Fi) with 'pertains to' can be

---

[64] See n. 62 above.

[65] See n. 5 above. *Opus Oxon*, IV, d. 12, q. 1, n. 5: '. . . contradictio est quod [respectus] sit sine subiecto et hoc actu, ita scilicet quod non actu inhaereat subiecto, extendendo subiectum ad fundamentum quod potest dici proximum subiectum respectus' (viii, p. 711); *Reportatio Paris*. IV, d. 12, q. 1, n. 2: '. . . praemitto unam distinctionem de accidentibus, quia quaedam sunt absoluta, quaedam respectiva. Si enim omnia accidentia essent respectiva, nullum esset, nec esse posset sine subiecto, quia accidentia relativa . . . impossibile et incompossibile est ista esse sine subiecto, quia incompossibile est aliquam relationem esse et non inter extrema ut inter terminos . . .' (xi, p. 677).

supported by (G). And I believe the relation of inherence R'
(though really simultaneous with R) is posterior in nature to R.
The formal notion of similarity does not logically imply the formal
notion of its inhering in something (as most philosophers today
would agree, one need not conceive of similarity as an inhering
accident); but the formal notion of R's inhering does imply the
formal notion of R.

The principle (Fi) is also the assumption behind the inference
from (iii) to (iv) in (H): since by (Hii) the relation R' of otherness
exists in R, and by (Hiii) R cannot exist without R', therefore by
(Fi) R and R' are really identical—and the infinite regress is
stopped.[66]

A third argument Scotus presents is not from Henry of Ghent
but is found repeatedly in the writings of Giles of Rome. It is
intended to show that a real relation cannot be other than its
foundation but is really identical with it: '. . . for a white thing that
is similar is not more composed than what is just white [and not
similar], and so the relation of similarity does not add a thing other
than the foundation; and so neither is it [i.e. a real relation] a thing
other [than its foundation]'.[67]

Oddly, it is in his reply to this argument of Giles of Rome that
Scotus finally discusses Henry of Ghent's real position. Giles's
major, though intuitively plausible, simply begs the question.[68]
Both Scotus and Henry of Ghent would object against Giles that
what is white and similar is indeed more composed than what is
only white. As Scotus says, 'This he [Henry of Ghent] also ought
to concede . . . For he himself concedes that there is never a difference of intention without composition, and that in creatures a relation differs from [its] foundation by a difference of intention.'[69]

---

[66] Scotus again uses (Fi) when he replies to another charge of infinite regress. Scotus
uses this formulation: if *b* formally inheres in *a*, and *a* cannot exist without *b*, then *a* and *b*
are really identical. Since R' inheres in R as in its foundation, and R cannot exist without
R', so they are really identical, and the regress is blocked. See *Ordin.* II, d. 1, q. 5, nn.
268–71 (vii, pp. 133–4); *Lectura* II, d. 1, q. 5, nn. 252–4 (xviii, pp. 85–6).

[67] *Ordin.*, ibid., n. 194 (vii, p. 97); *Lectura*, ibid., n. 216 (xviii, p. 72). For instances of
Giles of Rome's denial that 'aliquid esset compositius ex eo quod est album et simile quam
ex eo quod est album solum', see his *Quodlibet* IV, q. 3 (Louvain, 1646; repr. Frankfurt am
Main, 1966, fol. 206a); *In I Sent.*, d. 29, q. 2 (Venice, 1521, fol. 154ʳ A B); *Egidii Romani in
Libros de Physico Auditu Aristotelis Commentaria* (Venice, 1502, fol. 105ʳᵃ).

[68] *Lectura*, ibid., n. 217 (xviii, pp. 72–3).

[69] *Ordin.* ibid., nn. 232–3 (vii, pp. 116–17). For the intentional distinction involving
some composition, see Henry of Ghent, *Quodl.* V, q. 6, corp. (i, fol. 161 N).

Finally, concerning Henry's doctrine that a real relation is a mode, Scotus responds:

And if still someone heckles that although relations are not formally beings of reason, but something outside the intellect and not the same as the foundation, but not however things other than the foundation, but only proper modes of a thing—this heckling only seems to be fighting over the term 'mode of a thing'.[70]

Scotus can label this merely a verbal dispute since for him one and the same can be called both a thing and a mode.[71] He holds that (i) any categorical being can be called a 'thing', and he seems to hold that (ii) if *a* and *b* are categorical beings, if *b* depends on *a* for its existence, *b* is less perfect than *a*, and if *b* is less perfect than *a*, then *b* is a mode of *a*. So a quality with respect to substance can be called a mode, although it is a true thing. So also a relation with respect to its foundation is a mode. But, Scotus insists, it too is a true thing.

This view is amplified in the third question of his *Quodlibet*. There Scotus explains that the term 'thing' (*res*) has three meanings. Taken most generally a thing or being (*ens*) is anything that is not nothing.[72] This first meaning is subdivided into (a) that which includes no contradiction whether it can exist only in the intellect or also extra-mentally, and (b) that which has or can have existence outside the intellect. With sense (a), the term 'thing' refers to anything that is conceivable, i.e. non-contradictory. Among other things, sense (a) includes all concepts of second intention that refer to other concepts or *entia rationis* as logical entities, conceptual relations, etc. With the narrower sense (b), the term 'thing' refers to all real entities that can or do exist in the real, i.e. extra-mental, world.[73]

The second meaning of 'thing' includes only absolute things, i.e. substances, quantities, and qualities. ' "Thing" taken in this

---

[70] *Ordin.*, ibid., n. 228 (vii, p. 113); *Lectura* II, d. 1, q. 5, n. 210 (xviii, pp. 69–70).

[71] *Ordin.*, ibid. (vii, pp. 113–14).

[72] *Quodl.* q. 3, n. 3: 'Habemus ergo primum membrum sic, scilicet communissime, bipartitum in illud, scilicet, quod non includit contradictionem qualecunque esse habeat, et in illud quod habet, vel habere potest, proprium esse extra intellectum . . .' (xii, p. 67).

[73] Hence, Scotus' division of the meanings of 'thing' differs from Henry of Ghent's at least in this respect: the latter calls contradictory notions as goat-stag 'things', whereas Scotus does not. To be a thing for Scotus implies at least conceivability, i.e. absence of contradictory elements.

second or general sense, therefore, means something absolute in
contrast to a circumstance or mode which expresses a condition
of one to another.'[74] The final and narrowest meaning of 'thing'
includes only substances.[75] Scotus summarizes: 'Therefore the
first or broadest meaning includes conceptual being and any kind
of real being. The second signifies real and absolute being. The
third sense indicates a being that is real, absolute, and *per se*
existing.'[76]

Scotus contends that a real relation is not a thing in either the
second or third sense. Nor is it only a conceptual being, sense
(1a). But it is a thing in sense (1b), having its own proper entity
outside the soul, an entity which is not absolute but relative.

From what has been said it is clear what kind of thing this relation is. For
if it is a singular thing then it is either absolute or relative. Formally it is a
thing to another [i.e. a relative]. Nor does this determination 'to another'
militate against this meaning of 'thing', for this sense of 'thing' is not
contrasted with a mode or condition or circumstance of a thing, but it
covers them all.[77]

In summary: for Scotus, one and the same can be called a thing
and a mode. Calling it a thing stresses that it has its own proper

---

[74] *Quodl.* q. 3, n. 3: '. . . vult [Boethius] ergo distinguere rem contra circumstantiam, et
sic secundum eum sola tria genera, Substantia, Qualitas, et Quantitas rem monstrant, alia
vero rei circumstantias. Hoc ergo nomen *res*, in secundo membro acceptum, dicit aliquod
ens absolutum, distinctum contra circumstantiam sive modum qui dicit habitudinem
unius ad alterum' (xii, p. 67).

[75] Ibid.: 'Ens ergo sive simpliciter sive potissime dictum, et hoc sive sit analogum sive
univocum, accipit ibi Philosophus pro ente cui per se et primo convenit esse, quod est
substantia sola' (xii, p. 68).

[76] Ibid.: 'Sic ergo sub primo membro communisime continentur ens rationis et ens
quodcunque reale. Sub secundo, ens reale et absolutum. Et sub tertio, ens reale et
absolutum et per se ens.'

[77] Ibid: 'Ex ista distinctione patet quod quaestio, si relatio sit res, nullam difficul-
tatem habet de re tertio modo accipiendo, vel secundo modo, quia non est substantia
neque ad se. tantum ergo difficultas est de primo membro, sed nec de ente rationis, quia
patet quod relatio est intelligibilis sine contradictione. Est ergo hic sermo, si habeat esse
sive sit res habens entitatem realem propriam extra animam. Et de hoc dico, quod est res.
Secundo, quae res? Quod autem relatio sit res, probo: habitudo consequens extrema
realia, et realiter distincta, et hoc ex natura rei, est realis, quia entitas eius qualem habet
non est praecise in anima, et per consequens ipsa secundum entitatem propriam est res
suo modo; sed habitudo patris ad filium est talis, ut patet ex secunda quaestione ordinaria.
Ex hoc apparet quae res ipsa sit, quia si sit res singularis, vel est ad se vel ad alterum; ipsa
formaliter est res ad alterum. Nec ista determinatio, ad alterum, repugnat ei, quod est res
isto modo loquendo, quia isto modo res non distinguitur contra modum vel habitudinem
vel circumstantiam rei, sed includit eam.'

extra-mental reality, while calling it a mode emphasizes that it has less reality than that of which it is a mode.[78] This use of 'mode' also clarifies Scotus' frequent remarks that relation is a tiny being.[79]

His explanation of the various ways of taking 'thing' and 'mode' warns us that the differences between him and Henry of Ghent are in fact not merely verbal. Their differences on the specific issue of relation are rooted in their general ontologies. Henry draws a sharp distinction between things properly speaking and modes. Only entities of the first three absolute categories are things properly speaking. Only they have absolute natures, ultimately existing in *esse essentiae*. All other extra-mental entities are modes of these things. For Henry, then, a mode is not defined in terms of dependence and relative perfection, but as a way of existing. The only things in Henry's ontology are absolute things, and they can exist in various ways.

Scotus himself makes it clear that there is a real difference between the two positions. 'And if it is said that the genus of relation is a thing, not because of that mode that is a condition toward another, but because of that thing [i.e. the foundation] to which it pertains to be 'toward another'—this is not true.'[80] Scotus is criticizing Henry's position that the whole reality of a relation is derived from and is really identical with its foundation. The relation, Henry insists, does not have its own existence distinct from that of its foundation. Scotus disagrees and asserts repeatedly that a relation does have its own existence distinct from that of its foundation.[81]

The difference between the two positions can also be seen in

---

[78] See n. 77 above; also *Ordin.* II, d. 1. q. 5, n. 215 (vii, p. 108); *Lectura* II, d. 1, q. 5, n. 198 (xviii, pp. 65–6); *Quodl.* q. 3, n. 9 (xii, p. 76).

[79] *Ordin.*, ibid., n. 240 (vii, p. 119). Also *In Metaph* V. q. 6, n. 14 (iv, p. 612).

[80] *Ordin.*, ibid., n. 229 (vii, p. 114); *Lectura* II, d. 1, q. 5, n. 211 (xviii, p. 70). See also *Quodl.* q. 3, nn. 7–8 (xii, p. 75).

[81] *Ordin.*, ibid., nn. 219–20 (vii, p. 110). That a real relation has its own *esse-in* or accidentality other than that of its foundation, see nn. 222, 237, 238 (vii, pp. 110, 118–19); *Lectura*, ibid., n. 219 (xviii, p. 74). Also *Quodl.* q. 3, n. 15: '. . . concedo tamen quod relatio, quae est accidens in creaturis, propriam habet accidentalitatem, quia illa est per se res et non est illa res in qua fundatur, nec est res per se ens, sicut substantia. Ita oportet dare quod ipsamet per se sit res habens propriam accidentalitatem, quae non sit accidentalitas entis ad se sed accidentalitas entis ad alterum. Sicut enim non est eadem entitas ad se et ad alterum, sic nec eadem accidentalitas accidentis entis ad se et accidentis entis ad alterum' (xii, p. 81).

terms of their different criteria for a real distinction. Scotus'
separability criterion establishes a real distinction between some
relations and their foundations. He uses his criterion to construct
the elegant separation argument (A). The two realities denoted by
'white' and by 'similar' are two things (*res*) which, because they
are separable, are really distinct, each having its own reality.

Henry, on the other hand, offers both metaphysical and physical criteria for a real distinction. Metaphysically, he embeds his
position on relations within his general theory of the categories.
The two realities denoted by 'white' and 'similar' are not two
things, but one is a thing and the other is one of its modes. Since
the only things, metaphysically speaking, are absolute things, and
a real distinction holds only between such things, a foundation
and its relation cannot be really distinct, but are only intentionally
distinct. On the other hand, from the viewpoint of the physicist,
Henry can agree with Scotus' separation argument (A) that there
is a real distinction between a real relation and its foundation if
they are separable.

Without Henry's general ontology based on *esse essentiae*,
Scotus has no reason to refrain from doing what Henry warns
against: calling a real relation not a mode, but a thing, albeit a
relative thing.[82] This relative thing, as in Richard of Mediavilla's
theory, should not be thought of on the model of a little substance.
Both Richard and Scotus held that a real relation adds no
absolute thing to its subject, but only a relative thing. And both
talk of this relative thing as a condition (*habitudo*). But there is a
difference in their conception of this relative thing. Richard of
Mediavilla distinguishes absolute and relative accidents in terms
of the former inhering and the latter not inhering in their
foundations. Scotus, on the other hand, believes that a real
relation does inhere in its foundation; it has its own accidental
reality really distinct from that of its foundation.

Of all the thinkers considered so far, Scotus accords the
most ontological status to a real relation. He becomes the chief
representative in the fourteenth century of the strongly realist
position. Further, because of the battery of arguments he uses to
criticize others and to defend his own solution, he sets the stage

---

[82] *Ordin.* II, d. 1, q. 5, n. 215 (vii, p. 108). Cf. Henry of Ghent, *Summa*, a. 55, q. 6 (ii,
fols. 111 f.).

for the fourteenth-century debate on relations. Many of his successors will construct theories in support of or in opposition to his theory. And finally, as we have seen, his complex and rich teaching on relation is dependent upon particular tenets of his philosophy: the formal distinction in real identity, the separability criterion for a real distinction, and the notions of priority and posteriority of nature. To the degree that Scotus' successors reject these, to that degree will they reject his solution and seek other means of understanding what sort of being is to be accorded relations.

6

Relation as Condition

HENRY OF HARCLAY

HENRY OF HARCLAY (*c.*1270–1317) can perhaps rightly be called the first Scotist.[1] He had read the *Sentences* in Paris around 1300, at the time when Duns Scotus was teaching there, and this early influence is seen in Harclay's own commentary on the first book of the *Sentences*.[2] A later work, a series of questions, has been preserved in which he shows more independence and maturity.[3] This pattern of early dependence on Scotus and later independence is evidenced in his changing position on divine prescience

[1] For Henry of Harclay's life and works, and an overview of his philosophy in his Questions, see F. Pelster, 'Heinrich von Harclay, Kanzler von Oxford und seine Quästionen', *Miscellanea Francesco Ehrle*, i (Studi e Testi, 37; Rome, 1924), pp. 307–56; A. B. Emden, *A Biographical Register of the University of Oxford to A.D. 1500*, ii (Oxford, 1958), pp. 874–5; and references to Harclay in J. I. Catto (ed.), *The Early Oxford Schools* (The History of the University of Oxford, 1; Oxford, 1984). A. Maurer has edited a number of Harclay's Questions and has helped uncover Harclay's doctrine on a number of issues; see A. Maurer, 'Henry of Harclay's Question on the Univocity of Being', *Mediaeval Studies* 16 (1954), pp. 1–18; 'Henry of Harclay's Questions on Immortality', ibid. 19 (1957), pp. 79–107; 'Henry of Harclay's Questions on the Divine Ideas', ibid. 23 (1961), pp. 163–93; 'St. Thomas and Henry of Harclay on Created Natures', in *III Congresso internazionale di filosofia medioevale* (Milan, 1966), pp. 542–9; 'Henry of Harclay's Disputed Question on the Plurality of Forms', in *Essays in Honor of Anton Charles Pegis*, ed. J. R. O'Donnell (Toronto, 1974), pp. 125–59. In addition to the Question used as the basis for this chapter (see n. 5 below), I have edited two Questions: 'Henry of Harclay's Questions on Divine Prescience and Predestination, *Franciscan Studies* 40 (1980), pp. 167–243; 'Henry of Harclay on the Formal Distinction in the Trinity', ibid. 41 (1981), pp. 250–335. See also G. Gál, 'Henricus de Harclay: Quaestio de Significato Conceptus Universalis', ibid. 31 (1971), pp. 178–234; R. C. Dales, 'Henricus de Harclay: Quaestio "Utrum mundus potuit fuisse ab eterno"', *Archives d'histoire doctrinale et littéraire du Moyen Âge* 50 (1983), pp. 223–55; id., Henry of Harclay and the Infinite', *Journal of the History of Ideas* 45 (1984), pp. 295–301.

[2] The commentary is found in two codices: Vatican Library Lat. 13687, fols. 13ᵛ–97ᵛ, and Casale Monferrato, Biblioteca del Seminario Vescovile MS b 2, fols. 1ʳ–84ʳ. See C. Balić, 'Henricus de Harcley et Ioannes Duns Scotus', *Mélanges offerts à Étienne Gilson* (Toronto and Paris, 1959), pp. 93–121, 701–2.

[3] These Questions are found in three codices: Vatican Library Borghese 171, fols. 1ʳ–32ᵛ; Worcester, Cathedral Library F. 3, fols. 181ᵛ–215ᵛ; Assisi, Biblioteca Comunale

and predestination.[4] A similar pattern emerges in his handling of the problem of relations. In his *Sentences* commentary he follows Scotus in adopting a strongly realist position on real categorical relations, but in a lengthy later *Quaestio* he argues against this view and devotes much energy to defending his own position, one closer to that of William of Ockham.[5] Furthermore, Harclay is not afraid to take the non-traditional position that God is really related to creatures.

1. Harclay's Early Theory of Relations

As in his later Question on relations, Harclay asks in his earlier *Sentences* commentary whether there is in God a real relation to a creature.[6] In this context he discusses the ontological status of relations. He criticizes arguments offered by Henry of Ghent and Duns Scotus that God cannot be really related to creatures and then presents his own reason for this traditional opinion.

In the course of the discussion in his *Sentences* commentary, it becomes clear that although Harclay may object to certain specific arguments of Duns Scotus, he has the same ontology of relations. For example, he says it is false that a real relation can come to something without any change:

when it is said that a real relation can come to something without its changing, I say that if by change is understood all newness, the

172, fols. 125^r–131^v, 133^r–136^r, 149^r–153^v. For further information on these and other smaller Questions of Harclay in various manuscripts, see G. Gál, 'Quaestio de Significato', pp. 178–9. V. Doucet, 'Descriptio codicis 172 Bibliothecae Communalis Assisiensis', *Archivum Franciscanum Historicum* 35 (1932), pp. 502–4, notes that on fols. 116^v–117^v of this codex is found a chain of axioms dealing with relations entitled 'Fundamenta et propositiones notabiles Arcelini'. C. Balić has examined in detail whether the Arcelinus in question could be Harclay; in the Vatican edition of Duns Scotus' *Opera Omnia*, see Balić's 'Adnotationes . . . circa *Ordinationem* I. Duns Scoti' (Vatican iv, p. 32*, n. 1). I hope to do a study of this Assisi text at a later date.

[4] See M. Henninger, 'Questions on Divine Prescience', pp. 167–243.
[5] Henry's Question is found in only one codex: Vatican Library Borghese 171, fols. 3^v–7^v: 'Utrum Dei ad creaturam sit relatio realis.' The citations of it in my notes refer to the numbered paragraphs in my edition 'Henry of Harclay's Question on Relations', *Mediaeval Studies* 49 (1987), pp. 76–123.
[6] Henry of Harclay, *In I Sent.*, 'Utrum in Deo sit aliqua relatio realis ad creaturam' (Casale Monferrato MS b 2, fols. 67^{v}b–68^{v}b).

proposition is false, because a real relation is some thing although it is not an absolute [thing]. So if white Socrates is brought into being, some new thing is created in white Plato because similarity [is created] which is a true thing in the category of real relation.[7]

A relation, then, is not an absolute thing, but a relative thing that changes that to which it comes and makes its foundation more 'composite'.[8] In short, the early Harclay along with Duns Scotus believes a real categorical relation is an extra-mental relative thing that inheres in its foundation. Along with Scotus Harclay holds

(T7″)   Something can be accidentally changed by acquiring or losing an inherent accident whether it be an absolute or relative thing

and

(T9′)   If the foundation that is or is in *a* changes, then there is a change of *a*; and if only the foundation that is or is in *b* changes, there is a change of *a*, for *a* acquires or loses a relative thing.

This ontology is also behind Harclay's early acceptance of the knower–known relations as non-mutual. 'The known is not really referred to the occurrent act of knowledge . . . because altogether no thing is posited in the known by the fact that it comes to be known.'[9] This is so because the act of knowing is immanent in the knower and does not affect the thing known. Similarly, God is not

---

[7] Harclay, *In I Sent.*: '. . . cum dicitur relatio realis potest advenire alicui sine sui mutatione, dico quod si per mutationem intellegitur omnis novitas, falsa est propositio, quia relatio realis aliqua res est, etsi non sit absoluta. Ideo cum Socrates albus generatur, aliqua [aliter *MS*] res nova creatur in Platone albo quia similitudo, quae est vera res de genere relationis realis' (fol. 68ᵛa).

[8] Harclay, ibid.: '. . . dico quod necessitas praecise non excludit relationem realem, sed necessitas essendi cum simplicitate [Dei] excludit relationem novam quia illa faceret compositionem' (fol. 68ᵛb).

[9] Harclay, ibid.: 'Dicis saltem posita creatura necessario simpliciter est relatio Dei ad eam et relatio est magis realis. Dico quod non sequitur, quia plus requiritur, quia novitas realis in altero extremo; ideo scitum non refertur realiter ad scientiam, etsi posito uno ponitur reliquum, quia nulla res omnino ponitur in scito, per hoc, quod scientia cadit super ipsum' (fol. 68ᵛa–b). Also: '. . . etsi posito scito, necessario ponitur scientia et e contrario, tamen nulla res nova causatur in scito ex eo quod de non-scito sit scitum' (fol. 68ᵛa).

really related to creatures, because no new thing can be posited in God who is a necessary being and absolutely simple.[10] For Harclay, then, maintaining the traditional theological position that God is not really related to creatures depends on the viability of his and Scotus' ontology of categorical relations.[11]

In his later Question he rejects this ontology, but already in the *Sentences* commentary he is an independent critic of Scotus. Not only does he reject arguments of the Subtle Doctor, but at one point he proposes that it is sufficient for a real relation that *a* and *b* be really distinct and *a* have a condition by which it is apt to be referred to *b*.[12] His expression is not clear, and he does not elaborate on the ontological status of this condition (*habitudo*). But it exists in such a way that something can become really related without any change.[13] This line of thought is similar to his later theory in which a real relation is a mind-independent condition of one thing toward another, in no way changing its subject. Hence, God could become really related to creatures without any change. In his *Sentences* commentary, however, Harclay finally rejects these momentary innovative suggestions, reverting to his Scotistic ontology when he explains his own position, as outlined above.

---

[10] Harclay, ibid.: 'Dico ergo quod causa per se quare non est relatio realis Dei ad creaturas est illa quae dependet ex duabus propositionibus. Probatio. Una est: illa relatio non posset esse aeterna, quia res non est aeterna; ergo esset nova. Secunda propositio est: illa relatio si esset in Deo esset idem realiter, etsi non quidditative, cum Deo. Ex his duabus sequitur quod aliquid idem Deo sit novum, et per consequens non esse necesse. Consequens est falsum, non minor, ergo maior. Minor propositio probatur per divinam simplicitatem, sed falsitas conclusionis probatur per divinam necessitatem. Et hoc modo pertinet necessitas divina ad illam deductionem: quia quidquid est idem realiter cum Deo, est simpliciter necesse esse et aeternum' (fol. 68ᵛa). Cf. Duns Scotus, *Ordinatio* I, d. 30, q. 1–2, nn. 49–51 (Vatican vi, p. 192).

[11] Harclay, *In I Sent.*: 'Si ergo dicatur quod relatio non addit novam rem super fundamentum (relatio dico [addit] novam [rem]) non in Deo quod possit prohiberi quin Dei ad creaturam esset relatio realis, quia nihil aliud obstaret' (Casale Monferrato MS b 2, fol. 68ᵛb). I find the reading difficult; the sense, however, is that if a relation were not a thing added to the foundation, then there would be nothing to stop us from holding that God is really related to creatures.

[12] Harclay, ibid.: 'Et plus non requiritur ad relationem realem nisi quod posito uno extremo subiecto habitudine quam habet secundum quam natum est referri ad illud, et aliud ex hoc necessario ponitur, est relatio realis' (fol. 68ᵛa).

[13] Harclay, ibid.: 'Confirmatur: nova relatio realis potest convenire alicui sine sui mutatione. Sed non repugnaret Deo passio nisi propter mutationem et propter novitatem quam ponit in Deo. Et iam patet quod illud non obstat; ergo esset relatio realis.'

2. Harclay's Later Theory of Relations

In his *Quaestio*, Harclay is quite clear that his changed opinion on the theological problem is dependent on his new theory of relation:

it seems to me that it is not inconsistent that God have a real relation to a creature. I argue thus with common arguments that I do not know how to solve: nothing new is incompatible with God that does not bring about any change or newness in the divine nature. . . . But a new real relation, if it came to God, would posit no new change [nor] any newness in the divine nature, as I will prove. Therefore, it is not incompatible [with God that he become newly really related to a creature]. Proof of the minor: a real relation coming anew to a creature changes nothing concerning that nature, nor brings about any newness in that creature; and so much less in God if it came to [God]. The inference is plain: [for] that which is apt to bring about a change is more able to change that which is apt to be changed, as a creature, than that which is not apt to be changed, as is God. Now the proof of the antecedent—that a new [real] relation makes no change in a creature that comes to be related [by it]—[is] by the common way: Aristotle, in *V Physics*, proved that with respect to relation there is no *per se* motion, arguing thus: 'For it happens', he says, 'that while one thing is changed, the other is changed in nothing.' And yet that second thing takes on a new [real] relation; therefore a new [real] relation [comes to be] without any new change [in its subject].[14]

Harclay's new position, then, relies on the argument: nothing is incompatible with God unless it effects some change in Him. But if a new real relation came to God, it would not effect any change in Him. So, there is no reason why God cannot become newly really related to creation. Harclay uses or refers to this argument repeatedly throughout the question.[15]

The major is proved by an appeal to the authority of Anselm.[16] What is of more interest is the minor. It is shown by an *a fortiori* argument: if a creature can become newly really related without its being changed, how much more so God whose nature is immutable. The assumption that creatures can become newly really related without changing in any way is supported by the now familiar text from Aristotle's *Physics*: 'In respect of Substance

---

[14] Harclay, 'Henry of Harclay's Question on Relations', ed. Henninger, n. 9.
[15] See ibid., nn. 33, 40, 48, 56, 66, 100.   [16] Ibid., n. 16.

there is no motion, because Substance has no contrary among things that are. Nor is there motion in respect of Relation: for it may happen that when one correlative changes, the other can truly be said not to change at all, so that in these cases the motion is accidental.'[17]

Harclay uses this to support the main theses of his new ontology of categorical real relations. They are the principal theses of Thomas Aquinas' position:

(T7) Something changes only if there is a change *in* it if by 'in' is meant inherence;

(T8) *a* comes to be or ceases to be really related to *b* through some change of the foundation that is or is in *a* and/or of the foundation that is or is in *b*

and

(T9) If the foundation that is or is in *a* changes, then there is a change of *a*; but if only the foundation that is or is in *b* changes, there is no change of *a*, for there is no change *in* *a*.[18]

As we have seen, the intuition that things are not changed by becoming really related was widespread and strong. According to Sextus Empiricus, the Stoics used it to support their belief that all relations are subjective and do not have any existence outside the mind.[19] This is not Harclay's position, but he uses the same intuition to argue for a different conclusion: real categorical relations are not relative things really distinct from and inhering in their foundations.

By adopting (T7), (T8), and (T9) in place of (T7″) and (T9′), Harclay has reversed his position from that of his early agreement with Scotus in the *Sentences* commentary. To understand better the reasons for this change, I first investigate and evaluate his criticism of his early ontology of relation and then consider his new theory.

2.1. Criticism of Harclay's Early Theory

Harclay gives two types of arguments against the strongly realist ontology of relations. In the first, which seems to be original with

---

[17] Aristotle, *Physics* V, c. 2 (225^{b}10–14).
[18] Harclay, 'Question', n. 40. Also nn. 9–15a, 33.   [19] See n. 20 of ch. 1.

Harclay, he cleverly turns the separation argument back on its proponents. In the second, he presses the argument that the ontology of the strongly realist position commits one to an infinite regress.

2.1.1. *The Separation Argument* Bis

Recall that Scotus had used the following separation argument:

(A) (i) If *a* is identical with *b*, then it is contradictory that *a* exist but not *b*.
    (ii) In many cases of a relation R and its foundation F, it is not contradictory that F exist but not R.
    (iii) Therefore, in many cases of a relation R and its foundation F, R is not identical with F.

Harclay agrees with his opponent that it is possible that a white thing *a* exist without a relation R of similarity. But if this is true of one white thing *a*, it is certainly also true of another white thing *b*. But then it is logically possible (as Harclay says, through God's power) that two white things both exist without any real relations of similarity, which is absurd.[20]

Harclay records a reply: 'It is said to this that it does not follow. For something [i.e. a relation of similarity] is necessary in this white [*a*] when there is posited another white [*b*] that is not necessary in it [*a*], the other white [*b*] not posited.'[21]

One can interpret this response as drawing attention to Leibniz's distinction between possibility and compossibility. Hintikka expresses this distinction by comparing

(a) $M(\exists x)Ax \;\&\; M(\exists x)Bx$

and

(b) $M((\exists x)Ax \;\&\; (\exists x)Bx)$

where M = 'it is possible that'. (a) says that substances of kind A are possible and that substances of kind B are possible. (b) says that substances of both kinds can coexist.[22]

---

[20] Harclay, 'Question', n. 18.
[21] Ibid., n. 19.
[22] J. Hintikka, 'Leibniz on Plenitude, Relations and the "Reign of Law"', in *Leibniz: A Collection of Critical Essays*, ed. H. G. Frankfurt (New York, 1972), pp. 159–60. See also D. Wong, 'Leibniz's Theory of Relations', *The Philosophical Review* 89 (1980), pp. 251–3.

It might be argued that with non-relational monadic predicates (a) entails (b), possibility entails compossibility. For ((∃x)Ax & (∃x)Bx) is satisfiable if and only if (∃x)Ax and (∃x)Bx are both separately satisfiable. But in certain cases of complex, relational predicates this is not so. 'There exists everybody's master' and 'There exists nobody's slave' are separately satisfiable but incompatible.

So also here: 'There exists a white thing *a* without a relation of similarity R' and 'There exists a white thing *b* without a relation of similarity R'' are separately satisfiable but incompatible. In sum, the response to Harclay's argument would be: Scotus' doctrine of the possibility of separability (R from *a*) does not commit him to the compossibility of separability (R from *a* and R' from *b*).

This is also consistent with another aspect of Scotus' philosophy, the distinction between intrinsic and extrinsic advenience which distinguishes the category of relation from the other relative categories.[23] Things of the category of relation are intrinsically advenient in that the real existence of the really distinct relata and that of their foundations are necessary and sufficient conditions for the existence of the relation. This is not the case with the last six relative categories, as action and passion, etc. These he calls extrinsically advenient, because the relation does not necessarily arise given the relata and their foundations, but an additional extrinsic factor is required. For example, the existence of the agent and the patient and the foundations, i.e. the active and passive potencies, though necessary is not sufficient for an action and passion. In addition, some extrinsic factor is necessary, e.g. volition in a free agent, the lack of impeding factors, or spatial proximity. Hence, since things in the category of relation are intrinsically advenient, if two things actually white are posited, Scotus is committed to holding that necessarily there exist real relations of similarity.

Harclay agrees that two white things cannot both exist without the relations of similarity.[24] But he questions whether this is consistent with another part of Scotus' thought, the doctrine of natural priority and posteriority.

---

[23] See Scotus, *Opus Oxon.* IV, d. 13, q. 1, nn. 9–11 (viii, p. 791); d. 6, q. 10, nn. 3–4 (viii, pp. 351–2).

[24] Harclay, 'Question', nn. 22, 24–7.

the precise cause why a whiteness is able to exist without similarity is because it is prior by nature to that [similarity], or at least [natural priority is] a sufficient cause. For any prior absolute thing does not depend on anything posterior by nature for [its] being. Therefore, that which does not remove from this whiteness its priority with respect to another, does not prevent its [i.e. the whiteness's] being able to exist without that. But [another] white thing [*b*] caused just now does not remove from this white thing [*a*] that the whiteness [in *a*] be prior to the relation, i.e. the similarity [in *a*]. Therefore, because of this it is not prevented that the whiteness [in *a*] is able to exist without the similarity [in *a*] even with the other whiteness [in *b*] posited.[25]

Hence, according to Scotus' doctrine of natural priority and posteriority, *a* and *b* could exist simultaneously and *a* exist without its naturally posterior relation R of similarity to *b*. This Harclay finds absurd, and he could also point out that it is inconsistent with Scotus' doctrine of relations as intrinsically advenient.

Scotus could reply that Harclay has equated natural priority and posteriority with separability, as if from the fact that *a* is naturally prior to *b* one can conclude that *a* can exist without *b*. This is not Scotus' notion of natural priority and posteriority which, as noted in Chapter Five, is used in widely differing contexts. For example, the creature and its relation of dependence on God are really identical but formally distinct. In addition, the creature is naturally prior to its relation of dependence: the formal notion of any creature, say a stone, does not imply the formal notion of its relation to God; but not vice versa. Still they are inseparable. In short, for Scotus natural priority and posteriority do not imply separability. So Scotus would agree that the foundation *a* is naturally prior to R: the formal notion of R entails that of *a* its foundation, but not vice versa. This remains true, as Harclay has seen, whether *b* exists or not. But Scotus would deny Harclay's premiss that the natural priority of *a* with respect to R is a sufficient condition for *a*'s being able to exist without R.

Given this response, then, Harclay's clever argument fails to uncover incoherence in Scotus' theory of relations, either with his doctrine of priority and posteriority of natures or with his doctrine that relations are intrinsically advenient.

[25] Harclay, 'Question', n. 20.

In his Question, Harclay has his opponent take a second line of defence. His opponent defends the conclusion that two white things can exist without being really related to each other by similarity. With the courage of his convictions, he maintains that although there are two white things each without a real relation to the other, they are still similar. Harclay immediately replies that a real relation is intrinsically advenient: it arises necessarily with the positing in reality of the extremes with the foundations. So, if two white things are posited in reality, necessarily there will be real relations of similarity.[26]

The opponent tries to deny this last inference.[27] Take an example from Aristotle's second type of relations, those founded on things acting and being acted upon. *a* is fire, *b* is wood; R is the relation of burning, R' is the relation of being burned. It is true that if *a* and *b* both exist and are disposed to act and be acted upon, i.e. in close proximity, etc., then R and R' will follow. But this is a contingent fact based on the common law of nature. Since the denial of this law does not involve a contradiction, and so is logically possible, God can contravene this law. He can cause a miracle such that although *a* and *b* exist and are disposed to act and be acted upon, R and R' do not follow, since the action does not occur. This in fact happened, the objector reminds Harclay, as recorded in the Book of Daniel with the three youths in the fiery furnace.

So also with relations of Aristotle's first type. It is logically possible that two white things exist and though similar are not really related. And this is the case even if according to the common natural course of events it happens that two white things are always really related.

This strange argument is interesting in showing the ways in which the doctrine of God's absolute power was beginning to be put to use in the early fourteenth century. The suggestion is that it is only by God's ordained natural order that a real relation, an extra-mental relative thing, always inheres in those things which are similar. But remarkably, it is logically possible that two things be similar and not be really related, i.e. not possess these relative extra-mental things.

Harclay disagrees.[28] There is a difference between the two

---

[26] Ibid., n. 22.   [27] Ibid., n. 23.   [28] Ibid., nn. 24–5.

types of relations distinguished by Aristotle. Regarding those of the first type, he maintains one cannot hold that the two white things are similar, but not really related. This is to say that similarity is not a relation, which is absurd. Also, all agree that if two white things exist, even God cannot bring it about that they are not similar. What, then, of this similarity? If it is a relation, this is Harclay's conclusion. If it is some absolute thing, then it would be possible for it to exist alone, without its co-relative or the other white thing, which is simply impossible.

Regarding relations of the second type, Harclay continues, the action of burning and the passion of being burned are to be sharply distinguished from the relations of burning and being burned.

For the relation of what is active to what is passive or of an agent to a patient is not an action or a passion; indeed it [i.e. the relation] is of another category and posterior, founded upon action and passion (or at least upon passion), so that that relation necessarily presupposes action and passion already posited in being upon which it [i.e. the relation] may be founded or by which it may be founded; so that, in any case, the action posited in being is a necessary condition of the foundation of the relation in so far as it founds the relation. So even if God is able to make an agent and a patient without making the action, still with the action of the agent and the passion of the patient posited, it is impossible that [the agent and patient] exist without the relation of the agent and of the patient.[29]

In sum, as it is logically impossible that two white things exist without being really related by similarity, so also it is logically impossible that burning and being burned take place without the relations founded on them.

I think Scotus would agree with Harclay's response. In *Collatio* thirty-four the question is asked, 'Whether the relation of a creature to God be really that essence of the creature or a thing other than the essence of the creature.'[30] At one point in the argument, the text reads:

[29] Harclay, 'Question', n. 27.
[30] Duns Scotus, *Collationes seu Disputationes Subtilissimae, Collatio* 34 (Wadding iii, pp. 415–17). The commission editing Scotus' works has not yet attempted to determine the nature of these disputations. They may be a record of student exercises conducted in the Franciscan study house at Oxford, in which opponents and respondents were students and Scotus played the role of master. In this collation, as in many others, no definitive determination or answer to the question is presented. I thank A. B. Wolter for cautioning me about its authenticity and suggesting the interpretation of this particular passage.

For example, given the existence of two white things, immediately from the nature of the extremes the relation of similarity arises. Nevertheless, the nature of both white things can be understood and could exist by the power of God without there being the actual relation of similarity; and in this case similarity would be posterior naturally to the nature of the extremes, because it is an effect of the two extremes; however, it can neither by understood nor exist without the aptitudinal relation of similarity that stems, I believe, from whatever the potency, unless God were to change the nature of the white things and then they would not be white, because *ex natura rei* they are apt by nature to be the total cause of the similarity.[31]

If this passage does indeed reflect Scotus' own views, the first sentence tells us what we already knew of his opinion: things in the category of relation are intrinsically advenient. Scotus never claims that God could cause two actually white things to exist without their relations of similarity. But his claim here parallels Harclay's point regarding causal relations. According to some medieval theories of how colour is produced on an illuminated surface, the actual whiteness (or whatever colour) is an effect that is produced primarily by the nature of the body that is illuminated. It is this nature, or more precisely one of its active potencies, that is the principal cause of the effect, the colour. This effect, the colour, is really distinct from its cause and so separable. In this passage the author argues that this cause can exist without its effect. God, by a miracle, i.e. by not co-operating with the natural causal powers of the active potency, could prevent the colour from arising even as the body is struck with light. In this case, though struck with light, the body would not be white.

Through God's power, then, it is possible for two existing things having a white nature not to be actually similar. They would be of a white nature since they would have the active potencies to become white when struck with light (as opposed to the active potencies to become blue when struck with light). But

---

[31] Scotus, *Collationes*, 34: 'Exemplum: positis duobus albis statim ex natura extremorum oritur relatio similitudinis; et tamen posset natura utriusque albi intelligi et esse per potentiam Dei sine relatione actuali similitudinis; et ibi similitudo est posterior naturaliter natura extremorum, quia effectus eorum, nec tamen potest intelligi nec esse sine relatione similitudinis aptitudinali per quamcunque credo potentiam, nisi Deus mutaret alborum naturam et tunc non essent alba, quia ex natura rei sunt apta nata ut sint totalis causa similitudinis' (iii, pp. 416–17).

they would not be actually white, through God's miraculous intervention. Nevertheless, if they were to become white, then the actual relations of similarity would arise, relations of similarity being intrinsically advenient. Scotus would concur, then, with Harclay's response in his Question.

The passage in the *Collatio* also claims that God could not do away with the 'aptitudinal relation of similarity'. This aptitudinal relation is present in the active potency which is really identical with but formally distinct from the nature itself. Hence, if God destroyed that potency, He would be changing the nature of the white thing itself. So, although God miraculously can prevent the object when struck with light from actually becoming white (and so becoming actually similar), He cannot change the active potency (and aptitudinal relation) without changing the nature of the thing.

2.1.2. *Charge of an Infinite Regress*

Against the view that a real relation is an extra-mental relative thing really distinct from, but inhering in, its foundation, Harclay also argues that this thesis implies an infinite regress. He gives two such arguments, one leading to an infinite regress of foundations,[32] and the other leading to an infinite regress of relations.[33] Each infinite regress implies a simultaneously existing actual infinity of real things, which was commonly held to be impossible.

The second version runs as follows.[34] Take two really distinct things *a* and *b*. On the strongly realist position, if *a* is really distinct from *b*, then there would be some thing R, a real relation of distinction, really distinct from but inhering in *a*. But since R is really distinct from *a*, R is also really related to *a*. But then there must be some thing R′, a real relation of distinction, really distinct from but inhering in R. Hence, either there will be an infinite regress, or one will finally come to admit that something is really related to another, not through some third thing, but through itself.

The response of Harclay's opponents is disappointing. His opponent replies that identity and distinction are similar: as *a* is

---

[32] Harclay, 'Question', nn. 21, 28–9.
[33] Ibid., nn. 30–1.
[34] Ibid., n. 30.

identical with *a* without a relation R″, so *a* is distinct from *b* without R. There is no third thing to generate the infinite regress.[35]

Although Harclay would agree that there is no third thing, he does not agree with the alleged symmetry between identity and distinction.

That which is proposed, however, concerning identity is not to the question. For it is true that real identity is not a real relation since it lacks one condition of a relation that is necessary to a relation and impossible to the same [thing] and to identity, namely, a real distinction of extremes. And that [i.e. real distinction] is in distinct [things] and not in [what is] the same and one. So distinction is a relation but identity [is] not.[36]

It is for this reason that there is no R″ distinct from *a* by virtue of which *a* is identical with itself. But with real distinction this is not the case, for no reason has been given why it should not involve a real relation. There is certainly a real distinction of extremes. Indeed Harclay maintains that real distinction is a real relation. If so, then for the strong realist it is really distinct from its foundation and the infinite regress begins again. (Harclay himself, like Ockham, believes that a thing is both identical with itself and distinct from others through itself and not through something other than itself.)[37]

Harclay does not treat Scotus' main defence against the charge that his position involves an infinite regress, namely (H) supported by (F) and (G). Scotus would construct an argument in reply to Harclay showing that R′ is identical with R:

(i)   It is not possible without contradiction that R exist without its foundation *a*.

(ii) If R and *a* exist, then a relation of distinctness R′ to *a* exists in R.

(iii) So it is not possible without contradiction that R exist without R′. (i, ii)

(iv) If R′ properly inheres in R, and R cannot exist without R′, then R′ is really identical with R.

---

[35] Ibid., n. 31.

[36] Ibid., n. 32.

[37] Ibid., n. 21. William of Ockham, *Ordinatio* I, d. 2, q. 2 (*Opera Theologica*, vol. ii, ed. S. Brown and G. Gál (St Bonaventure, NY, 1970), p. 63).

(v) But R' properly inheres in R, and R cannot exist without
     R'. (ii, iii)
(vi) So R' is really identical with R. (iv, v)

and the infinite regress is stopped.

The crucial premiss (iv) is an instance of premiss (i) of
argument F, which had been supported by (G) using the notions
of natural priority and posteriority. These are the arguments and
notions that need to be examined and were finally examined by
William of Ockham. In summary, Harclay is not successful in
challenging Scotus' separation argument nor in pressing the
charge of an infinite regress.

2.2. Harclay's Later Theory of Categorical Real Relations

In considering Harclay's mature theory, I treat two questions:
first, what is it for two things to be really related, that is, what are
the truth conditions for sentences of the form 'aRb'? Second,
what is a real relation, that is, what are the truth conditions for
sentences of the form 'R-ness exists'?

What is it for two things to be really related? For Harclay,
sentences of the form 'aRb' are true if and only if (i) a and b are
really distinct extra-mental things, (ii) there is a real foundation in
a for R to b, and (iii) there exists a non-inhering condition in a
toward b. Two points should be noted: there is no need to posit a
third thing really distinct from, but inhering in, a; and the
condition of a's being related to b is mind-independent.

To illustrate this, Harclay uses the example of the sentence
'Socrates is seen by an ox'. This humble example is well chosen.
Socrates is the thing sensed and the ox is the one sensing. It is a
clear case of Aristotle's third type of relations. Recall that for a
number of scholastics, the one knowing or sensing is really related
to the known or sensed, while the latter is related to the former
only by a relation of reason. As mentioned earlier, Christian
theologians such as Thomas Aquinas and Duns Scotus had
seized on this third type of Aristotelian relation as a model for the
God–creature relations. A creature is really related to God, but
God is only related by reason to it.

Harclay breaks with tradition and maintains that God is really
related to creatures, but this no more implies a change in God
than Socrates' being seen by an ox implies a change in Socrates.

In effect, Harclay argues that the sentence 'Socrates is seen by an ox' has a logical structure different from 'Socrates is six feet tall' or 'Socrates is white'. The truth conditions for the latter sentences are that Socrates exist and that there exist an absolute thing (as specified in each sentence) inhering in Socrates. But this is not the case with all affirmative categorical sentences. This is one of the keys to Harclay's position: predicates behave in logically different ways, since there are different types of accidents. As he says '. . . among the nine accidents there are some to which it pertains to inhere in a subject and to inform a subject. There are others to which it does not pertain to inhere in a subject nor to inform a subject, but only to be conditions of the subject with respect to another.'[38]

He maintains that only absolute accidents, i.e. those in the categories of quantity and quality, inform or inhere in a subject. He believes that the other accidents are 'in' in their own way. i.e. other than by inhering or informing.[39] To illustrate this, he discusses numbers. He believes that numbers are accidental properties of things. But if there are two stones, where could the numerically one accident of being two (*dualitas*) inhere? It is understood that it does not inhere in only one or the other stone, for neither stone is two. And the two stones are certainly not one subject in which the accident might inhere. Nor, I would add, could the accident inhere in each stone taken separately, for it is numerically one accident. 'And so it [the accident of being two] is not in two subjects, but is only the separateness [*discretio*] of two subjects or of two unities which in reality have no unity. And number is in things numbered; so 'to be in' can pertain to something without being [in] as in a subject.'[40]

There are predicates that ascribe an accident to a subject or subjects, but do not name a thing, an accident, that inheres. If 'There are two stones' can be put into subject–predicate form as 'These stones are two', Harclay shows the difficulty, if not absurdity, of taking the predicate in the latter sentence in the same way as the predicate in 'These stones are white'. This latter can be analysed as 'This stone is white and that stone is white', where each conjunct is true if and only if a stone exists and a

[38] Harclay, 'Question', n. 49.
[39] Ibid., n. 80. See also nn. 53–6.
[40] Ibid., n. 81.

whiteness exists that inheres in the stone. But neither 'This stone is two' nor 'These stones are two' can be so analysed.

On the other hand, Harclay insists that numbers are mind-independent. They are in some sense 'in' their subjects. As with his treatment of relations, he tries to steer a middle course between positing numbers as absolute or relative things that inhere in subjects and, on the other hand, reducing them to entities dependent on the mind.

Harclay writes paragraph after paragraph, using arguments and authorities, defending this distinction of two types of accidents.[41] Those accidents that inform are predicated of their subjects by intrinsic denomination. Those that do not inform, such as relations, are predicated of their subjects by extrinsic denomination.[42]

Returning to the sentence 'Socrates is seen by an ox', Henry argues:

I intend to speak of Socrates absolutely, and I call him by the absolute name 'Socrates'. Again, I intend to speak of Socrates in some circumstance; for example, let us posit that now Socrates is seen by an ox [and] that the ox sees him. It is certain that [even] with no intellect considering, there is a distinction between Socrates [taken] absolutely and Socrates [as] seen. For neither the existence of Socrates nor the vision of the ox by which it sees Socrates depends on a considering intellect. Further, neither does Socrates depend on the seeing ox nor on its vision, for even if no intellect considers, Socrates may certainly cease to be seen by the ox, and it is not necessary that he be seen by it. Therefore [even] with no intellect considering, this being-seen is not altogether the same thing as Socrates. And still, 'being-seen' does not bespeak in Socrates any form inhering in him, nor anything existing in him that previously was not [in him]. For all concede that what can be sensed is not referred by a real relation to the power of sense, nor is it necessary that it be referred by a real relation. And besides, the vision of the ox is an action remaining in the one seeing, and it causes no thing in the object that is seen; and yet Socrates would now be seen and [later] would cease to be seen, with no intellect considering.[43]

The sentence, then, is not true either (i) by virtue of the predicate 'seen by an ox' naming a thing, an inherent accidental

[41] Harclay, 'Question', nn. 16–18, 49, 79–83, 101–20.
[42] Ibid., n. 117. See also nn. 118–19.
[43] Ibid., n. 51.

form, or (ii) by virtue of some mind thinking it. Why, then, is it true? Harclay finds this difficult to express. He continues:

So extending 'thing' to all that does not depend on the intellect, it is necessary that some new thing is able to come to something and be verified of something, which thing does not inform that to which it comes, but only bespeaks a condition (*habitudo*) or association (*societas*) or concurrence (*simultas*) or coexistence (*coexistentia*) or however we intended to call [it]. For 'human communication labours with truly a great scarcity', according to Augustine, *V De Trinitate*.[44]

Harclay concedes that one could say that when Socrates becomes really related by being seen by an ox, some new thing comes to Socrates. But here 'thing' is taken in a very broad sense, covering all that is not made by the mind. He is not affirming that Socrates acquires some inherent relative thing named 'seen by an ox'. Not even Scotus had held this, for the Subtle Doctor had taught that the thing sensed is related to what senses only by a relation of reason. Harclay is rather affirming that Socrates is now associated with the ox in some mind-independent way in which he was not previously.

Harclay insists that the new real relation does not inhere in Socrates. He says that the relation does not have the property of 'in-ness' (*initas*).[45] He speaks of the new real relation as a 'toward-ness' (*aditas*). But again, this toward-ness is not some absolute or relative thing as in Scotus' ontology, nor is it only a being of reason. Rather, 'toward-ness' is Harclay's way of pointing out the essential characteristic of all relations. '*aRb*' affirms something of *a*: that it is associated with *b* in some mind-independent way. It is this toward-ness or association that is essential to a relation, not that it inheres in a subject. I believe this is true. Taking 'thing' in a very broad sense, he says: 'this name "relation" is imposed to signify only the thing of toward-ness (*rem aditatis*) and not the thing of in-ness (*rem initatis*), if I may so speak'.[46]

With his theory of relations Harclay answers the original theological question that prompted his inquiry. Departing from tradition, he maintains that there is a real relation of God to

---

[44] Ibid.
[45] Ibid., n. 50. See also n. 49.
[46] Ibid., n. 50.

creatures: 'But the relation of God to a creature is nothing other than His coexistence with the creature.'[47] Furthermore:

I say, however, that that accident [i.e. a real relation] posits nothing in God, no more than a relation of reason posits [something] in God. . . . Nor does a real relation differ from a relation of reason in this, that one, namely a real relation, posits something in that of which it is, [and] a relation of reason [does] not, but in this, that one, namely a real relation, would be in extra-mental reality if no intellect were considering, but a relation of reason [would] not.[48]

He also departs from the traditional interpretation of Aristotle's third type of relations, for he believes that they are not necessarily non-mutual, but can be mutual real relations.[49]

We can now finally ask: what according to Harclay is a real relation? In other words, what are the truth conditions for sentences of the form 'R-ness exists'? On the one hand, he has rejected an ontology of relations by which substitutions for 'R-ness' name some extra-mental relative thing that inheres in a foundation. On the other hand, he does not have an ontology, as Peter Aureoli, in which sentences of this form are true only if there exists some being of reason. Harclay insists repeatedly that real relations exist independently of the mind. Neither of these ontologies is his: 'So a relation posits nothing in [its] foundation, and yet it is a thing not made by the intellect.'[50]

Harclay explains his own view on the being of relation:

Now I say that 'relation' signifies only such conditions or concurrences and association. So a relation posits nothing in [its] foundation, and yet it is a thing not made by the intellect. So I say that when a quality is alone, I call it 'whiteness'. When, however, there is another [quality of] whiteness with it in reality, the same is called 'similarity'. And whiteness no more differs from similarity than whiteness absolutely speaking differs from whiteness when it has a partner. And so that association is the relation. Whiteness and similarity, however, are not the same, but rather radically different. For that condition of association and concurrence is of a nature different from whiteness. And I say that a relation has no stronger being than has that concurrence or association. And that association posits nothing in it [i.e. the subject], but only bespeaks a condition of it with respect to another.[51]

---

[47] Harclay, 'Question', n. 66.   [48] Ibid., n. 102. See also n. 80.
[49] Ibid., nn. 70–8, 87–100.   [50] Ibid., n. 52.   [51] Ibid.

Here, Harclay is clearly struggling to express the way relations exist. He is very much an heir of his medieval Aristotelian background. He still talks of the relation as being 'in' one subject and 'toward' another. But the aspect of being-in has been reduced from Scotus' emphasis on inherence and the relation having its own accidentality. For Harclay, statements of the form 'R-ness exists' are true if and only if there exists a mid-independent condition in (non-inherence) one thing toward another. But although a real relation is not an extra-mental relative thing that inheres in its foundation, neither is it identical with its foundation. Rather the foundation is of a nature different from the relation, the former being an absolute accident, the latter being a condition or association of two or more things. Harclay further argues that a relation is not to be identified with both foundations.[52] Despite the difficulty in expression, Harclay's intuition is that a real relation has an extra-mental ontological status that is not reducible to that of absolute things.

Finally, Harclay is ambiguous on the semantics of relational terms. On the one hand, he holds that the term 'similarity' signifies only the condition itself. On the other hand, he says that 'similarity' signifies this whiteness when there exists another whiteness. Here a relational term is connotative: although it primarily signifies one absolute thing, i.e. this whiteness, it connotes another white thing and that they are associated in a certain way, i.e. by colour.[53]

3. Conclusion

The theories of Henry of Harclay and Duns Scotus on real categorical relations can be contrasted in the following way. According to Scotus, if R is a real relation, then sentences of the form '*a*R*b*' are true if and only if (i) *a* and *b* are really distinct extra-mental things, (ii) there is a real foundation in *a* for R to *b*, and (iii) there exists an extra-mental relative thing R inhering in *a* which is really distinct from its foundation. And sentences of the

---

[52] Ibid., nn. 46–7.
[53] Ibid., n. 50 (for 'relation' as directly signifying the condition of toward-ness) and n. 52 (for 'similarity' as connotative).

form 'R-ness exists' are true if and only if there exists an extra-mental relative thing really distinct from, but inhering in, its foundation.

Harclay held this ontology in his *Sentences* commentary, though even there he voices reservations. But in his later Question he develops his own theory holding that if R is a real relation, then sentences of the form '*a*R*b*' are true if and only if (i) *a* and *b* are really distinct extra-mental things, (ii) there is a real foundation in *a* for R to *b*, and (iii) there exists a real relation R, a non-inhering condition of *a* toward *b*. And sentences of the form 'R-ness exists' are true if and only if there exists a mind-independent condition in (non-inherence) one thing toward another.

Harclay's Question is evidence of his hard struggle to work his way out of his early Scotist position. He took the bulk of authoritative texts and arguments that had grown up around the problem of relations, worked through them very carefully, and developed his own novel position. It is probably because of the vastness of the task and his unconventional teaching that this question is the second longest of his twenty questions preserved in the Vatican codex Borghese 171.

He was perhaps the first to challenge the arguments Scotus had marshalled for his theory, concentrating on the separation argument and the charge of an infinite regress. Although I do not think Harclay's criticism was successful, his ways of attacking the separation argument and the charge of an infinite regress were taken up by a contemporary who was familiar with Harclay's teaching in other areas as well, William of Ockham.

Harclay's position on relations also looks back—to Thomas Aquinas. Both agree on (T7), (T8), and (T9). Further, both claim that a real categorical relation does not have its own inherent accidental reality distinct from that of its foundation. Aquinas, however, teaches that its accidental reality is identical with that of its foundation, while Harclay teaches that its accidental reality is non-inhering. Both deny that a real relation changes its subject. Finally, Harclay, without Thomas's argument from different orders, finds no reason to follow theological tradition: for him, God is as really related to creatures as they are to Him.

7

Relative Terms as Connotative

WILLIAM OF OCKHAM

WILLIAM OF OCKHAM (1285–1347/9) wrote extensively on the ontological status of relations, his teaching being carefully articulated and consistent with other of his philosophical and theological doctrines.[1] On the one hand, he believed that reason unaided by revelation does not lead one to affirm that any real categorical relation is an extra-mental thing really distinct from its foundation.[2] In this, he considers Duns Scotus his most distinguished adversary. On the other hand, the authorities of Sacred Scripture and the Church lead him to conclude that in certain cases there are such relative things.

In this chapter, I first present certain key arguments of Ockham against Scotus' strong realism. I then present Ockham's doctrine according to natural reason unaided by revelation. Third, I discuss his distinction between real relations and relations of reason. I then briefly consider exceptional cases in which he is forced to assume the existence of extra-mental relative things really distinct from absolute things.

---

[1] Ockham treats relations in many places throughout his works. The following are the most important and extensive discussions (I use the new critical edition of Ockham, *Opera Theologica* (OT) and *Opera Philosophica* (OP) of St Bonaventure, NY): *Ordinatio* I, dd. 30, 31, and 35, q. 4 (OT iv, pp. 281–407, 463–79); *Reportatio* II, qq. 1, 2 (OT v, pp. 3–49); *Quodlibeta* VI, qq. 8–30; VII, qq. 1, 8 (OT ix, pp. 611–706, 726–30); *Summa Logicae* I, cc. 49–54 (OP i, pp. 153–79); *Expositio in Librum Praedicamentorum Aristotelis*, cc. 12–13 (OP ii, pp. 238–68). All page references are to the respective editions and volumes. For secondary literature, see M. Adams, *William Ockham*, 2 vols. (Notre Dame, Ind., 1987), vol. 1, c. 7, pp. 215–76; G. Martin, *Wilhelm von Ockham: Untersuchungen zur Ontologie der Ordnungen* (Berlin, 1949); id., 'Ist Ockhams Relationstheorie Nominalismus?', *Franzis-kanische Studien* 32 (1950), pp. 31–49; P. Doncœur, 'Le Nominalisme de Guillaume Occam: La Théorie de la relation', *Revue néo-scolastique de philosophie* 23 (1921), pp. 5–25; H. Greive, 'Zur Relationslehre Wilhelms von Ockham', *Franziskanische Studien* 49 (1967), pp. 248–58.

[2] Ockham, *Ordinatio* I, d. 30, q. 1: 'Immo etiam dico quod rationes, quae non innituntur Scripturae et dictis Sanctorum, ad probandum talem rem in nullo penitus sunt efficaces' (OT iv, p. 307:1–4).

1. Ockham's Criticisms of Scotus' Strong Realism

In his *Summa Logicae*, chapter forty-nine, when speaking of
Scotus' opinion, Ockham remarks: '. . . many theologians are of
this opinion which at one time I even believed to have been the
opinion of Aristotle, but now it seems to me that the contrary
opinion follows from his principles'.[3] This remark indicates there
may have been a time when Ockham held a position on relations
like that of Scotus, and in Section Four we shall see why in certain
special cases he himself posited *res relativae*. But throughout his
writing he consistently criticizes and rejects Scotus' doctrine
as applied to categorical real relations, the subject of this
section.[4]

I present and evaluate three different arguments illustrating
various strategies that Ockham used against Scotus. The first (I)
illustrates a fundamental ontological difference between the
thought of the two Franciscans. The second (J) centres around
Scotus' use of (Fi) and (G) in support of (H), his defence against
the charge of an infinite regress. The third (K) is Ockham's attack
on the Subtle Doctor's separation argument.

Recall that in order to stop an infinite regress of relations R, R',
R", etc., Scotus had replied that if R is a real relation inhering in
its foundation F, then

(H) (i) It is not possible without contradiction that R exists
         without its foundation F.
   (ii) If R and F exist, then a relation of otherness R' to F
         exists in R.

---

[3] *Summa Logicae* I, c. 49 (OP i, p. 154:10–15). It would not be surprising if when
Ockham began his philosophical studies he believed categorical real relations were *res
relativae*, following Scotus. This was the case with Henry of Harclay who still held Scotus'
views when he wrote his own *Sentences* commentary. But if Ockham did hold such views
very early, he changed his mind by the time he wrote his commentary. Concerning the
remark in *Summa Logicae*, the editors of his *Expositio* surmise: 'Probabiliter hoc dictum
referendum est ad tempus quo Ockham studiis philosophicis et theologicis vacabat et non
ad aliquod opus prius scriptum' (OP ii, p. 242, n. 9). See also L. Baudry, 'A propos de la
théorie occamiste de la relation', *Archives d'histoire doctrinale et littéraire du Moyen Âge* 9
(1934), pp. 199–203.

[4] Ockham's principal objections against Scotus are found in *Ordinatio* I, d. 30, q. 1
(OT iv, pp. 287–306, 310–19); q. 2 (ibid., pp. 321–2); q. 5 (ibid., pp. 378–81, 388–93);
Reportatio II, q. 2 (OT v, pp. 32–43); *Quodl.* VI, qq. 8–19 (OT ix, pp. 611–55).

(iii) So it is not possible without contradiction that R exists without R'. (i, ii)

(iv) Therefore, R and R' are really identical.

The critical step between (iii) and (iv) is made via the first premiss of his argument (F):[5]

(Fi) If *b* properly inheres in *a*, and *a* cannot exist without *b*, then *b* is really the same as *a*.

Applying (Fi) to the step from (iii) to (iv) in (H): since (ii) the relation of otherness R' properly inheres in R, and (iii) R cannot exist without R', therefore R' is really identical with R. Thus Scotus attempts to stop the regress by arguing that R is related to F, not through another thing really distinct from it, but through R' which is really identical with R.

In support of (Fi), recall that Scotus had argued

(G) (i) If *a* cannot exist without *b*, then either (a) *b* is naturally prior to *a*, or (b) *b* is naturally simultaneous with *a*, or (c) *b* and *a* are really identical.

(ii) But if *b* properly inheres in *a*, then not (ia) nor (ib).

(iii) So if *b* properly inheres in *a*, and *a* cannot exist without *b*, then (ic) *b* is really the same as *a*.

1.1. Ockham's First Argument

In the first argument that I have chosen (I), Ockham attacks Scotus' defence against the charge of an infinite regress, specifically the assertion that a real relation R is not really distinct from its relation R' of otherness to its foundation, as argued in (H).[6] Ockham argues

(I) (i) Distinct terms imply distinct relations.

(ii) The term of *a*'s relation R of similarity is another thing *b*.

(iii) The term of R's relation R' of otherness is the foundation in *a*.

(iv) *b* and the foundation in *a* are distinct.

---

[5] See sects. 2 and 4 in ch. 5 for Scotus' discussion of (F), (G), and (H).

[6] *Ordinatio* I, d. 30, q. 1 (O T iv, p. 293:8–16). For Ockham using other formulations of the charge of an infinite regress, see *Reportatio* II, q. 2 (O T v, pp. 32:14–34:26); *Quodl.* VI, q. 10 (O T ix, pp. 622:40–624:80); *Expositio*, c. 12 (O P ii, p. 241:75–87).

    (v) So the terms of R and R′ are distinct. (ii, iii, iv)

    (vi) So R and R′ are really distinct relations. (i, v)

And if they are really distinct, an infinite regress is generated.

    Scotus is committed to some form of (i). In fact, he makes the more general claim that 'it cannot be the same relation unless it is between the same extremes'.[7] But he might deny that distinct terms imply *really* distinct relations, holding that relations with really distinct terms can be really the same but formally distinct.[8] Hence, although R and R′ are really the same, they are not the same in every way. Rather, they are formally distinct, and each can and does have a really distinct term, *b* and *a*'s foundation. This reply, of course, rests on the acceptability of Scotus' formal distinction *a parte rei*. Ockham denies any such distinction in creatures as leading to ontological paradoxes.[9]

    This more fundamental ontological disagreement illumines Ockham's rejection of Scotus' defence. Ockham strikes at the heart of the defence by rejecting formalities and an objective formal order of priority and posteriority among them within one really identical thing. Specifically, Ockham rejects (Fi) as contradictory, and instead holds that 'where one properly inheres in another, one is really distinguished from the other, for nothing properly inheres in itself'.[10] The consequent of (Fi) cannot be true if the antecedent is true. One key reason for this denial is Ockham's denial of the formal distinction.

    Scotus had also argued in (G) that although *a* and *b* are really identical, there is an objective formal order of priority and posteriority obtaining between them. But in Ockham's ontology, there are in creatures no formalities *a parte rei*, nor any order of priority and posteriority among such formalities. Ockham denies that *a* and *b* can be really identical and yet prior and posterior. Without the ontology needed for the soundness of (G), not only does (G) not go through, but it cannot be used to support (Fi), Scotus' bulwark against the charge of an infinite regress in (H).

---

[7] Scotus, *Ordinatio* I, d. 30, qq. 1–2, n. 17 (Vatican vi, p. 176).

[8] For this possible reply, see Ockham, *Ordinatio* I, d. 30, q. 1 (OT iv, pp. 293:20–294:10); *Quodl.* VI, q. 11 (OT ix, pp. 625–9).

[9] *Ordinatio* I, d. 2, qq. 4–8 (OT ii, pp. 99–292).

[10] *Ordinatio* I, d. 30, q. 1 (OT iv, p. 297:15–20).

1.2. Ockham's Second Argument

In the second argument that I consider (J), Ockham argues that in affirming (Fi) Scotus must deny his own doctrine that real relations are really distinct from their foundations. Ockham begins by stating his own version of (Fi), doubling the number of entities involved:[11]

(Fi′)   If *c* and *d* properly inhere in *a* and *b* respectively, and it is logically impossible that *a* and *b* exist without *c* and *d* respectively, then *c* is really identical with *a*, and *d* is really identical with *b*.

Hence, if there are two white things, *a* and *b*, with their respective relations of similarity, R and R′, Ockham argues:

(J)   (i)   R and R′ are relations of similarity properly inhering in *a* and *b* respectively.
   (ii)   It is logically impossible that *a* and *b* exist without R and R′ respectively.
   (iii)   So, R is really identical with *a*, and R′ is really identical with *b*. (i, ii, Fi′)

Scotus agrees with (i), and (ii) purports to be a formulation of Scotus' doctrine that relations of similarity are intrinsically advenient: given two actually white things *a* and *b*, it is logically impossible that there not be real relations of similarity R and R′ inhering in *a* and *b* respectively.

Ockham argues for (Fi′) in two ways. First, the same reason can be given for holding (Fi′) as is given for holding (Fi), namely, the separability criterion for a real distinction. '. . . there is no greater reason that something really distinct from another can exist without the other, than that things really distinct from other things are able to exist without them.'[12] According to (Fi), if *b* properly inheres in *a*, and *a* cannot exist without *b*, then *b* is really identical with *a*. If, on the contrary, *b* were said to be really distinct from *a*, then they would be separable, which contradicts the second conjunct of the antecedent. So also for (Fi′): if *c* and *d*

---

[11] Ibid. (OT iv, pp. 298:19–299:6). See also *Quodl.* VI, q. 9 (OT ix, pp. 619:15–620:43).
[12] *Ordinatio* I, d. 30, q. 1 (OT iv, p. 299:7–13).

were really distinct from *a* and *b* respectively, they would be separable, which contradicts the second conjunct of the antecedent.

Scotus would reply first by denying, rightly, that the separability criterion is the reason he has for holding (Fi). Rather, the reason (Fi) holds is (G), using the notions of natural priority and posteriority. This difference is evidenced by the fact that in (J) Ockham makes no mention of natural priority and posteriority, but only uses premiss (ii) and the separability criterion for a real distinction.

Second, Scotus would point out the ambiguity involved in premiss (ii) above. In similar fashion to the reply I brought against Harclay, he could distinguish between possibility and compossibility. It is not compossible that *a* exist without R and also that *b* exist without R′, real relations being intrinsically advenient. But it is still logically possible that *a* exist without R, and it is logically possible that *b* exist without R′. Hence, R is really distinct from *a*, and R′ is really distinct from *b*.

The second reason Ockham offers for holding (Fi′) is based on Scotus' (G). If (G) is valid in support of (Fi), so also is the following argument valid in support of (Fi′):[13]

(G′) (i) If *a* and *b* cannot exist without R and R′, then either (a) R and R′ are naturally prior to *a* and *b* respectively, or (b) R and R′ are naturally simultaneous with *a* and *b* respectively, or (c) R and R′ are really identical with *a* and *b* respectively.

(ii) But R and R′ are not naturally prior to nor simultaneous with *a* and *b* respectively.

(iii) *a* and *b* cannot exist without R and R′.

(iv) So R and R′ are really identical with *a* and *b* respectively.

The reason for (ii), presumably, is that R and R′ properly inhere in *a* and *b* respectively.

In similar fashion to the response in the previous argument, Scotus could question (iii). It is true that it is not compossible that *a* exist without R and also that *b* exist without R′. But that *a* exist without R is still logically possible, i.e. if no other white thing existed; and so also for *b*'s existing without R′.

Alternatively, in *Quodlibet* III Scotus states: 'For it is always the

[13] *Ordinatio* I, d. 30, q.1 (OT iv, pp. 299:14–300:6); *Quodl.* VI, q. 9 (OT ix, p. 619:28–35).

case that whatever pertains to something in such a way that it would be a complete contradiction for the latter to exist without the former, then the former is really identical with the latter. And, by contrast, where there is no such contradiction, there is no need for it to exist at all.'[14] It is not a 'complete contradiction', i.e. it is not logically impossible, that a exist without R, for it is not necessary that b exist. Nor is it logically impossible that b exist without R', for it is not necessary that a exist.

Scotus would deny, then, that Ockham has given good reason for accepting (Fi'). If one wished to double the number of entities involved in (Fi), this could be done innocently and clearly: If c properly inheres in a, and d properly inheres in b, and it is logically impossible for a to exist without c, and it is logically impossible for b to exist without d, then c is really identical with a, and d is really identical with b. This is the case with two creatures a and b and their really identical yet formally distinct relations of dependence on God c and d.

1.3. Ockham's Third Argument

I do not believe the line of attack against Scotus in (J) is successful. Ockham, however, is not without further resources. Against Scotus' separation argument, he follows Harclay and maintains that if the argument works with one thing, there is no reason why it should not work with two things:[15]

(K) (i) God can make any absolute thing without anything really distinct and naturally posterior to it.

    (ii) God can make two white things without their relations of similarity. (i)

    (iii) But the two white things would still be similar.

    (iv) So similarity is not an extra-mental thing really distinct from its foundation. (ii, iii)[16]

---

[14] Scotus, *Quodl.* q. 3, n. 15 (Wadding xii, p. 82); *God and Creatures*, trans. Alluntis and Wolter, pp. 73–4.

[15] Ockham, *Ordinatio* I, d. 30, q. 1 (OT iv, pp. 291:21–292:2); *Quodl.* VI, q. 8 (OT ix, p. 614:73–83). The qualification 'really distinct' in premiss (i) is found in *Ordinatio* I, d. 30, q. 4 (OT iv, pp. 367:18–368:18) and *Reportatio* II, q. 2 (OT v, p. 35:1–9).

[16] For other arguments using God's absolute power and the separability criterion for a real distinction, see *Quodl.* IV, q. 11 (OT ix, pp. 349–52) and *Reportatio* II, q. 2: 'Item, Deus potest facere omne absolutum sine quocumque alio positivo facto in quocumque alio, sed non potest facere duo alba nisi sint similia. Igitur similitudo non est aliquid positivum additum albedini' (OT v, p. 37:1–4).

Ockham does advance beyond Harclay's attack against the separation argument, for here, in contrast to Harclay, he does not rely solely on the notions of natural priority and posteriority. In two versions of the argument he does seem to do this, but in two other versions he inserts the important phrase in premiss (i) 'really distinct'. I believe he would have done well to drop all reference to natural priority and posteriority, for it is real distinction and separability in (i) that supports (ii).

I do not see how Scotus or a follower of Scotus could reply to this without difficulty. Given the real distinction and so the separability of these real relations from their foundations, what reasons can be brought forward to block (ii)? It might be replied, as to Harclay, that Scotus' separability criterion does not commit him to the compossibility of separability (*a* from R and *b* from R′). But Ockham would ask, why not? Scotus could claim in reply to Ockham's arguments (I) and (J) that with *b* existing, *a* is really distinct from R. But if so, and if real distinction implies separability, then with *b* existing *a* is separable from R and can exist without it. Scotus' criterion of separability is at odds with his doctrine that real relations are intrinsically advenient.

Ockham perhaps shows traces of reading or hearing Harclay when he records a reply on behalf of Scotus that we have already seen in Harclay's Question: in the case at hand, the two white things will be similar, but not by virtue of real relations of similarity.[17] The suggestion is that although it is logically impossible that two white things exist and not be similar, it is logically possible for them to exist without the relative things, the relations of similarity. Ockham agrees with Harclay in rejecting this response:

On the contrary, if similarity were a thing other [than its foundation], then similarity and a similar thing will be related as whiteness and a white thing. Therefore, as it is impossible for something to be white without whiteness—which is a thing other [than its subject]—so it is impossible that something be similar without similarity which is a thing other [than its foundation].[18]

The purpose of positing whiteness as a thing really distinct from its subject is to account for the subject's being white. So the purpose of positing a relation of similarity really distinct from its

---

[17] *Ordinatio* I, d. 30, q. 1 (OT iv, p. 292:3–4).
[18] Ibid. (OT iv, p. 292:4–7).

foundation is to account for the subject's being similar. If it is possible that they be similar without such an additional relative thing, why posit it in the first place? Using his razor Ockham argues: 'Similarly, it would be in vain to suppose that similarity is a thing other [than its foundation] if without such an other thing some things could be similar, as it would be in vain to suppose whiteness to be a thing other than its subject if the subject could be white without such an other thing.'[19]

In sum, I believe Ockham's criticisms of Scotus are more damaging than Harclay's. Arguments (I) and (J) do not show that Scotus' theory of relation is internally incoherent or incompatible with other parts of his philosophy. But it is clear that Scotus' defence against an infinite regress of relations in (F), (G), and (H) is dependent on his doctrines of formal distinction *a parte rei* and natural priority and posteriority, both denied by Ockham. Argument (K), I believe, reveals difficulties within Scotus' theory, particularly between the doctrines of intrinsic advenience and his separability criterion.

2. Ockham's Own Theory according to Natural Reason

Ockham's response to Scotus' separation argument (A) provides a transition from his critique of Scotus to his own teaching.[20]

Ockham agrees with the major: If *a* is identical with *b*, then it is contradictory that *a* exist but not *b*. According to Ockham, if *a* is and *b* is not, it follows that they are not really the same. But are there, as the minor states, some relations such that their foundations can exist without them apart from any contradiction? There are, but just because real relations are only intentions or concepts in the soul. Hence, since they are obviously not extra-mental things, one cannot conclude from the major and the minor that (iii) some real relations are extra-mental things not identical with their foundations.

His statement here that real relations are concepts or intentions in the soul is part of his response to Scotus' separation argument and should not be taken as his whole theory.[21] His

---

[19] Ibid. (O T iv, p. 292:8–11).   [20] Ibid. (O T iv, pp. 310–12).

[21] As the editors of Ockham's *Opera Theologica* iv remark: 'Porro, qui crederet veram et completam opinionem Guillelmi ex uno aliove paragrapho elici posse, graviter falleretur. Uno enim loco loquitur proprie, alio improprie; et quod uno loco explicat minus plene, alio loco explicat plenius' (O T iv, pp. 16*–17*).

statement does, however, serve to emphasize how Ockham differs from Scotus: according to natural reason, there are no relative things in the category of relation really distinct from and inhering in absolute things.

Ockham explains his own theory in terms of his semantics of absolute and connotative terms. Relational terms do not directly signify any extra-mental thing distinct from the relata. Rather, relational terms are connotative and signify both relata (or signify one relatum directly and the other connotatively), and also connote that the relata exist in a certain way.[22]

This is illustrated in his replies to Scotus' arguments (D) and (E) that a denial of his strongly realist position involves a denial of all composition and of all secondary causality.[23] For Ockham, '"composition" does not signify precisely two absolute things *a* and *b*, as matter and form, but signifies them and that nothing corporeal is a medium between them'.[24] And '"cause" and "active production" signify the absolute nature of the cause and connote [its] effect. And conversely concerning "effect" and "passive production", because they signify principally the effect and connote [its] cause.'[25] So also with similarity: '"similarity" signifies two white things immediately without any intervening relation, or one thing principally and the other connotatively'.[26]

Furthermore, Scotus' separation argument (A), as (D) and (E), depends on the principle:

> There can be no passage from contradictory to contradictory apart from the generation or corruption of some thing.[27]

Ockham replaces this with:

> It is impossible that contradictories be successively true about the same thing unless because of the locomotion of

---

[22] *Reportatio* II, q. 2: '... similitudo unius albedinis ad aliam significat primam albedinem et connotat aliam, et quamdiu simul exsistunt, dicuntur et denominantur similia sine aliqua relatione. Et hoc quia hoc nomen vel conceptus 'similitudo' significat ista duo alba quo ad totale significatum coexistentia, et non significat unam nisi coexistat alteri. Et ideo destructa una albedine non dicitur prima albedo similis, sed hoc propter solam destructionem secundae albedinis connotatae' (OT v, p. 39:8–15). See also *Ordinatio* I, d. 30, q. 1 (OT iv, p. 314:14–21); *Quodl.* VI, q. 8 (OT ix, pp. 616:123–617:132). [23] See sect. 1 of ch. 5.
[24] *Ordinatio* I, d. 30, q. 1 (OT iv, p. 312:18–20). See also his remarks on spatial proximity, ibid. (OT iv, p. 313:1–15). [25] *Reportatio* II, q. 1 (OT v, pp. 25:25–26:3).
[26] Ibid. (OT v, p. 16:13–15). See also *Ordinatio* I, d. 30, q. 4 (OT iv, p. 368:12–16).
[27] *Ordinatio* I, d. 30, q. 1 (OT iv, p. 282:6–12). See Scotus, *Ordinatio* I, d. 30, qq. 1–2, n. 41 (Vatican vi, p. 186); Aristotle, *Physica* V, c. 1, t. 7 (225ª12–20).

something, or because of the passage of time, or because of the production or destruction of something.[28]

An example of change in truth-value through the generation or corruption of some thing is seen in Ockham's treatment of the separation argument. Ockham believes that 'this white [thing] that now is not similar is able to become similar not through the coming of some thing to it, but only through the becoming of one other white [thing]. For that something be similar that previously was not similar only requires that something now be white that previously was not white.'[29]

This is a clear statement of (T8), first encountered in Thomas Aquinas and subsequently in Henry of Harclay:

(T8) *a* comes to be or ceases to be really related to *b* through some change of the foundation that is or is in *a* and/or of the foundation that is or is in *b*.[30]

For *a* to become similar to *b*, it is not necessary that any relative thing come to inhere in *a*. Rather it is only necessary that something become white which previously was not white, i.e. that there occur a change 'of the foundation that is or is in *b*'. Ockham also uses the citation from Aristotle's *Physics*, book five, chapter two, that one relatum can change without any change in the other. From this he concludes that (T8) is true.[31]

---

[28] *Ordinatio* I, d. 30, q. 4 (OT iv, p. 369:7–9). See also *Reportatio* II, q. 1 (OT v, pp. 14:21–15:3).

[29] *Ordinatio* I, d. 30, q. 1 (OT iv, p. 311:6–10); *Quodl.* VI, q. 8 (OT ix, pp. 617:151–618:158). See also *Reportatio* II, q. 1: 'Nec est transitus a contradictorio in contradictorium sine adquisitione vel perditione alicuius positivi vel in eo de quo dicuntur contradictoria successive vel in alio' (OT v, p. 16:8–10). Also *Summa Logicae* I, c. 51 (OP i, pp. 165:95–9; 166:112–18).

[30] See sect. 3 of ch. 2.

[31] *Ordinatio* I, d. 30, q. 3: 'Praeterea, quod dicit quod mutatio est in ad aliquid, non videtur secundum principia Philosophi. Quia dicit Philosophus, V *Physicorum* sic: "Convenit altero mutato verum esse alterum nihil mutans", hoc est dictu, per mutationem alterius extremi dicitur vere alterum extremum ad aliquid sine omni mutatione sui ipsius. Sicut si Sortes sit primo albus, si postea fiat Plato albus, Sortes est similis Platoni de novo sine omni mutatione sui ipsius' (OT iv, p. 347:14–21). Also ibid. (OT iv, pp. 346:5–8; 357:16–21); *Ordinatio* I, d. 24, q. 2 (OT iv, p. 112:4–13); *Reportatio* II, q. 2 (OT v, pp. 39:7–40:4); *Quodl.* VI, q. 17 (OT ix, pp. 646:14–647:19); ibid., q. 16 (OT ix, p. 640:14–17); *Expositio*, c. 12 (OP ii, pp. 245:184–246:209), c. 13 (OP ii, p. 250:21–31); *Summa Logicae* I, c. 49 (OP i, pp. 157:107–158:111). Like Harclay, Ockham uses Anselm's *Monologion*, c. 25, in support of (T8); see *Summa Logicae* I, c. 51 (OP i, p. 169:198–203).

Put in terms of the connotation of relative terms:

when some name signifies one principally and another connotatively, with only that connoted destroyed and with nothing real destroyed in the principal significatum, that name will not denote the principal significatum, because it only signifies that principal [significatum] as it coexists with the connoted. So with the connoted destroyed that denomination does not pertain to it; and the connoted being posited so that it coexists with the principle significatum of that name or concept, immediately without the acquisition of anything real in the principle significatum that name or concept denominates both, so that there is in this case a transition from contradictory to contradictory because of only a change of the connoted.[32]

In other cases, there can be a passage from contradictory to contradictory, not because something is generated or corrupted, but because at $t1$ one exists in one way and at $t2$ it exists in another way.

the fact that a thing proximate to another can act on it and a thing not proximate cannot act on it is not because the thing which is proximate has some true thing in it formally that it does not have when it is not proximate; rather this is because when it is proximate, no impeding thing is in the way; when however it is not proximate, some impeding thing is in the way. For even air of a great quantity will be able to impede sometimes if it is between.[33]

Ockham's position, then, can be contrasted with Scotus' in the following way. According to Scotus, if R is a real categorical relation, then sentences of the form 'aRb' are true if and only if (i) a and b are really distinct extra-mental things; (ii) there is a real foundation in a for R to b; and (iii) there exists an extra-mental relative thing R inhering in a which is really distinct from its foundation.

For Ockham, the truth conditions for sentences of the form 'aRb' are quite different. First, as will be shown in Section Three, he denies that a and b must be really distinct; for him, numerical

---

[32] *Reportatio* II, q. 2 (OT v, pp. 38:17–39:6). On relational terms being connotative, see *Ordinatio* I, d. 30, q. 3 (OT iv, pp. 351:22–365:14); *Reportatio* II, q. 1 (OT v, pp. 8:13–11:8); *Quodl.* V, q. 25 (OT ix, pp. 582–4); *Quodl.* VI, q. 16 (OT ix, pp. 642:67–643:99). On the distinction between absolute and connotative terms, see *Summa Logicae* I, cc. 10, 49–51 (OP i, pp. 35–8, 153–71).

[33] *Ordinatio* I, d. 30, q. 1 (OT iv, p. 313: 16–23). See also *Quodl.* VII, q. 8 (OT ix, pp. 728:56–730:106).

identity is a real relation. According to Ockham, then, sentences of the form '*a*R*b*' are true if and only if *a* and *b* exist in the way connoted by the substitution for 'R'.[34] Nothing other than the two absolute things need be posited extra-mentally.

Although Ockham denies Scotus' strong realism, he does not go to the other extreme, i.e. he does not believe that sentences of the form '*a*R*b*' depend for their truth-value on some intellect thinking them.

against one way of positing that a [real] relation is not a thing other [than an absolute thing], but is only in the intellect, I say it is not to be imagined according to that opinion that a relation in that way be only in the intellect such that nothing truly would be such [i.e. really related] except because of an act of the intellect or because of something caused in the intellect, as that Socrates not be similar to Plato except because of an act of the intellect, as 'Socrates' cannot be said to be subject or predicate except because of an act of the intellect. But it is to be so imagined that the intellect does no more [to bring it about] that Socrates be similar than that Socrates be white.[35]

He is arguing against a conceptualist theory of relation that I have encountered only in the works of Peter Aureoli. Ockham illustrates his own position which has a commitment neither to the *res relativae* of Scotus nor to the concepts of Aureoli:

And so Socrates is similar to Plato because of absolute things only, all else excluded—whether in extra-mental reality or in the intellect. And so in extra-mental reality there is nothing besides the absolute things. However because there are in extra-mental reality many absolute things, the intellect can express them in diverse ways: in one way expressing precisely that Socrates is white, and so it has precisely absolute concepts; in another way that Plato is white; in a third way by expressing that both Socrates and Plato are white. And this [last] it can do through a relative concept or intention saying, 'Socrates is similar to Plato according to whiteness', because altogether the same is implied by these propositions, 'Both Socrates and Plato are white' and 'Socrates is similar to Plato according to whiteness'.[36]

Hence, Ockham agrees with Scotus' denial that real relations are mind-dependent. Scotus had argued that such a position

[34] *Ordinatio* I, d. 30, q. 1 (OT iv, pp. 309:15–310:13); *Quodl.* VI, q. 25 (OT ix, p. 678:9–14); ibid. q. 20 (OT ix, pp. 656:12–657:28).
[35] *Ordinatio* I, d. 30, q. 1 (OT iv, p. 316:3–12).
[36] Ibid. (OT iv, p. 316:14–24). See also *Quodl.* VI, q. 25 (OT ix, p. 679:27–32).

cannot account for the real unity of the universe nor for real composition and spatial proximity; it also makes mathematical knowledge radically subjective.[37] Ockham agrees: '. . . the intellect does nothing that the universe be one or that a whole be composed or that causes in spatial proximity [to their effects] cause or that a triangle have three [angles], etc. . . . any more than [the intellect] brings it about that Socrates be white or that fire be hot or water cold'.[38]

It is one thing to ask what it is for *a* and *b* to be really related, i.e. the truth conditions for sentences of the form '*aRb*'. It is another to inquire into the ontological status of a real relation, i.e. the truth conditions for sentences of the form 'R-ness exists'. For Scotus, sentences of the form 'R-ness exists' are true if and only if there exists an extra-mental relative thing really distinct from its foundation. For Aureoli, to anticipate, sentences of this form are true if and only if there exists a concept of a certain kind. While denying both of these ontologies, Ockham does not believe a real relation is simply identical with its foundation. He also denies that a real relation of, say, similarity is properly speaking *in* the white thing. His formula is: 'This white thing is really similar, although similarity is not really in this white thing.'[39]

What, then, is a real relation? Ockham claims to be following Aristotle in holding that the term 'relation', along with '*ad-aliquid*' and 'relative', is a term of second intention. In propositions, they supposit significatively only for relative concepts, not for extramental things.[40] He holds that the propositions 'Father is a

---

[37] See sect. 3 of ch. 5.

[38] *Ordinatio* I, d. 30, q. 1 (OT iv, pp. 316:24–317:4; see also pp. 317:5–319:10); *Quodl.* VI, q. 25 (OT ix, p. 679:18–26); *Summa Logicae* I, c. 36 (OP i, p. 103:120–4).

[39] *Ordinatio* I, d. 30, q. 1 (OT iv, pp. 312:3–7; 311:14–17; 315:1–15). See n. 43 below.

[40] *Summa Logicae* I, c. 49 (OP i, pp. 155:44–159:143); *Quodl.* VI, q. 17 (OT ix, p. 648:62–5 and n. 11); ibid., q. 27 (OT ix, pp. 688:76–689:83; 689:89–99). For the difference between the second intentions '*relatio*' on the one hand, and '*ad-aliquid*' and '*relativus*' on the other, see *Ordinatio* I, d. 31, q. un. (OT iv, pp. 403:2–404:4). In *Quodl.* VI, q. 22 (OT ix, pp. 666:15–667:29), he talks of the opinion that 'relation' is a term of first intention as being reasonable, but it is not that of Aristotle. See also *Quodl.* V, q. 21 (OT ix, p. 559:11–16); *Summa Logicae* I, c. 36 (OP i, p. 103:122–4). Furthermore, according to theology 'relation' can be used as a term of first intention, for it signifies a true relation outside the soul, i.e. one of the divine relations of the Trinity; see *Quodl.* VI, q. 27 (OT ix, p. 689:84–7); ibid., q. 30 (OT ix, pp. 700:46–701:60); *Summa Logicae* I, c. 49 (OP i, p. 155:44–6). For first and second intentions, see *Summa Logicae* I, c. 11 (OP i, p. 40:61–71); *Quodl.* IV, 35 (OT ix, pp. 470:38–471:63).

relation', 'Son is relative', and 'Similarity is a relation' are true when the subjects supposit *simpliciter*, i.e. stand for relative concepts, and the predicates supposit personally, i.e. stand for the same relative concepts.[41]

Again following Aristotle, Ockham asserts that relation is a real predicament or *genus generalissimum*, not because 'relation' 'signifies things outside [the mind] which are not signs, but because its species [i.e. specific relational concepts] signify such things outside [the mind] and supposit for them'.[42]

What is the ontological status of these 'species' of relation, i.e. of similarity, paternity, etc.?

I say that whiteness does not contain similarity or dissimilarity according to perfect identity, because whiteness is neither similarity nor dissimilarity. But I say that either similarity is a relative concept signifying many taken together, or it is many absolute things taken together. As a people is many human beings and no human being is a people, so similarity is many white things and no white thing is similarity.[43]

Taken in one way (A), similarity is a relational concept, while taken in another way (B), it is the extra-mental things taken together which are signified connotatively by the relational concept.

I believe Ockham is not ambiguous about his ontology here. One is free to understand a real relation as either a relational concept or as the things signified by the concept. But on either option, what exists outside the mind is clear: only individual absolute things. Hence, sentences of the form '*a*R*b*' are true if and only if *a* and *b* exist in the way connoted by substitutions for 'R'. On (A), sentences of the form 'R-ness exists' are true if and only if (i) the relata *a* and *b* exist in the way connoted by substitutions for 'R-ness' and (ii) the relevant relational concept exists. On (B), sentences of the form 'R-ness exists' are true if and only if the relata *a* and *b* exist in the way connoted by substitutions for 'R-ness'.

---

[41] *Quodl.* VI, q. 22 (OT ix, p. 669:80–6).

[42] Ibid. (OT ix, p. 669:87–90).

[43] *Quodl.* VI, q. 15: '. . . dico quod albedo non continet similitudinem nec dissimilitudinem secundum perfectam identitatem, quia albedo nec est similitudo nec dissimilitudo. Sed dico quod vel similitudo est conceptus relativus significans plura coniunctim, vel est plura absoluta coniunctim. Sicut populus est plures homines et nullus homo est populus, ita similitudo est plura alba et nullum album est similitudo' (OT ix, pp. 638:67–639:73). Also *Ordinatio* I, d. 30, q. 1 (OT iv, p. 314:14–21).

When dealing with the ontology of relation, I believe that Ockham was not much concerned about the options between (A) and (B). Which is the more appropriate way of speaking is a question for logic.[44] One of his primary ontological concerns is to maintain that two white things *a* and *b* are similar, and this is not dependent on any mind.[45] When no mind is involved, whether or not the proposition 'There is a real relation of similarity' is true simply depends on whether one opts for sense (A) or sense (B). If sense (A), the proposition is false; if (B), it is true. I believe the latter, in fact, more clearly represents Ockham's ontology.

Taking real relations in sense (B), he elaborates his position using the distinction between abstract and concrete terms. For example, (i) 'similarity', 'paternity', and 'equality' are abstract relational terms, and (ii) 'the similar', 'father', and 'the equal' are concrete relational terms.

Regarding (i), Ockham holds that the proposition 'Two white things are similarity' is true, for the predicate 'similarity' taken with personal supposition stands for the same as the subject, i.e. the two white things.[46] Regarding (ii), Ockham holds that terms like 'father' and 'the similar' can be said truly of only one relatum, not of both:

so it is to be conceded that Socrates is similar [or] Socrates is equal, but that Socrates is similarity [or] Socrates is equality is denied; however, that Socrates and Plato are equality [or] two white things are similarity is conceded. In sum, such abstract names of relations are collective names.[47]

---

[44] *Ordinatio* I, d. 30, q. 1 (O T iv, p. 314:19–21). In *Ordinatio* I, d. 31, q. un. (O T iv, pp. 404:11–405:8), Ockham briefly notes, with little concern, a peculiarity if one takes sense (A): it is possible that two things be equal without the relation of equality, i.e. on the assumption that no mind thinks the relevant relational concept. Greive, 'Zur Relationslehre', is wrong in not taking alternative (B) seriously and so in asserting that Ockham only held (A): 'Es bleibt somit dabei, dass die Beziehung für Ockham eine Sache des Verstandes ist' (p. 254), which is the thesis of Doncœur, 'Le Nominalisme de Guillaume Occam'; see n. 1 above.

[45] See nn. 35–8 above.

[46] *Quodl.* VI, qq. 23 and 25 (O T ix, p. 672:70–1; p. 679:18–23); *Ordinatio* I, d. 30, q. 1 (O T iv, p. 315:3–6); ibid., d. 31, q. un. (O T iv, p. 404:11–23).

[47] *Quodl.* VI, q. 25 (O T ix, p. 681:82–7); *Ordinatio* I, d. 30, q. 2 (O T iv, p. 334:10–23); ibid., q. 3: '. . . dico quod nomina relativa non proprie significant ad aliquid nisi accipiendo "ad aliquid" secundum quod potest stare pro ipsis rebus extra. Et tunc idem est dicere ac si diceretur: nomen relativum significat ad aliquid, hoc est, significat diversas res quarum una est similis vel aequalis alteri, et sic de aliis. Et tunc talia nomina non significant alias res a substantiis et qualitatibus, sed significant ipsas substantias vel qualitates, non tamen

There is, however, another way to treat these terms.[48] In this way, both the concrete and abstract relational terms can always be predicated truly of the same things.[49] This is true, in fact, in all the genera other than substance and quality. In those two genera, the abstract and concrete terms do not signify the same thing and so cannot be predicated truly of the same thing. 'The just' signifies a particular human being, e.g. Socrates, while 'justice' signifies a really distinct quality inhering in Socrates. Hence, 'the just is justice' is false. But for those, like Ockham, who deny that quantity, relation, and all respects of the other genera are really other than substance and quality, the abstract and concrete terms signify altogether the same thing.[50] As it is true that 'whiteness is similar', so also 'whiteness is similarity'; as it is true that 'Socrates is a father', so also 'Socrates is paternity', for in all cases the subject and predicate supposit for the same thing.[51] But again, however one chooses to take these abstract and concrete relational terms, Ockham claims such terms taken significatively only denote absolute things existing extra-mentally.[52]

Finally, on (B), when these specific relational terms, whether concrete or abstract, are taken with simple supposition in propositions, and so stand for relative concepts, 'relation' can be truly predicated of them. Hence 'this proposition is true, "similarity is a relation", as "similarity" supposits simply'.[53]

divisim ita quod possint verificari de aliquo uno per se sumpto, sed magis quasi coniunctim quasi possint verificari de multis simul sumptis et de nullo per se, illo modo quo dictum est prius quod ista potest aliquo modo concedi "duo similia sunt similitudo", et tamen haec est falsa "unum simile est similitudo". Sicut conceditur quod "multi homines sunt populus", et tamen haec est falsa "aliquis homo est populus"' (OT iv, p. 355:13–26). See also *Summa Logicae* I, c. 9 (OP i, pp. 34–5). Ockham holds that this way of taking relational terms is probably to be held for cases where the relation and co-relation are of the same type, i.e. denoted by the same name, as 'similar'. But this does not hold where the relation and co-relation are not of the same type, for he finds it odd affirming 'a father and son are paternity' or 'God and the creature are active creation'. *Quodl.* VI, q. 25 (OT ix, p. 682:88–93); ibid., q. 20 (OT ix, pp. 656:12–657:28).

[48] *Quodl.* VI, q. 25 (OT ix, p. 682:94–112).
[49] *Summa Logicae* I, c. 6 (OP i, pp. 19–22, esp. 21:65–77).
[50] In *Quodl.* VI, q. 17 (OT ix, p. 648:53–61), Ockham denies the proposition 'No quality is a relation or similarity'. Here he is taking 'relation' as a term of first intention (see p. 648: 62–4), and 'similarity' in the way discussed here, i.e. it signifies altogether the same thing as 'similar' which can be predicated of *qualitas*.
[51] *Quodl.* VI, q. 25 (OT ix, p. 682:106–12).
[52] *Ordinatio* I, d. 30, q. 2 (OT iv, p. 334:10–23).
[53] *Quodl.* VI, q. 23 (OT ix, p. 672:69–70).

3. Relations of Reason and Real Relations

Ockham does not remember reading in Aristotle's writings of the distinction between relations of reason and real relations, and he claims 'relation of reason' is not a philosophical term.[54] But one can maintain this distinction for the sake of common usage understanding it in the following way:[55]

(T12) There exists a relation of reason R concerning *a* if and only if (*a* is of the sort to be denoted by 'relation' or a concrete relative term only if there is an act of intellect).

The relative characteristic ascribed to *a* by the relative term depends upon an act of some intellect. For example, Ockham calls signification a relation of reason.[56] No written or spoken word signifies except through institution, an act of intellect. Hence, some mental act of institution is necessary for the spoken sound 'man' to be of the sort to be denoted by the relative term 'sign'. So also for the value of a coin.[57] It too is a relation of reason, for the value depends on a 'voluntary institution', which volition is preceded by an act of the intellect. Hence, such an act of institution is necessary for the coin to be of the sort to be denoted by the relative term 'valuable'.

Or again, without an act of intellect, the written, spoken, or mental term 'white' would not be of the sort to be denoted by the relative term 'predicate'.[58] For the written or spoken term 'white' to be a predicate, there is required some act of intellect. And since the mental term 'white' would not exist without an act of intellect, *a fortiori* it would not be the sort to be denoted by the relative term 'predicate'. But Ockham's intention is that if the mental term did exist, then another act of intellect is necessary for it to be of the sort to be denoted by the relative term 'predicate'.

[54] *Ordinatio* I, d. 30, q. 5 (O T iv, p. 385:16–20); *Quodl.* VI, q. 30 (O T ix, p. 699:9–13); *Expositio*, c. 13 (O P ii, pp. 266:63–267:65).
[55] *Ordinatio* I, d. 30, q. 5 (O T iv, pp. 385:21–386:13); ibid., d. 31, q. un. (O T iv, p. 396:13–16); *Quodl.* VI, q. 30 (O T ix, p. 699:14–16); ibid., q. 26 (O T ix, p. 684:35–7).
[56] *Quodl.* VI, q. 30 (O T ix, pp. 699:21–700:33); *Ordinatio* I, d. 30, q. 5 (O T iv, p. 386:3–6).
[57] *Quodl.* VI, q. 30 (O T ix, p. 700:34–8); *Ordinatio* I, d. 30, q. 5 (O T iv, p. 386:7–13).
[58] *Quodl.* VI, q. 30 (O T ix, p. 699:16–20); *Ordinatio* I, d. 30, q. 5 (O T iv, pp. 385:24–386:2).

Regarding relations of reason he makes a number of precisions. Similar to the two ways in which a real relation can be understood, Ockham distinguishes two ways of understanding a relation of reason: '[A] in one way for that spoken sound or concept conveying something or some things; [B] in another way for the things signified'.[59]

If (A), then relative names or concepts such as 'value', 'sign', 'subject', and 'predicate' are relations of reason. If (B), a relation of reason is identical with the things signified by such relative names. Ockham is explicit about what the things signified are. Speaking of what is signified or conveyed by the relative term 'sign' he says: 'But such relative [terms] convey absolute things together with an act of intellect and of will, as for this spoken sound "man" to signify men is only, or conveys, the spoken sound and the men and the present or past act of will by which we wish to use this spoken sound for men.'[60]

In addition, on (B), it is not a necessary condition for a relation of reason that there exist terms such as 'value' and 'sign'. The relation of reason is the things signified, i.e. the absolute things including an act of will or of intellect. The term 'sign' is needed only to express that the spoken sound 'man' is a sign. As Ockham says, 'But truly this ["Socrates"] is a sign and that other [Socrates] the signified, although without such relative names [e.g. "sign"] this cannot be expressed.'[61]

He distinguishes between two ways of understanding a relation of reason as a relative name. According to the first,

(T13) Any name is said to be a relation of reason concerning *a* if and only if (*a* is of the sort expressed by that name only if there is an act of intellect whether in act or in potency).[62]

In this way, 'intelligible', 'subject', and 'predicate' can be called relations of reason, for without some actual or potential act of intellect, nothing would be intelligible, a subject, etc., and so be of the sort expressed by 'intelligible', 'subject', etc.

[59] *Ordinatio* I, d. 35, q. 4 (O T iv, pp. 470:13–16; 477:15–17).
[60] Ibid. (O T iv, p. 471:4–8).
[61] Ibid. (O T iv, p. 471:15–17).
[62] Ibid. (O T iv, p. 472:4–10).

One can understand relation of reason in a more restricted way:

(T14)   Any name is said to be a relation of reason concerning *a* if and only if (*a* is of the sort expressed by that name only if there is at present an act of intellect or of will, or there was an act of intellect or of will and there has been no contrary act of intellect or of will).[63]

In this sense, 'value', 'sign', 'lordship', and 'servitude' are relations of reason. Nothing could be of the sort expressed by these terms without the relevant acts of intellect or of will *actually performed* either in the past or in the present.

For a spoken sound is a sign and a coin is money or wealth only because, with a previous act of intellect, we wish to use the spoken sound or coin in this way. And given that there is such a volition in us—or there was and there was no contrary volition—immediately, without anything else added, the spoken sound is a sign and the coin is money.[64]

So also for the relations of lordship and servitude between creatures. Since they depend upon conventionally established (and not contravened) property laws instituted by past acts of intellect and will, they also are relations of reason in this strict sense.

When contrasting real relations with relations of reason, Ockham holds

(T15)   There exists a real relation R concerning *a* if and only if *a* is of the sort to be denoted by 'relation' or a concrete relational term irrespective of any act of intellect.[65]

The relative character ascribed to *a* by the relative term is not dependent on an act of intellect.[66] On (T15), there is a real relation of God to creatures:

Not that some thing comes to God, as neither does some imaginable thing come to white Socrates by his becoming similar to Plato newly

---

[63] *Ordinatio* I, d. 35, q. 4 (OT iv, pp. 472:11–473:5). For another formulation of this strict meaning of relation of reason, see p. 476:7–12).

[64] Ibid. (OT iv, p. 472:17–21).

[65] *Ordinatio* I, d. 30, q. 5 (OT iv, pp. 386:14–20; 394:12–15); ibid., d. 31, q. un. (OT iv, p. 397:5–22); *Quodl.* VI, q. 30 (OT ix, p. 700:39–45); ibid., q. 26 (OT ix, p. 684:28–32).   [66] *Ordinatio* I, d. 30, q. 5 (OT iv, p. 386:17–20).

existing as white. But as similarity is called a real relation because one white thing in reality is similar to another white thing, and for this—that one be similar to another—the intellect does no more than it does that Socrates be white or that Plato be white, so in the case at hand the created intellect does nothing that God be creating.[67]

With Harclay, Ockham breaks with tradition that ascribed only a relation of reason in God to creatures. He argues that God could create a stone without any created intellect existing and so without any relation of reason. Instead, He would be really related to it.[68]

As with relations of reason, there can be real relations obtaining both between real extra-mental things and between mental entities.[69] An example of the latter would be the similarity relations between two qualities or absolute things in the soul, as two acts of the intellect or habits of knowledge. Hence, the phrase 'irrespective of any act of intellect' in (T15) should be understood as referring to an act of intellect other than any required for bringing one or both of the relata into existence.

With the understanding of real relation in (T15), Ockham holds that numerical identity is a real relation: '. . . I say briefly that numerical identity is a real relation in the same way as similarity and equality, because Socrates is really identical with himself and the intellect does nothing to bring this about'.[70] Here too Ockham breaks with the common opinion that had taken numerical identity as a relation of reason,[71] and he also eliminates a commonly held necessary condition for a real relation, i.e. that the extremes be really distinct.[72]

A counter-example against Ockham's theory is that on this account of real relation, 'something would be really related to a non-being, as matter is really related to a form to which it is in potency, because without any operation of the intellect matter is truly in potency to form'.[73]

---

[67] Ibid. (OT iv, pp. 385:1–8; cf. 381:19–22).
[68] Ibid. (OT iv, p. 385:8–15).
[69] *Quodl.* VI, q. 25 (OT ix, p. 678:11–14).
[70] *Quodl.* VI, q. 27 (OT ix, p. 685:8–11).
[71] See nn. 14 and 17 of ch. 1.
[72] For further discussion of numerical identity as a real relation, see *Ordinatio* I, d. 31, q. un. (OT iv, pp. 400:4–402:19). Also see *Reportatio* II, q. 1 (OT v, pp. 3:15–4:2; 26:15–16), where he holds that the extremes' being really distinct is one among three jointly sufficient conditions for a real relation but does not say it is a necessary condition.
[73] *Ordinatio* I, d. 30, q. 5 (OT iv, p.387:6–9); *Quodl.* VI, q. 25 (OT ix, p. 679:34–9).

For Ockham, the difficulty is more verbal than real. One could hold that the relata must actually exist in reality, and then matter's relation of being in potency to a non-existent form is not real. But one could expand (T15) to read:

(T16) There is a real relation R concerning *a* if and only if *a*—whether in act or in potency—is of the sort to be denoted by 'relation' or a concrete relational term irrespective of any act of intellect.[74]

The basic intuition remains: the relative character—whether in act or in potency—ascribed to *a* is not mind-dependent: '. . . the intellect does no more to bring it about that matter be in potency to form than that one ass generate [another] ass'.[75]

4. Exceptional Cases

According to Ockham, 'followers of natural reason' conclude that it is more reasonable to deny than affirm the existence of relative things really distinct from their foundations. Nevertheless, there are cases in which he is constrained to dissent from such elegant reasonableness.

The Christian doctrine of the Trinity of persons in God is a case of doing with more what other religions do with less. Following Augustine, Ockham holds that 'the Father is not the Father by that by which he is God'.[76] So also for the other persons. Each person is constituted as that person by a relation to the other persons. The theological conclusion for Ockham was that the Father is constituted by the relation of paternity, the Son by that of filiation, and the Holy Spirit by that of passive spiration.[77] While these three real relations are really distinct

---

[74] *Ordinatio* I, d. 30, q. 5 (OT iv, p. 387:10–20); *Quodl.* VI, q. 25 (OT ix, p. 680:49–58).

[75] *Ordinatio* I, d. 30, q. 5 (OT iv, p. 387:18–19); *Quodl.* VI, q. 25 (OT ix, p. 680:56–8). Ockham mentions that if (T16) is not adopted and one holds fast to requiring the real actual existence of the relata, then 'it would be necessary to posit something between a real relation and a relation of reason, which some call a potential or aptitudinal relation, although perhaps not properly'. See *Ordin.* I, d. 30, q. 5 (OT iv, p. 387:21–4).

[76] *Ordinatio* I, d. 30, q. 4 (OT iv, p. 366:19–22). Augustine, *De Trinitate* VII, c. 6, n. 11 (PL 42, 943; *Corpus Christianorum Latinorum* 50, p. 262).

[77] See the discussion by the editors of Ockham's *Opera Theologica* iv, pp. 5*–7*.

from each other,[78] they are really the same as, though formally distinct from, the divine essence. In this case, there exist three relative things really distinct from each other.

Furthermore,

> concerning certain special respects there is a special difficulty. If some [such] respects are to be assumed, they are these: evidently the union of a human nature to the divine [nature], the union of matter to form and vice versa, the union of accident to subject . . . And for all these, there is only one reason which is this: it is impossible that contradictories be successively true of the same thing unless because of the locomotion of something, or because of the passage of time, or because of the production or destruction of something.[79]

Ockham is clearly influenced by the arguments involving the Incarnation and transubstantiation that Scotus had used to support his strong realism.[80] Ockham's arguments, however, rely on the principle

> It is impossible that contradictories be successively true about the same thing unless because of the locomotion of something, or because of the passage of time, or because of the production or destruction of something.[81]

For example, with regard to the Incarnation Ockham argues:[82]

(L) (i) It is possible that a human nature first not be united and afterward be united to the Divine Word without any locomotion.

(ii) The mere passage of time cannot account for this change.

(iii) Hence, there must be the production or destruction of something.

(iv) The production or destruction of any absolute thing cannot account for this change.

---

[78] *Ordinatio* I, d. 30, q. 4 (O T iv, pp. 366:16–367:9; 366:12–14; 374:5–13).

[79] Ibid. (O T iv, p. 369:2–9); *Reportatio* II, q. 1 (O T v, pp. 14:21–15:3). See Aristotle, *Physica* V, c. 1, t. 7 (225ª12–20). In the same place in the *Ordinatio* I, d. 30, q. 4 (O T iv, p. 369:5–6), Ockham mentions another case, that of the union of one part of a continuum with another. But he later denies there is reason to posit relative things distinct from absolute things in this case; ibid., p. 470:7–10). See also *Reportatio* II, q. 10 (O T v, pp. 190:4–191:10); ibid., q. 2 (O T v, pp. 40:20–41:5).

[80] See ch. 5, sects. 1.2, 1.3.   [81] See n. 28 above.

[82] *Ordinatio* I, d. 30, q. 4 (O T iv, p. 369: 16–20); *Reportatio* II, q. 1 (O T v, p. 15:3–10).

(v) Hence, there must be the production or destruction of some relative thing.

Concerning the doctrine of transubstantiation Ockham argues:[83]

(M) (i) God can bring it about that an accident simply present to the same subject first inform the subject and afterward not inform it without any locomotion.

   (ii) The mere passage of time cannot account for this change.

  (iii) Therefore, there must be the production or destruction of something.

  (iv) The production or destruction of any absolute thing cannot account for this change.

   (v) Hence, there must be the production or destruction of some relative thing.

By 'simply present' in (Mi) Ockham means to affirm that after the change the accident is as present locally to the subject as before, so that no locomotion has taken place.

Hence, by (L), there exists in the human nature of Christ a real relation of union to the Divine Word, which relation is really distinct from that human nature. By (M), at each occurrence of transubstantiation there ceases to exist a real relation of inherence of an accident of quantity to its subject, which real relation is a relative thing really distinct from the absolute thing, the quantitative accident. He argues in the same way that one must posit a real relation of union of a substantial form with its matter, and vice versa.[84]

Ockham mentions two ways one might try to deny the need to posit such relative things: the first deals with the theological cases, the second with the philosophical cases.

The first is to insist on Ockham's doctrine 'according to natural reason' that denies there are any things other than absolute things. With regard to the Trinity, one might hold

[83] *Ordinatio* I, d. 30, q. 4 (O T iv, pp. 369:21–370:7); *Reportatio* II, q. 1 (O T v, p. 15:10–16). Remarkably, he goes on to argue similarly (ibid., p. 15:16–19) that spatial proximity is a relative thing really distinct from the relata, a view he denies later in the same question (ibid., p. 24:4–13). See also *Reportatio* II, q. 2 (O T v, p. 36:5–11); *Ordinatio* I, d. 30, q. 1 (O T iv, p. 313:16–23).

[84] *Ordinatio* I, d. 30, q. 4 (O T iv, pp. 369:21–370:6).

that in God there would be three absolute [things] really distinct that would not be formally the divine essence, and that one of them would be really the Father and not the Son, and another of those absolute [things] would be really the Son and not the Father, in such a way, however, that 'Father' no more would convey anything in reality besides that absolute thing than 'the one creating' conveys anything on the part of God other than God who creates.[85]

With respect to the Incarnation, one denies (iv) in (L) and accounts for the change by positing the production of an absolute thing:

concerning the union of a human nature to the [Divine] Word, some perhaps would say that just as according to others it is only because a respect informs a human nature that it can be said 'God is a man', so perhaps they would say it is because of some absolute form (much more perfect than would be such a respect and much more fitting for the divine nature informing human nature) that it can be said truly that God is a man, and this is not other than to say that a human nature is united to the [Divine] Word or to God.[86]

Oddly, he does not respond to these alternatives which are more consonant with his stated position that there are only absolute things.[87] There may be at least two reasons for this. First, in the previous question, the third of distinction thirty, he clearly states that the intention of Aristotle was to deny all such relative things. In this fourth question, he asks the same question 'according to the truth of the matter', i.e. according to theology. The tension is seen in the two initial principal arguments that many scholastics traditionally used to begin their discussions. The first, given against positing such relative things, is a statement of Ockham's razor: everything 'can be saved' without such entities. The second argument, for positing such entities, is the traditional assertion that in God 'it is manifest that paternity is a relation'.[88] I believe that Ockham, at least with regard to the Trinity, felt the pull of a very strong tradition going back to Augustine for interpreting the divine persons as constituted in some way by real relations. In addition, he perhaps took the

[85] Ibid. (OT iv, pp. 370:14–371:5).
[86] Ibid. (OT iv, p. 371:15–23).
[87] For more on Ockham's analysis of arguments that fail to establish the necessity for positing relative things, see *Quodl.* VI, q. 15 (OT ix, p. 637:20–32); *Ordinatio* I, d. 30, q. 1 (OT iv, pp. 307:12–308:6).
[88] *Ordinatio* I, d. 30, q. 4 (OT iv, p. 366:8–14).

positing of three absolute things as compromising God's simplicity.[89]

The second way of denying relative things deals with the philosophical cases. 'But if it were not possible for an accident to be separated from its subject nor a form [to be separated] from its matter without separation by place, then I would not posit any relation there because I would save everything by local motion that you save by a respect.'[90]

On this suggestion, (Mi) is false, for God cannot bring it about that an accident simply present to the same subject first inform the subject and afterward not inform it without any locomotion. The union or non-union of subject and accident (or of matter and form) would be explained as Ockham explains other real relations. The term 'union' is connotative: it only signifies the extremes, connoting the negation of an intervening space.[91] No third relative thing need be posited. Again, it is not clear to me why Ockham did not adopt this alternative.

To summarize, Ockham believed that 'it is clear that we cannot save everything without all of these respects. However, we can save everything without any relation which is posited in the genus of relation. . . . But [we cannot save everything] without paternity in God, nor without the respect of union, etc.'[92]

The divine personal relations of the Trinity, being really identical with the infinite divine essence, do not fall under any of the ten categories. The inherence relation of form to matter and that of an accident to its subject are not considered to be relations in the category of relation. They are not examples of one of the three modes of relation mentioned by Aristotle in his lexicon of philosophical terms in chapter fifteen of *Metaphysics* V.[93] Hence, whatever doubts Ockham may have had, he finally posits as relative things (a) the personal relations constituting the divine persons, and if any others,[94] they are (b) relations of union,

---

[89] *Ordinatio* I, d. 30, q. 4 (O T iv, p. 367:8).

[90] *Reportatio* II, q. 2 (O T v, p. 40:13–16); *Ordinatio* I, d. 30, q. 4 (O T iv, p. 372:1–4); *Reportatio* II, q. 1 (O T v, pp. 23:17–24:19).

[91] *Reportatio* II, q. 2 (O T v, p. 40:16–17).

[92] *Ordinatio* I, d. 30, q. 4 (O T iv, pp. 373:21–374:3); *Reportatio* II, q. 1 (O T v, pp. 14:17–21; 16:3–5; 17:12–15).

[93] Aristotle, *Metaph.* V. c. 15 (1020^{b}25–1021^{b}11).

[94] Note the conditional phrasing in *Ordinatio* I, d. 30, q. 4: 'Unde si aliqui respectus sint ponendi, sunt isti: scilicet unio naturae humanae ad divinam . . .' (O T iv, p. 369:3–4). But see *Reportatio* II, q. 2 (O T v, p. 40:19–20).

specifically (i) of Christ's human nature to the Divine Word, (ii) of matter to substantial form, and vice versa, and (iii) of an accident to its subject.

5. Conclusion

The central parts of Ockham's theory of relation can be summarized as follows: sentences of the form '*a*R*b*' are true if and only if *a* and *b* exist in the way connoted by substitutions for 'R'. Sentences of the form 'R-ness exists' are true if and only if either (A) the relata *a* and *b* exist in the way connoted by substitutions for 'R-ness', and the relevant relational concept exists; or alternatively (B) the relata *a* and *b* exist in the way connoted by substitutions for 'R-ness'.

Also, regarding real relations as distinct from relations of reason:

(T12) There exists a relation of reason R concerning *a* if and only if (*a* is of the sort to be denoted by 'relation' or a concrete relative term only if there is an act of intellect)

and

(T15) There exists a real relation R concerning *a* if and only if *a* is of the sort to be denoted by 'relation' or a concrete relational term irrespective of any act of intellect

or

(T16) There is a real relation R concerning *a* if and only if *a*—whether in act or in potency—is of the sort to be denoted by 'relation' or a concrete relational term irrespective of any act of intellect.

Other parts of his doctrine can be summarized by comparison with rival theories. Against Scotus, Ockham denies there exist any relative things in the category of relation really distinct from absolute things. Hence, with categorical relations he denies Scotus'

(T7″) Something can be accidentally changed by acquiring or losing an inherent accident whether it be an absolute or relative thing and

(T9′)   If the foundation that is or is in *a* changes, then there is a
        change of *a*; and if only the foundation that is or is in *b*
        changes, there is a change of *a*, for *a* acquires or loses a
        relative thing.

His argument against Scotus' separation argument is strong,
while his attacks regarding an infinite regress are less successful.
His most fundamental criticism is to reject the formal distinction.
In this regard, Ockham asserts that the source of many errors by
his contemporaries regarding relations is

that many are deceived so that whenever something is predicated of
something [else], they desire that there be some abstract [term] conveying that thing coming to the other for which reason it is called
such-and-such. Indeed they desire that there be as many distinct things
as there are significative spoken sounds, so that there are as many
distinctions between things signified as between spoken sounds
signifying.[95]

I find surprising, however, the extent to which Ockham is
forced to assume the reality of relative things really distinct from
absolute things, as in the special cases mentioned in Section
Four. Also, importantly, both Scotus and Ockham concur that
real relations are not mind-dependent. Nevertheless, Ockham's
overall discussion of relations moves in a philosophical world
quite different from that of Scotus. It is securely grounded in his
own semantics of absolute and connotative terms, his use of
signification and supposition, and his interpretation of Aristotle's
doctrine in the *Praedicamenta* as dealing with terms, not extra-
mental things.

Ockham's doctrine can be further clarified by contrast with
Harclay's. Harclay was Chancellor at Oxford (1312–17) when
Ockham was studying there, and Ockham quotes verbatim from
Harclay's Question on universals which is critical of Scotus.[96] As
noted earlier, Ockham may have held a Scotist position on
relations as he began his philosophical career, but changed very
soon afterward during his course of studies. I believe that as
Harclay's work on universals influenced Ockham, so also it is very
probable with relations.

[95] *Ordinatio* I, d. 31, q. un. (O T iv, p. 405:9–14).
[96] *Ordinatio* I, d. 2, q. 7 (O T ii, pp. 227–9). Regarding Harclay, see G. Gál, 'Quaestio
de Significato', pp. 178–234, esp. 216–17, no. 79.

Ockham uses a version of Harclay's clever separation argument *bis* against Scotus. In both their writings this is followed by the infinite regress argument.[97] In their positive teachings on relations, they agree on a number of particulars. Both reject Scotus' (T7″) and (T9′) in favour of

(T8)   *a* comes to be or ceases to be really related to *b* through some change of the foundation that is or is in *a* and/or of the foundation that is or is in *b*

and

(T9)   If the foundation that is or is in *a* changes, then there is a change of *a*; but if only the foundation that is or is in *b* changes, there is no change of *a*, for there is no change *in a*.

Both use Aristotle's passage in *Physics* V and Anselm's *Monologion*, chapter twenty-five, to support (T8) and (T9); both hold that God is really related to creatures, and for the same reason: His immutability is not threatened. By becoming really related, on (T8), no new thing is posited in God that changes Him.[98] Further

[97] For Harclay, see 'Question', nn. 18–27; for Ockham, *Ordinatio* I, d. 30, q. 1 (O T iv, p. 291:21 ff.).

[98] For Ockham, see nn. 67 and 68 above. Not all were pleased with this innovation. John Lutterell, successor of Harclay as Chancellor at Oxford (1317–22), drew up a list of philosophical doctrines culled from Ockham's works along with a list of their supposed theological consequences. See John Lutterell, *Libellus contra Doctrinam Guilelmi Occam*, ed. F. Hoffmann, in *Die Schriften des Oxforder Kanzlers Iohannes Lutterell* (Leipzig, 1959); for Hoffmann's discussion of Ockham's theory of relation and Lutterell's objections, see pp. 187–203. See also A. Pelzer, 'Les 51 Articles de Guillaume Occam censurés, en Avignon, en 1326', *Revue d'histoire ecclésiastique* 18 (1922), pp. 240–70; J. Koch, 'Neue Aktenstücke zu dem gegen Wilhelm Ockham in Avignon geführten Prozess', *Recherches de théologie ancienne et médiévale* 7 (1935), pp. 353–80; 8 (1936), pp. 79–93, 168–97. In Lutterell's list are found: Article 11: 'Quod non sunt quattuor relationes in divinis'; consequence: 'Ad 11m, quod non sunt tres personae in divinis.' Art. 38: 'Quod nulla est relatio rationis Dei ad creaturam'; consequence: 'Ad 38m, quod Deus non est dominus nec refugium nec aliquod tale.' Art. 50: 'Quod equalitas, similitudo et aliae relationes in creaturis sunt nomina significantia res distinctas absolutas nec est aliquid imaginabile a parte rei nisi absolutum, quamvis nomina vel conceptus sint diversi'; consequence: 'Ad 50m quod nulla sit dependentia creaturae ad Deum nec ad aliud.' Art. 52: 'Quod equalitas et similitudo in divinis significant divinas personas habentes essentiam eandem numero'; consequence: 'Ad 52m quod sunt plures personae in divinis quam tres.' (Koch, 'Aktenstücke' (1935), pp. 375–80; Hoffmann, *Schriften*, pp. 3–7.) John XXII gave the list to James Concoz, the Dominican archbishop at Aix-en-Provence, for preliminary evaluation, and Concoz discarded nearly half of Lutterell's list, including all of the above except article 11. See C. K. Brampton, 'Personalities at the Process against Ockham at Avignon, 1324–26', *Franciscan Studies* 25 (1966), pp. 4–25.

similarities include their agreement on the difference between real relations and relations of reason, even their formulations being very similar.[99] Both insist that a real relation is not identical with its foundation.[100] Both distinguish real relations of Aristotle's first and second mode from those of the third mode: the former are simultaneous by nature, while the latter are not. Hence, both reject the long-standing distinction that relations of the first and second mode are mutual, while those of the third mode are not. All such relations are mutual.[101]

However, there are real differences. Ockham's ontology of relation is more parsimonious than Harclay's. Ockham maintains there exists nothing outside the mind but absolute things, and he specifically denies that a real relation is some type of condition (*habitudo*).[102] Harclay, on the other hand, talks of a real relation principally as an extra-mental condition; sentences of the form 'R-ness exists' are true if and only if there exists a mind-independent condition in (non-inherence) one thing toward another. Harclay, then, holds that a real relation is in its subject, though in a non-inhering way, while Ockham denies that properly speaking a real relation is in its subject.[103] Further, while Ockham denies that a real distinction of extremes is a necessary condition for a real relation, Harclay maintains the tradition holding that the relata must be really distinct. Hence, while Ockham can hold that numerical identity is a real relation, Harclay denies it is.[104] In addition, Harclay's theory is not as firmly grounded in a broad semantic theory and lacks the clarity and precision of Ockham's theory, as seen in their discussions of relational terms as

---

[99] See n. 48 of ch. 6; for Ockham, see sect. 3 above.

[100] See n. 51 of ch. 6; for Ockham, see n. 39 of this chapter, and *Ordinatio* I, d. 30, q. 3 (OT iv, p. 355:6–7).

[101] See ch. 6, sect. 2.2 for Harclay's example of 'Socrates is seen by an ox'. For Ockham, see *Ordinatio* I, d. 30, q. 3 (OT iv, pp. 358:17–359:24); ibid., q. 5 (OT iv, pp. 378:6–380:7; 388:13–391:8; 393:9–12); *Quodl.* VI, q. 19 (OT ix, pp. 653:24–655:101).

[102] For Ockham, see *Reportatio* II, q. 1: 'Ad quaestionem igitur dico—de relatione rationis sicut de relatione reali—quia relatio realis nihil aliud positivum dicit reale nisi extrema relata et non aliquam habitudinem vel rem mediam inter correlativa' (OT v, p. 9:7–10).

[103] For Ockham, see *Ordinatio* I, d. 30, q. 1 (OT iv, pp. 311:11–17; 312:3–7); *Quodl.* VI, q. 8 (OT ix, p. 617:133–49).

[104] See ch. 6, n. 36; for Ockham, see *Ordinatio* I, d. 31, q. un. (OT iv, pp. 400:4–8; 401:13–16).

connotative.[105] Finally, Harclay remains in the tradition distinguishing two aspects of a relation, as Thomas Aquinas and others had done. Harclay formulates the distinction in terms of *initas* and *aditas*, identifying the real relation with the *aditas*.[106] Ockham makes no such distinction.

In sum, Harclay remains much more firmly planted in the medieval tradition regarding relations, particularly in still conceiving of a relation as 'in' one relatum and 'toward' the other. Ockham does not conceive a real relation in this traditional medieval way, and he was not alone. His fellow Franciscan Peter Aureoli also denied that properly speaking a real relation is in its subject; his ontology of relation is the least medieval of all.

[105] Similar remarks should be made regarding a work on relations edited by G. E. Mohan, 'The *Quaestio de Relatione* Attributed to William Ockham', in *Franciscan Studies* 11 (1951), pp. 273–303. Mohan and Boehner are right in doubting that it is authentically Ockham. I believe it is the work of a compiler who misunderstood Ockham's position or of an author who took various arguments of Ockham against Scotus, put them into his own words, and used them to help establish his own position. My reasons are: (i) the basic thesis of the author is that a real relation in creatures is really the same thing as its foundation; (ii) the author denies that in the case of the Incarnation one need posit any relation or *res relativa* really distinct from the relata (both (i) and (ii) are contrary to Ockham's doctrine); (iii) the author never talks of connotative terms; and there are (iv) differences in vocabulary and (v) a lack of sophistication in the author's handling of the problem.

[106] See ch. 6, nn. 45 and 46.

8

Relation as Concept

PETER AUREOLI

AMONG the outstanding characteristics of Peter Aureoli (*c*.1280–1322) were his outspoken criticism of contemporaries and independence from the revered authorities of the past: 'A great nothing it is to do what has already been done.'[1] In his theory of universals he was a resolute opponent of both nominalism and realism, finding his own middle way in a conceptualism of a strongly psychological character with an emphasis on the role of the will.[2] He was one of the first to break radically with traditional forms of medieval realism, anticipating the concern with ideas and psychology of the early modern period. This break with the past is shown clearly in his theory of relations, quite different from any other studied so far.

He treats relations in his chief work, the commentary on the first book of the *Sentences*, distinctions thirty and thirty-one. He probably began writing this *opus magnum* during his teaching at

---

[1] *Petri Aureoli Verberii Ordinis Minorum Archiepiscopi Aquensis . . . Commentariorum in Secundum Librum Sententiarum* (Rome, 1605), d. 14, q. 2, art. 1: '. . . factum facere est magnum nihil' (p. 434.1 F).

[2] See the very helpful and foundational work by R. Dreiling, *Der Konzeptualismus in der Universalienlehre des Franziskanererzbischofs Petrus Aureoli* (Beiträge zur Geschichte des Philosophie des Mittelalters, 11/6; Münster, 1913). For a good overview of Peter Aureoli, his life, works, and thinking, see Am. Teetaert, 'Pierre Auriol', in *Dictionnaire de théologie catholique* (Paris, 1935), vol. 12, cols. 1810–81. For Aureoli's philosophical and theological positions, see ibid., cols. 1846–77; F. A. Prezioso, 'Il nominalismo ambiguo di Pietro Aureolo', *Sapienza* 25 (1972), pp. 265–99. For a presentation of Peter's theory of relations along with a criticism by Thomas of Strassburg, see B. Lindner, *Die Erkenntnislehre des Thomas von Strassburg* (Beiträge zur Geschichte der Philosophie des Mittelalters, 27/4–5; Münster, 1930), pp. 111–28. The beginning of a critical edition of Peter's first book on the *Sentences* based on the Vatican MS Borghese 329 is found in *Peter Aureoli Scriptum super Primum Sententiarum*, ed. E. M. Buytaert (St Bonaventure, NY), vol. i (1952); vol. ii (1956). Buytaert's first volume contains the text of the prologue, distinction 1, and much information on Aureoli. Vol. ii contains distinctions 2 to 8. For a description of MS Borghese 329 see A. Maier, *Codices Burghesiani Bibliothecae Vaticanae* (Studi e Testi, 170; Vatican City, 1952), pp. 373–4.

Toulouse in 1314, and after reworking it for a few years he completed it in 1316. Very fortunately there has survived a beautiful artistic codex, Vatican Borghese 329, completed 19 May 1317. Although it is not an autograph, it comes very close to the original, and I have used it as the basis for my research.[3]

Unlike his contemporaries, Peter does not begin his investigation by asking whether a real relation is distinct from its foundation. Rather, he enquires 'Whether any relation exists in extra-mental reality without any activity of the intellect, or if every relation exists only in [sensitive or intellectual] apprehension.'[4] From this unusual *status quaestionis* he proceeds to elaborate an equally novel conceptualist theory, arrived at after explaining and criticizing the opinions of others such as Thomas Aquinas, Henry of Ghent, Durand of Saint Pourçain, and Duns Scotus.[5] He is fair in presenting these opinions, giving a good description of Henry of Ghent's theory as well as that of Aquinas, stressing the two aspects of a real relation, its *esse-in* and *esse-ad*.[6] His initial arguments against any kind of mind-independent status for relations, however, reveal best his break with the past.

1. Arguments against the Mind-Independence of Real Relations

Peter opens his discussion by giving a few quick initial arguments against any mind-independent existence for relations.[7] Like

[3] *Scriptum super Primum Sententiarum*, distinctions 30–1, (MS Borghese 329, fols. 317ᵛ–345ᵛ). I follow Buytaert, who based his edition entirely on the text of Burghese 329, which is in fact better than the flawed sixteenth-century edition of the first book of Peter's commentary, *Commentariorium in Primum Librum Sententiarum Pars Prima Auctore Petro Aureolo Verberio Ordinis Minorum Archiepiscopo Aquensi* (Rome, 1596), pp. 659–718 being the corresponding passage dealing with relations in distinctions 30–1. When referring to the first book of his commentary, I cite the folios of MS Borghese 329, followed by the page references to the more accessible 1596 edition. The first is referred to as '*Scriptum*', the second as '*In I Sent*'. When referring to books II–IV of his commentary, I use the 1605 edition cited in n. 1 above. Peter produced at least two redactions of his *Sentences* commentary. My research is based entirely on the 'great *Scriptum*' represented in MS Borghese 329 and the printed edition of 1596. For more on this vexed question of the double redaction see Buytaert's introduction to vol. i of *Scriptum*, and A. Maier, 'Zu einigen Sentenzenkommentaren des 14. Jahrhunderts', in id., *Ausgehendes Mittelalter*, vol. 1 (Rome, 1964), pp. 265–305, esp. 265–89.

[4] *Scriptum*, d. 30: 'Utrum aliqua relatio sit in rerum natura circumscripto omni opere intellectus vel sit omnis relatio in sola apprehensione' (fol. 317ᵛa; *In I Sent*., p. 660.1 A).

[5] *Scriptum*, d. 30, fols, 318ᵛb–321ʳa; *In I Sent*., pp. 662.2 E–667.2 D.

[6] *Scriptum*, d. 30, fols. 318ᵛb–319ʳa; *In I Sent*., pp. 662.2 E–663.1 E.

[7] *Scriptum*, d. 30, fol. 318ᵛa–b; *In I Sent*., p. 662.1 C–662.2 C.

much of Peter's writing, they all suffer from vagueness and
ambiguity. His terminology is at times not clear, and he has a
tendency to repeat his thought in different ways in an often vain
attempt to clarify his position. These arguments are valuable,
however, in revealing the basic assumptions supporting his own
theory.

According to the first argument,

it seems that relation is only in apprehension, having no being in things.
For that what is one and simple reach two really distinct [things] only
seems to come about by the work of the intellect, otherwise the same
simple and indivisible [thing] will be in many [that are] separated from
each other. But it is clear that a relation reaches two distinct [things], one
as a foundation and the other as a term. If, however, it is something
indivisible and simple, then it cannot be posited in [an extra-mental]
thing, but only in the consideration [of the intellect].[8]

In conceiving of a relation as an entity simple and indivisible,
Peter opposes those like Aquinas, Giles of Rome, and Henry of
Ghent who affirm two aspects of a real relation, its *esse-in* and
esse-ad. The first aspect is the accidentality of a relation, its being
in a subject, while the second is its specifically relational character. This distinction plays no role in Peter's ontology of relations.[9]

---

[8] *Scriptum*, d. 30: 'Sed in oppositum videtur quod relatio sit in sola apprehensione
nullum esse habens in rebus. Illud enim quod unum existens et simplex attingit duo
realiter distincta non videtur esse nisi ex opere intellectus, alias idem simplex et
indivisibile erit in multis ad invicem separatis. Sed manifestum est quod relatio attingit
duo distincta, unum tamquam fundamentum et reliquum tamquam terminum. Cum
tamen sit indivisibile quid et simplex, ergo non potest poni in re sed in sola consideratione'
(fol. 318ᵛa; *In I Sent.*, p. 662.1 C).
[9] Peter explicitly argues against the view that a real relation has two ontological
constituents. According to this view, a real relation with respect to its accidentality is
already in a white thing in the east before a white thing in the west is produced. After the
production, a real relation is now in the first white thing also with respect to its having a
condition or respect to a term. This view is similar to the position of Thomas Aquinas and
Henry of Ghent. Peter argues: 'Nec valet si dicatur quod tota realitas similitudinis
praeerat in albedine nihilominus deficiebat terminus, et idcirco producto termino non
consurgit realitas similitudinis quantum ad id quod ponit in fundamento, sed ex ea parte
qua terminum exigebat. Non valet quidem . . . quia habitudo non intelligebatur in esse
orientali albedini ante productionem albedinis accidentalis [*lege*: occidentalis]. Cum ergo
tota ratio relationis consistat in esse habitudinem, manifeste apparet quod nihil praefuit de
similitudine quantum ad id quod importat in recto, nec solum deficiebat terminus immo
formale importatum in recto . . .' (fol. 324ʳa; *In I Sent.*, p. 673.2 CD).

Further, the argument takes for granted that no one, simple extra-mental thing can exist in many really distinct spatially separated subjects. This accords with Peter's strong intuition that what exists extra-mentally must be particular. This intuition guides his discussion of universals where, for example, he argues against Scotus' theory that there exist natures common to many individuals of the same species.[10]

In the second argument, Peter reasons: '. . . the formal effect of a relation is not other than that one thing be carried to another. But it is clear that nature does not carry one thing to another, but only the intellect. Therefore neither does a relation have being in nature but only in the intellect.'[11] Like the first argument, this one suffers from the use of metaphor: what is the force of 'carry' here? Still, one can discern the beginning of the post-medieval difficulty in conceiving a relation as an accident in one thing and somehow 'toward' another. Because of this difficulty, Peter resorts to metaphor: if a relation did exist extra-mentally, it would somehow have to 'reach' from one thing to another or 'carry' one thing toward another. Remarkably in the year 1316, Peter can make little sense of the traditional view of relation.

In the third argument he writes:

Besides, that one existing [thing, i.e. a real relation], which is to be imagined as a kind of interval between two [things], does not seem to be in extra-mental reality but only in the intellect. [This is so] not only because nature does not make such intervals, but also because such a medium or interval does not seem to be in any one of them [i.e. the two extra-mental things] as in a subject, but between them where it is evident that there is not some thing that can be the subject [of the relation]. So it is necessary that such an interval is only objectively in the intellect. But the Commentator [i.e. Averroes] says, in the third book of his *Physics* commentary, comment twenty, that a relation is one disposition existing between two; and it is evident even without him that paternity is conceived as a kind of medium connecting a father with a son, and so

[10] For Peter's teaching that all extra-mental reality is particular, see *In II Sent.*, d. 9, q. 3, a. 3 (p. 114.1 F–114.2 A); Dreiling, *Konzeptualismus*, pp. 159–72; and see ibid., pp. 87–93, 150–5 for his arguments against Duns Scotus on common nature.

[11] *Scriptum*, d. 30: 'Praeterea formalis effectus relationis non est aliud nisi rem unam ad alteram ferri. Sed manifestum est quod natura non fert rem unam ad alteram sed tantummodo intellectus. Ergo nec relatio habet esse in natura sed solum in intellectu' (fol. 318^{v}a; *In I Sent.*, p. 662.1 D).

with the other relations. Therefore, a relation can be posited only in apprehension.[12]

A clearer view of Peter's way of conceiving relations emerges from this argument.[13] He does not think of a real relation primarily as an accident existing or being founded in one thing as its subject; it is imagined as an entity that exists between two things. Peter himself stresses this property of relations. He conceives of a relation as an 'interval', and he believes 'it is necessary that besides the foundation and term, a relation be conceived as a medium'.[14] It has the property of 'being in the middle'[15] or 'connecting'[16] two things; it is a disposition, condition, or something existing between two things.[17] As seen

---

[12] *Scriptum*, d. 30: 'Praeterea illud quod unum existens est imaginandum quasi intervallum inter duo non videtur esse in rerum natura sed in solo intellectu: tum quia natura non facit talia intervalla, tum quia huiusmodi medium vel intervallum non videtur subiective esse in aliquo illorum, sed inter illa ubi constat quod non est aliqua res quae subici possit. Unde necesse est quod tale intervallum sit solummodo in intellectu obiective. Sed Commentator dicit, tertio *Physicorum* commento 20, quod relatio est una dispositio existens inter duo; et apparet etiam sine ipso quod paternitas concipitur quasi per modum medii connectentis patrem cum filio, et sic de aliis relationibus. Ergo non potest poni relatio nisi in apprehensione sola' (fol. 318ᵛa–b; *In I Sent.*, p. 662.1 DE).

[13] In another place Peter argues: 'Quarta demum propositio est quod relationi repugnat in communi ex sua ratione quod sit res in natura existens. Dicitur enim de ea quod acquiritur et oritur in fundamento sine sui mutatione, sola mutatione facta in termino. Illud igitur non est res quod acquiritur in subiecto ullo agente ipsum attingente. Sed manifestum est quod albo existente in oriente, si fiat album aliud in occidente similitudo intelligitur inesse albo quod praefuit in oriente absque hoc quod aliquod agens ipsum attingat praeterquam intellectus qui ipsum comparat ad album aliud quod de novo producitur in occidente. Non enim dealbans in occidente actionem suam protendit usque in oriens ut ibi similitudinem imprimat, nec coelum aut aliquid aliud potest imprimere eam nisi solus intellectus. Ergo poni non potest quod aliqua talis res fuerit acquisita, et per consequens relationi ex sui natura repugnat habere existentiam in natura' (fol. 324ʳa; *In I Sent.*, p. 673.2 A–C).

[14] *Scriptum*, d. 30: 'Sed praedicti modi dicendi non videntur posse stare. Aut enim intelligunt sic ponentes quod relatio non importet in recto aliquam habitudinem quae concipiatur per modum medii et intervalli cuiusdam inter fundamentum et terminum . . .' (fol. 319ʳb; *In I Sent.*, p. 663.2 F). '. . . ergo necesse est quod ultra fundamentum et terminum concipiatur relatio tamquam medium' (fol. 319ᵛa; *In I Sent.*, p. 664.1 C).

[15] *Scriptum*, d. 30: '. . . ergo necessario concipit eam tamquam aliquod medians inter illa, quod fundetur in uno et terminetur in alio' (fol. 319ʳb; *In I Sent.*, p. 664.1 AB).

[16] See nn. 18, 39, and 46 below.

[17] *Scriptum*, d. 30: '. . . ergo necesse est quod relatio concipiatur per modum cuiusdam habitudinis quae sit dispositio una existens inter illa. . . . Ergo ultra fundamentum et terminum relatio est aliqua medians habitudo, unde hoc habet vocabulum "ad-aliquid". Nam ultra aliquid quod est terminus, ponit "ad" quod exprimit habitudinem mediantem. Praeterea impossibile est quod intellectus concipiat aliqua mutari in suo conceptu de non tali ad tale nisi addendo aliquid secundum rationem; sed concipiens duo alba simul

in the first argument stressing the simplicity of a relation, the *esse-in* or accidental character of a relation has been entirely discarded.

Furthermore, Peter is convinced that no extra-mental thing can have this peculiar property of connecting two subjects: if a relation were an accident inherent in one subject, it could not perform its function of connecting two subjects. He even goes beyond Richard of Mediavilla and Henry of Harclay who admitted real relations into their ontologies as non-inhering accidents. According to them, a real relation is an extra-mental non-inhering condition. However they still spoke of it as somehow in one thing and toward another. Peter can make no sense of this language. In fact, Peter's emphasis on a relation's connecting or intervening between two things and his conviction that no extramental thing can have this peculiar property are two of the principal assumptions leading him to conclude that a relation is an entity that exists only in apprehension.[18] As will be shown in Section Two, Subsection Two, only the cognitive powers of sense and intellect can 'reach' two things at once, connecting or joining them together.

Peter offers other less original reasons against the extra-mental reality of real relations, many being formulations of arguments common to the debate. He uses the often cited text from the fifth book of Aristotle's *Physics* which states that there is no change in the category of relation. Peter quickly concludes that a relation has no extra-mental reality or 'natural existence'.[19]

He also argues against the extra-mental reality of real relations

existere, nondum concipit ut similia. Ergo dum concipit ut similia aliquid addit in conceptu ad illa, utpote habitudinem et connexionem mutuam inter ipsa' (fol. 319ᵛa; *In I Sent.*, p. 664.1 B–E).

[18] See another argument of Peter's: 'Praeterea omnis realitas coniungens aliqua duo impeditur per distantiam illorum, ut patet quod actio et passio requirunt approximationem et habent ex distantia impediri. Sed relatio est habitudo connectens extrema secundum quod Simplicius dicit hypostasim relationis in diversis existere cum sit ad alterum habitudo. Constat autem quod haec connexio per nullam distantiam impeditur. Unde quantumcumque duo alba sint distantia vel propinqua, nulla variatio sit in albedine nec erit vigorosior aut debilior sicut contingit in actione et passione. Ergo impossibile est quod relatio sit res aliqua in natura quae connectat extrema' (fol. 324ʳb; *In I Sent.*, p. 674.1 BC).
[19] *Scriptum*, d. 30: 'Praeterea id quod advenit alicui seipso quiescente non potest dici habere realitatem et existentiam naturalem in illo. Sed Philosophus, V *Physicorum*, sic dicit de relatione quod advenit alteri relativorum absque hoc quod transmutetur' (fol. 324ᵛa; *In I Sent.*, p. 674.1 F).

by using a version of the infinite regress argument.[20] In this argument and throughout his discussion, it is clear that he considers a thing (*res*) whatever exists outside the soul.[21] He does not distinguish various types of real entities as Scotus had done, and he is content to call both the intentions of Henry of Ghent and the formalities of Duns Scotus things. Peter is against positing any such realities as intentions, quiddities, formalities, modes, or the like.[22] They all are things, and all lead to an infinite regress.[23]

He argues that if relations were real things there would be fantastic consequences.

For if equality were a thing in act, it would follow that there would be innumerable realities in one subject. For one man is unequal to all the grains of sand that are in the sea and to all the leaves and to the entire collection of flowers, and so with other innumerable things; and so innumerable inequalities [i.e. relations of inequality] will be in one man. If therefore whatever relation is a thing in act, one man will be adorned [and loaded down] with innumerable realities. Similarly if the face of whatever man is of a different form to the faces of all [other] men, the man's face will be burdened with innumerable realities, because he will have as many real dissimilitudes and differences of form in [his] face as in a subject as there are [other] men.[24]

---

[20] *Scriptum*, d. 30 (fol. 321ʳb; *In I Sent.*, p. 668.1 AB).

[21] *Scriptum*, d. 30 (fol. 320ᵛa; *In I Sent.*, p. 666.2 BC).

[22] *Scriptum*, d. 30 (fol. 320ᵛb; *In I Sent.*, p. 667.1 B–D).

[23] *Scriptum*, d. 30 (fol. 322ʳa; *In I Sent.*, p. 669.1 F–669.2 A).

[24] *Scriptum*, d. 31: '. . . nec similitudo nec relatio alia est in rebus in actu, sed earum reductio in actum sit per aliquam apprehensionem. Si enim aequalitas esset res in actu, sequeretur quod innumerabiles realitates essent in uno subiecto. Nam unus homo inaequalis est omnibus arenis quae sunt in mari et omnibus foliis et universis floribus et sic de aliis innumerabilibus rebus; et ita innumerabiles inaequalitates erunt in uno homine. Si ergo quaelibet [relatio] sit res in actu, erit unus homo innumerabilibus realitatibus honeratus. Similiter cum facies cuiuslibet hominis faciebus omnium hominum sit diffor-mis, erit honusta facies hominis innumerabilibus realitatibus, quia quot sunt homines tot habebit reales dissimilitudines et difformitates in facie subiective. Similiter etiam si sunt decem albedines, erunt in qualibet novem similitudines, et ita tot realitates in actu. Habet enim qualibet albedo novem similitudines ad novem albedines et resultabunt in universo nonaginta; vel si fiunt centum albedines, necesse est in actu ponere decem millia realitates. Unde cum talis rerum infinitas omnino irrationalis sit, non debet in mentem alicuius venire quod similitudo vel dissimilitudo sint in rebus nisi in potentia et quod tunc fient in actu dum anima illas reducit' (fol. 343ʳa–b; *In I Sent.*, pp. 713.2 E–714.1 A). In this century, J. E. M. McTaggart embraced just such a view as criticized here by Aureoli, holding that if any one substance changes, all substances must change by gaining or losing a relation of similarity. See J. Passmore, *A Hundred Years of Philosophy* (London, 1957), p. 78.

Peter, who employs the principle of parsimony frequently throughout his writings, finds these consequences altogether irrational.[25]

Finally, Peter gives his formulation of a principal argument used by Harclay at about the same time, *c.*1315, and by Ockham a few years later. They all argue against Scotus' strong realism: if relations of similarity were extra-mental things really distinct from their white foundations, an omnipotent God could keep two white things in existence while destroying their really distinct and so separable relations of similarity—which is absurd. Peter gives this argument his own conceptualist twist:

But that, without any apprehension, similarity and equality are not in nature is clear in this way: for if similarity were a thing existing in a white [thing] with another white [thing] posited, or if equality were a thing existing in a line, having posited another line of the same quantity, it would follow that the omnipotent one without contradiction would be able to conserve the two whitenesses while annihilating the thing of similarity; and he would conserve the two lines while annihilating the thing of equality. But it is clear that God is not able to do this, because supposing that God destroyed the reality of equality or of similarity, still an intellect considering two whitenesses finds them similar just as before. Therefore, it is superfluous and impossible that some reality be added to the whitenesses that would be called 'similarity' or to the quantities that would be called 'equality'.[26]

In his version Peter does not use the notions of natural priority and posteriority as found in Harclay. He is closer to Ockham's stronger version, (K) in Section One, Subsection Three, of

---

[25] For his use of the principle of parsimony, see *In II Sent.*, d. 14, q. 1, a. 2: '. . . multitudo ponenda non est nisi ratio evidens necessaria illud probet aliter per pauciora salvari non posse. Deus enim et natura nihil faciunt frustra' (p. 189.1 C). See also Dreiling, *Konzeptualismus*, pp. 204–7.

[26] See ch. 6, sect. 2.1.1, and ch. 7, sect. 1.3. Peter Aureoli, *Scriptum*, d. 30: 'Quod vero similitudo et aequalitas non sint in natura absque apprehensione quacumque, sic patet. Si enim similitudo esset res existens in albo posito alio coalbo, aut si aequalitas esset res existens in linea posita linea alia quantitatis eiusdem, sequeretur quod omnipotens sine contradictione posset duas albedines conservare adnihilando rem similitudinis. Et conservaret duas lineas adnihilando rem aequalitatis. Sed manifestum est quod hoc Deus facere non potest quia dato quod realitatem aequalitatis aut similitudinis Deus deleret, adhuc intellectus considerans duas albedines aeque invenit eas similes sicut ante. Ergo superfluum est et impossibile quod realitas aliqua addatur albedinibus quae appelleretur similitudo aut quantitatibus quae dicatur aequalitas' (fol. 321ᵛa; *In I Sent.*, p. 668.2 DE). Peter gives a number of other arguments against the extra-mental reality of relations of Aristotle's second and third types; see fols. 322ᵛb–324ʳa; *In I Sent.*, pp. 671–3.

Chapter Seven, but he introduces the activity of the intellect as Ockham does not. This is characteristic of a difference between the two Franciscans in the treatment of relations: Aureoli is interested in the psychological aspects of his conceptualist theory and does not make use of a semantics of connotative terms as Ockham does.

2. Peter Aureoli's Doctrine of Relations

Peter taught that no relations really exist in extra-mental reality; all relations exist only 'objectively in the soul'.[27] His ontology of relations can be understood only by first examining what he means by 'objective existence', and this can be approached by considering his doctrine of universals as concepts, for these also exist objectively in the soul.

2.1. Objective Existence and Universals

Peter's doctrine of universals is not without ambiguity. Problems arise not only from his vague terminology and his desire to mediate widely differing positions,[28] but also from the fact that he treats universals in two places, and the accounts, though similar in some respects, are not fully compatible.

The first account (i) is found in the second book of his *Sentences* commentary, distinction three, question two, articles one to five, and the second account (ii) is found in the second book, distinction nine, question two, articles one to four. The differences can briefly be summarized as follows: in (i) one object suffices for the formation of many universal concepts; in (ii) many objects are required. Regarding the content of a universal concept, i.e. what it represents, in (i) a universal concept represents particular things; in (ii) it is constituted by a qualitative resemblance existing between many particular objects. In both (i) and (ii) the difference

---

[27] *Scriptum*, d. 30: 'Ex praedictis igitur colligitur evidenter quod relatio non habet esse nisi in anima obiective et quod hoc competit cuilibet trium modorum ex sua propria ratione et omni relationi ex proprietate et rationi communi . . .' (fol. 324ᵛb; *In I Sent.*, p. 674.2 F).

[28] On Peter's attempts at mediation, see Dreiling, *Konzeptualismus*, pp. 203–4; on Peter's terminology, pp. 125–7, 146.

between universal concepts, say between 'man' and 'animal', is accounted for by a difference in clarity and determination. But in (i) the more or less clear and determined concepts represent one and the same thing, e.g. Socrates. In (ii) they represent the resemblance between various things, e.g. between Socrates and Plato or between Socrates and Brownie the donkey. Finally, in (i) universal concepts are only unclear concepts of individuals; in (ii) universal concepts differ in kind and number from concepts of individuals.[29]

Instead of trying to account for these differences or even attempting to reconcile them, I use only the second discussion. It is more helpful as an introduction to Peter's theory of relation, for it sheds light not only on his doctrine of objective existence, but also on the different ways the unity characteristic of a universal exists both within the soul and in external reality. This last parallels the different ways a real relation exists both within and outside the soul.

According to Peter, only singular and particular objects exist in extra-mental reality.[30] In distinction nine, question two, article four of the second book of his *Sentences* commentary, he explains the psychological process by which we form universal concepts from these individual objects.[31] Peter believes that some individual objects produce by means of our senses similar impressions of the same type in the intellect. The objects cause similar sensible impressions of the same type first in the senses. From the senses, impressions or *species* of the same type are

---

[29] See Dreiling, *Konzeptualismus*, pp. 147–9; Teetaert, 'Pierre Auriol', cols. 1851–3.

[30] For Peter's teaching that only particulars exist in extra-mental reality, see n. 10 above.

[31] *In II Sent.*, d. 9, q. 2, a. 4: 'Dico quod partim est in re, partim in specie, partim in actu, partim in conceptu. Ubi considerandum est quod ille est ordo, quia res illa particularis est apta nata facere in intellectu similes impressiones et eiusdem rationis. Ideo causant in intellectu species eiusdem rationis. Ad species autem eiusdem rationis sequitur in intellectu actus unus eiusdem rationis (sive species sit actus ille sive non, non curo modo). Ideo individua quae possunt communicare in una specie communicant in uno actu. Ad unum autem actum sequitur in intellectu unus conceptus, ita quod si actus sit perfectus et terminatus, conceptus obiectivus erit perfectus et terminatus; et ideo quae possunt communicare in uno actu communicant ex consequenti in uno conceptu obiectivo. Conceptus autem obiectivus non est aliud quam res apparens obiective per actum intellectus, qui dicitur conceptus quia intrinsece includit ipsum concipi passivum; et ideo secundum aliud et aliud concipi est alius et alius conceptus, cum identitate rei' (p. 109. 1 A–109.2A).

produced in the intellect; the intellect in turn produces a corresponding intellectual act. Peter is not concerned here with whether
the intellectual act and the *species* are identical or distinct. And for
our purposes, we need not puzzle over the ontological status of
the *species*. The intellectual act, however, is a real quality in the
soul. Finally, the intellectual act produces a universal concept
which is common to the many particular individuals at the
beginning of the causal chain. In short, certain individuals cause
impressions of the same type in the senses which produce
corresponding impressions or *species* in the intellect. The intellect, in turn, produces an intellectual act which produces a
universal concept existing 'objectively' in the soul.

Without dwelling on particulars of the psychological process,
two points are important: the unity of the universal and its
ontological status.

Peter says that the unity characteristic of the universal exists in
different ways at different parts of the causal chain.[32] In the many
extra-mental particular things, this unity does not exist actually,
but only in potency and inchoatively. The many extra-mental
things have the capacity or aptitude to produce impressions which
can bring about the numerically one universal concept. Perhaps
one can say more aptly that this unity exists virtually outside the
mind, since the extra-mental things have the power or *virtus* of
affecting the senses and intellect in such a way that they produce a
universal concept.[33]

---

[32] Ibid.: 'Tunc ad propositum, dico quod unitas specifica habitudinem aliquam habet
ad conceptum obiectivum in intellectu, et aliam ad actum intellectus, aliam autem ad
speciem et aliam ad rem extra. Est ergo unitas specifica in conceptu obiectivo formaliter, et
hoc est in re, in quantum objicitur intellectui et includit intrinsece concipi. Ideo si quaeras:
"Unitas specifica humanitatis in quo est formaliter?" dico quod in humanitate, non in
animalitate, sed ut concepta est, et hoc modo idem est quod conceptus obiectivus hominis.
Sed illa unitas est in re extra in potentia et inchoative in quantum nata est causare in
intellectu impressionem perfectam consimilem alterius rei, ex qua sequitur unitas actus et
ex consequenti unitas unius conceptus obiectivi. Sed in specie (si ponatur alia ab actu et
causa actus) dico quod talis unitas esset unitas sicut in causa. Nam eo modo quo species est
causa actus est causa conceptus obiectivi, [cuius] est formaliter talis unitas. Sed ad
alterum, quam habitudinem habet talis unitas, dico quod habitudo ista reducitur ad
habitudinem quam habet actus ad ipsum conceptum obiectivum sive ad rem positam in
esse apparenti et intellectu, de quo dictum est in primo et alias' (p. 109.2 A–C).

[33] He himself talks of one thing virtually containing a number of impressions, *In II
Sent.*, d. 3, q. 2, a. 4: '... dico quod habet ortum [*scil.* diversitas rationum generis et
differentiae] a re eadem simplicissima quae virtualiter continet duas impressiones, non
quod hoc quod dico "virtualiter duae impressiones" ponat in re aliquam diversitatem, sed
idem est ac si dicerem eandem rem continentem duos effectus' (p. 68.2 E F).

In addition, the unity of the universal is in the *species* and the intellectual act 'as in a cause', since they are the immediate causes of the concept. Finally, the unity of the universal is formally in the concept produced by the intellectual act, since it is only in this concept that the unity characteristic of the universal actually exists.

Second, regarding the ontological status of the universal concept, Peter distinguishes between the ontological status of the act of apprehension, whether sensitive or intellectual, and that of the object of the act. The act of apprehension really exists and is a quality in the soul, but the object of the act has a non-real mode of existence. It exists only as an object of apprehension, and so is said to exist 'objectively' or 'intentionally'. Hence, when a thing is sensed or understood, in addition to really existing, it begins to exist in the soul intentionally or in a diminished way. Depending on what type of act produces it, Peter uses different terms to designate this being: *esse intentionale, esse apparens, esse visum,* or *esse iudicatum.* Another term he uses, in discussing both universals and relations, is *esse obiectivum,* the being a thing has as an object of apprehension whether sensitive or intellectual.

Peter advances a number of arguments for holding that in both sensitive and intellectual apprehension, whether of a singular or of a universal, one must posit the term of the apprehension as the thing existing in objective being. He provides eight cases of sensory illusion to show that in intuitive cognition the extramental objects are apprehended in *esse apparens.*[34] In one case a circle appears when a stick is swung rapidly. I do not know why, but he assumes that the circle is no thing really existing in the air. And neither does it really exist in the stick which is straight. Finally the circle does not really exist in the eye or the act of vision, for it appears to be in the air where the eye and act of vision are not. Peter concludes that the circle does not really exist at all. It only has objective existence as an object of the sense of sight. He uses other examples of sensory illusion such as a stick appearing broken in water, cases of double vision in which a candle appears twice, and images created by mirrors. All these purport to show that the sense and imagination produce their objects in a non-real mode of existence. From these and other considerations, Peter argues that not only non-veridical acts of sense perception but

---

[34] *Scriptum,* d. 3, sect. 14, nn. 31–5, 55–8 (ed. Buytaert, vol. ii, pp. 696–700, 712–15).

also veridical acts of sense, imagination, and intellect produce some object in a non-real mode of existence.[35]

Although at the time some argued that Peter's doctrine of objective existence led to sceptical consequences, the object of knowledge and sense being an entity other than the extra-mental object, I believe Peter himself advocated a direct realism in epistemology.[36] When one apprehends an extra-mental object, Peter denies that there is any really existing *species* that is produced in the soul as term of the apprehension. He argues against Thomas Aquinas on this point, precisely because such entities would cause our knowledge to be of these really existing things in the mind and not of the extra-mental things themselves.[37] On the other hand, he argues against those who believe that one need posit only the extra-mental real thing and the really existing mental act.[38] Instead, Peter teaches that the object acquires a

[35] *Scriptum*, d., n. 31: 'Prima quidem quod in actu intellectus de necessitate res intellecta ponitur in quodam esse intentionali conspicuo et apparenti. Non est enim magis formativus sensus interior aut exterior quam sit actus intellectus; sed actus exterioris sensus ponit rem in esse intentionali, ut patet in multis experientis' (ed. Buytaert, vol. ii, p. 696). He then gives the eight cases of sensory illusion.

[36] For a clear and helpful discussion of this objective-existence theory of Aureoli and Ockham's criticisms, see M. Adams, 'Ockham's Nominalism and Unreal Entities', *Philosophical Review* 86 (1977), pp. 144–76. For the objections of Walter Chatton and Adam Wodeham in addition to those of Ockham, see R. Wood, 'Adam Wodeham on Sensory Illusions with an Edition of "Lectura Secunda", Prologus, Quaestio 3', *Traditio* 38 (1982), pp. 213–52. See also Teetaert, 'Pierre Auriol', col. 1853; Ph. Boehner, '*Notitia Intuitiva* of Non-Existents according to Peter Aureoli, O.F.M. (1322)', *Franciscan Studies* 8 (1948), pp. 388–416; F. A. Prezioso, 'La teoria dell'essere apparente nella gnoseologia di Pietro Aureolo, O.F.M. (1322)', *Studi francescani* 22 (1950), pp. 15–43.

[37] *Scriptum*, d. 9: 'Tertia autem propositio est quod nulla forma realis existens subiective in intellectu vel phantasmate ponenda est ad quam aspiciat intellectus. . . . Praeterea si sit forma aliqua specularis realiter inhaerens intellectui ad quam terminetur aspectus intellectus, aut in illam ultimate quiescit aut per illam ad res extra procedit; sed non potest dari istud nec illud. Primum quidem non, quia tunc scientiae non essent de rebus sed de talibus idolis quod omnino est aestimandum absurdum' (fol. 167[va–b]; *In I Sent.*, p. 319.1 F–319.2 A).

[38] *Scriptum*, d. 23: 'Secundo vero deficit quia imaginatur quod res concepta denominatur tantummodo ab actu intellectus et non capiat aliquod esse intentionale plus quam Caesar qui pingitur capiat a pictura. Hoc enim est impossibile. Manifestum est siquidem quod denominari praesupponit nomen aut adeo vocabulum; sed conceptus qui lucet in acie cogitantis et qui formatur et concipitur obiective nullius linguae est, immo ab omni nomine et omni vocabulo abstrahit secundum Augustinum, XV *De Trinitate*, cap. X. Ergo res quae concipitur capit esse aliud quam solum denominari. Praeterea, Commentator dicit IX *Metaph.*, commento VII. quod entia quae non sunt extra animam non dicuntur esse simpliciter, sed esse in anima cogitativa. Sed manifestum est quod per solum denominari non dicerentur esse in ea, alioquin Caesar sculptus aut pictus aeque erit in pictura sive sculptura sicut res intellectae erunt in anima. Ergo res concepta capit aliquod aliud quam denominari, utpote esse intentionale et diminutum' (fol. 260[va]; *In I Sent.*, p. 531.1 D–F).

non-real mode of existence when it is apprehended. Whatever the problems with his theory, his intention was that the object of sense and intellect is not some really existing thing other than the extra-mental thing, but rather that same extra-mental thing, only as existing in objective being.

2.2. The Objective Existence of Relations

With this background, we can examine Peter's teaching on the ontological status of relations. He gives a good summary:

relation taken formally and directly—namely as a condition which exists in a foundation and is between the foundation and term and which is nothing but being-toward and a respect—that [relation] certainly as such does not have being in things aside from any intellectual and sensitive apprehension, but it has being in the soul objectively, so that in things there are only foundations and terms, and the condition and connection between those [things] is from the cognitive soul.[39]

Like universals, relations do not really exist apart from the activity of the soul; they only come to exist objectively or intentionally by the activity of sense or intellect. When examining Aristotle's first type of relations based on number, Peter says that a relation of specific identity or of equality or of similarity is identical with an objective apprehension. He specifically distinguishes this from the real act of apprehension.[40] The objective

[39] *Scriptum*, d. 30: 'Circa secundum vero considerandum est quod sumendo relationem pro eo quod dicit formaliter et in recto (videlicet pro habitudine quae inexistit fundamento et mediat inter fundamentum et terminum et quae non est aliud quam esse-ad et respectus), ipsa quidem ut sic non habet esse in rebus circumscripta omni apprehensione intellectiva et sensitiva, sed habet esse in anima obiective, ita quod in rebus non sunt nisi fundamenta et termini; habitudo vero et connexio inter illa est ab anima cognitiva. Hoc autem poterit ex propositione quadruplici apparere' (fol. 321ʳa–b; *In I Sent.*, p. 667.2 EF). The four-part proposition is the following: 'Prima quidem relationes quae dicuntur modo numeri vel unius non sunt in re extra sine opere intellectus' (fol. 321ʳb; *In I Sent.*, p. 667.2 F); 'Secunda vero propositio est quod paternitas et filiatio et universaliter respectus de secundo modo qui fundantur super producere et produci non possunt esse res extra animam existentes' (fol. 322vᵇ; *In I Sent.*, p. 671.1 A); 'Tertia quoque propositio est quod relatio scientiae ad scibile et sensus ad sensibile et sic de omnibus quae referuntur ut mensuratum ad mensuram non sunt in rebus' (fol. 323ʳb; *In I Sent.*, p. 672.1 B); 'Quarta demum propositio est quod relationi repugnat in communi ex sua ratione quod sit res in natura existens' (fol. 324ʳa; *In I Sent.*, p. 673.2 A).
[40] *Scriptum*, d. 30: 'Unde non est aliud similitudo duarum albedinum quam earum apprehensio indistincta. Non quidem apprehensio actus, sed apprehensio obiectiva. Haec autem apprehensio indistincta incipit ab una albedine et terminatur ad alteram aut econverso' (fol. 322ʳb; *In I Sent.*, p. 670.1 BC).

apprehension (or judgement as he sometimes calls it) corresponds to and is the result of the act of apprehension (or judgement), whether sensitive or intellectual.[41]

Although Peter moves the relation from outside to within the mind or sense, he preserves yet transforms its traditional character as 'a condition which exists in a foundation and is between the foundation and its term'. He explains that with the relation of colour similarity, three concepts are involved: 'A particular white thing is apprehended in its singularity, and besides this another singular white thing, and with this a certain indistinction of one from the other.'[42] The three concepts are: (i) a particular white thing as apprehended, (ii) an objective apprehension of its indistinction in colour from (iii) a second particular white thing as apprehended. The first white thing apprehended functions as a foundation, while the other is the term of the relation.

For clarity through contrast, compare these two cases. (i) A person simultaneously apprehends two real white things *a* and *b*. The really existing apprehensive act produces *a* and *b* in objective being. (ii) A person simultaneously apprehends two real white things *a* and *b* and judges them to be indistinct with respect to colour. There is not only the apprehensive act producing *a* and *b* in objective being, but also a judgement that produces a third entity. This latter is the relation of similarity, an entity distinct from the really existing act of judgement that produced it.

One could have the act of apprehension in (i) and not the judgement of indistinction in (ii). One could apprehend two white things and not advert to their indistinction in colour.[43] For instance, one's job could be to take inventory by counting white filing cards. One's attention is on the number of cards, not on their colour, and so one does not make any judgement with

---

[41] *Scriptum*, d. 30: 'Actui enim apprehensivo correspondet apprehensio obiectiva, propter quod cum intellectus duas albedines iudicat indistinctas, correspondet obiective inter illas iudicium indistinctum. Cum vero iudicat eas dissimiles, correspondet quoddam iudicium discrepans et diversum, et haec vocatur dissimilitudo' (fol. 322ᵛa; *In I Sent.*, p. 670.1 E).

[42] *Scriptum*, d. 30: 'Et ideo est habitudo respiciens pro fundamento illam a qua incipit et pro termino reliquam, et similiter econverso. Unde sunt ibi tria concepta, videlicet particularis albedo, et indistincta apprehensio obiectiva ab alia albedine, et tertium alia albedo. Apprehenditur quidem particularis albedo in sua singularitate, et ultra hoc alia singularis albedo, et cum hoc quaedam indistinctio unius ab altera' (fol. 322ʳb; *In I Sent.*, p. 670.1 CD).

[43] See n. 17 above.

respect to their indistinction in colour. In such a case, one does not produce a corresponding objectively existing entity, i.e. the relation. In order for there to actually exist a relation, a judgement of the type in (ii) is necessary. In a very strong sense, then, all real relations are dependent on the activity of intellect or sense.

What precisely are the foundation and term of the relation of similarity? Peter argues that the relation cannot be founded upon an extra-mental common nature. One argument he gives is that if it were, then imagination and sense would be unable to apprehend similarity and dissimilarity of bodies, for the purported common nature is only accessible to the intellect. But by experience we see that this is not the case. Animals are drawn to members of their own species and avoid members of other species and so apprehend similarity, even if they cannot apprehend a common nature.[44]

Nor are the foundation and term the two extra-mental white things. If so, 'it would follow that [something that is] one [i.e. the relation] would be necessarily in two subjects even very distant [from each other]. For one whiteness can be in the north and another in the south.'[45] In this argument, the assumptions found in his opening arguments in Section One above are in evidence. He interprets the property of a relation by which it 'connects' two things in such a way that if a relation were extra-mental, it would be an 'intervening thing' and, in Leibniz's phrase, have its foot in two things. Second, he assumes that no extra-mental thing can exist in two spatially distant things. Hence, because of its very

---

[44] *Scriptum*, d. 31: 'Si utique sic dicatur, non valet . . . quia sequeretur quod similitudo non posset ab animalibus aliis apprehendi nisi ab homine, cum solus homo apprehendat universale et naturam specificam in communi, cuius oppositum docet experientia, cum alia dissimilia fugiant et sibi similibus coniungantur, iuxta illud sapientis: Omne animal suo simili coniungetur. Unde patet quod avis cognoscit aliam suae speciei nec tamen abstrahit specificum conceptum' (fol. 342^{r}b; *In I Sent.*, p. 712.1 BC). See also n. 45 below.

[45] *Scriptum*, d. 30: '. . . identitas, similitudo, aequalitas non sunt aliud quam quaedam unitates. Unitas vero non est indivisio et indistinctio. Haec autem indivisio quam importat identitas non est in natura communi fundata, alioquin non esset relatio sed idempcatio [*sic*] in natura communi quidditativa et essentiali in qua non includeret aliquid relativum. Et iterum imaginatio et sensus non iudicaret [*sic*] similitudines corporum aut dissimilitudines cum naturam communem non apprehendant. Et tamen quod de similitudinibus iudicent experimur. Nec potest dici quod ista indistinctio fundetur super duas albedines numeraliter distinctas prout sunt in re extra, alioquin sequeretur quod una necessario esset in duobus subiectis etiam distantissimis. Nam albedo una potest esse in aquilone et altera in meridie. Relinquitur ergo quod fundetur super apprehensione' (fol. 322^{r}b; *In I Sent.*, p. 670.1 AB).

nature as 'connecting two things', a relation cannot exist extra-mentally.

Instead, the foundation and term are the two white things, but as apprehended and existing in objective being. For it is the act of apprehension of two white things that is the condition of possibility and so foundation for the act of apprehension of their indistinction with respect to colour. It is this really existing act that has the character of 'connecting' or 'reaching' both foundation and term and produces the corresponding objectively existing apprehension, i.e. the relation which also 'connects' or 'reaches' both the foundation and term: '. . . similarity is a certain unity of this quality with that which indeed is not other than the unity of judgement, since distinct [things] are apt by nature to be judged as one and so as liable to a certain unity of judgement and to indistinction which, in the way of an interval, connects them'.[46] Similarity and dissimilarity 'are intervals between qualities, certainly not existing in reality, but only objectively in the soul, since they [i.e. relations] are only certain apprehensions or judgements, indistinct with respect to similarity and conformity, but distinct with respect to dissimilarity and difference of form'.[47]

The objects of these real acts of apprehension vary according to the type of indistinction or distinction grasped by the intellect or sense.[48] The type of indistinction apprehended between two white things is different from that apprehended between two six-foot things. For this reason, these relations are of different types, i.e. similarity and equality.

A further parallel obtains between Peter's treatments of relations and of universals. Real relations are not the mere products of imagination to which there corresponds nothing in extra-mental reality. Like universals, real relations can be said to really

---

[46] *Scriptum*, d. 30: 'Unde similitudo est quaedam unitas huius qualitatis ad illam, quae quidem non est aliud quam unitas iudicii pro eo quod distincta sunt apta nata iudicari ut unum, et ita ut substrata cuidam unitati iudicii et indistinctioni quae per modum intervalli ea connectit. Et ideo tale iudicium obiectivum connectens duas albedines appellatur similitudo, connectens vero duas quantitates vocatur aequalitas' (fol. 325^{r}b; *In I Sent.*, p. 676.1 D).

[47] *Scriptum*, d. 30: 'Secundum hoc igitur patet quod similitudo et dissimilitudo sunt intervalla inter qualitates, non quidem in re existentia sed solum in anima obiective, cum non sint nisi quaedam apprehensiones seu iudicia indistincta quidem quantum ad similitudinem et conformitatem, distincta vero quoad dissimilitudinem et difformitatem. Variatur autem haec indistinctio et iudicium indistinctum secundum diversas qualitates. Alia enim est conformitas alborum et alia nigrorum et sic de aliis qualitatibus' (fol. 322^{v}a; *In I Sent.*, p. 670.1 EF). [48] See n. 47 above.

exist outside the mind—potentially and inchoatively. They become actual only through the activity of the soul. Speaking of how on his theory the predicate in 'Socrates is a father' can truly be said of the really existent extra-mental Socrates, he explains that

those [entities, as relations] that are in extreme potency in things are said to denominate really because there is an imperceptible reduction of them to act through the intellect. And because the intellect does not perceive this, so they seem to be in things without the work of the intellect and to denominate them. And again, when there is set aside every operation of the intellect, and then it is expressed that still Socrates remains a father, some act of intellect now is left remaining, namely that one which expresses this; but that is [the one] that reduces paternity to act.[49]

As with universals outside the soul, the particular extra-mental objects have the aptitude or capacity to stimulate the senses and intellect in such a way that a relation is produced in objective existence. Because this process is imperceptible to the intellect and sense, we are normally deceived into reading into extra-mental reality what we ourselves have 'constructed'.

the intellect is deceived regarding those which it itself constructs when those are in things in potency so near, because it immediately imperceptibly reduces them to act. For then it seems to itself that it had not now constructed such things but had found [them] in things in act, and so it is concerning numbers and time and regarding genus and difference. For those seem to be in things because the intellect imperceptibly works on them.[50]

---

[49] *Scriptum*, d. 30: 'Secundo vero idem apparet ratione, propter hoc enim ea quae sunt in potentia ultimata in rebus dicuntur realiter denominare quia imperceptibilis est reductio eorum in actu ut per intellectum. Et quia non percipit hoc intellectus, ideo videntur esse in rebus sine opere intellectus et ipsas denominare. Et iterum cum circumscribitur omnis operatio intellectus et deinde enunciatur quod adhuc remanet Socrates pater, iam relinquitur aliquis actus intellectus, utpote ille qui hoc enunciat; ille autem est qui reducit paternitatem in actu' (fol. 332^{r}a; *In I Sent.*, p. 689.2 D). See also n. 24 above.

[50] *Scriptum*, d. 30: 'Ad undecimum dicendum quod intellectus decipitur circa ea quae ipsemet fabricat quando illa sunt in rebus in potentia sic propinqua, quod statim imperceptibiliter reducit ea in actu. Tunc enim sibi videtur iam non talia fabricasse sed in rebus reperisse in actu, et ita est de numeris et tempore et de genere et differentia. Videntur enim ista esse in rebus propterea quod intellectus ista imperceptibiliter operatur. . . . Secundum hoc ergo similitudo videtur generari et corrumpi in albo generato termino vel corrupto sine opere intellectus. Non sic autem, nec corrumpitur eius actualitas sed eius potentia propinqua, ita ut posito termino intellectus cogatur ad reducendum in actum similitudinem dum scilicet intelligit album et aliud coalbum' (fol. 331^{r}b; *In I Sent.*, p. 688.1 E–688.2 A).

Again, the real relation can be said to exist virtually in extra-mental particulars, i.e. the particulars have the power or *virtus* to act on the intellect and senses in a certain way. The potential but real existence of a relation outside the mind is completely reducible to the really existing particular objects that are capable of acting on the senses and intellect in a certain way. Hence, just as Peter denies that there is any real thing distinct from extra-mental particulars that has the property of being universal, i.e. common to many, so he denies that there is any distinct real thing that is relational, i.e. 'connects' many. Peter follows the logic of his position in holding that without apprehension two white things are not more similar in act than a black and a white thing.

For without apprehension, there is not a greater conformity in act between two whitenesses than between a whiteness and a blackness. Indeed it is a contradiction in terms, since a conformity is not other than a certain indistinct apprehension falling between the two whitenesses. So taking away the apprehension and having remain the conformity (which is a certain indistinct apprehension) is incoherent. Nevertheless, apart from all apprehension, two whitenesses are said [to be] more similar than a blackness and a whiteness on account of the near potency ultimately necessitating the cognitive power to have in act such an indistinct apprehension that is called 'similarity'.[51]

The ontological distinction between real/potential and objective/actual is important for understanding Peter's position and how it differs from those of others. His doctrine that real relations exist potentially outside the soul allows him to avoid the position of the Stoics, i.e. that real relations have no existence outside the soul whatever.[52] Also because of this doctrine, J. Paulus sees Peter's position to be basically that of Henry of Ghent.[53] As we have seen, Henry taught that there is an intentional distinction

---

[51] *Scriptum*, d. 31: 'Non valet etiam quartum. Nam sine apprehensione inter duas albedines non est magis conformitas in actu quam inter albedinem et nigredinem. Immo est contradictio in terminis cum conformitas non sit aliud quam quaedam apprehensio indistincta intercidens inter duas albedines. Unde tollens apprehensionem et cum hoc conformitatem relinquens, quae est quaedam apprehensio indistincta, repugnantiam ponit. Dicuntur nihilominus duae albedines magis conformes quam nigredo et albedo circumscripta omni apprehensione propter propinquam potentiam ultime necessitantem virtutem cognitivam ad habentem in actu apprehensionem huiusmodi indistinctam quae dicitur similitudo' (fol. 343^{r}b; *In I Sent.*, p. 714.1 D–F); also *Scriptum*, d. 30 (fol. 331^{r}b; *In I Sent.*, p. 688.2 A); *In II Sent.*, d. 3, q. 2, a. 3 (ii, p. 66.1 A B).

[52] Lindner, *Thomas von Strassburg*, p. 119.

[53] Paulus, *Henri de Gand*, p. 192.

between a real relation and its foundation. He believed that one real thing is apt to cause distinct concepts. An intentional distinction is potential in the thing prior to the mind's activity and becomes actual in the mind only when the mind reflecting on these concepts conceives one apart from the other.[54]

Despite this parallel between the two theories, we should not lose sight of the real differences, for the ontological world of Henry of Ghent is quite different from that of Aureoli. At the centre of Henry's ontology is his doctrine of *esse essentiae* which plays a key role in his theory of relations, and nothing like it is even suggested by Aureoli. Second, central to Henry's theory is the distinction between mode and thing; Peter eschews this distinction and denies that real relations are real modes of things. Further, Peter identifies real relations with entities in objective existence; Henry does not. Finally, Henry of Ghent conceives of a real relation as a mode *of one thing*, while Peter conceives of it as an entity connecting or *between two things*.

Peter uses the distinction between the actual and potential existence of a real relation in a number of ways. It provides him with a response to a classic objection against the thesis that relations are mind-dependent: there would be no order in the universe if there were no apprehending intellect or sense—which seems absurd. Peter responds:

And if it is said that apart from all intellect there will not be an ordered universe, on the contrary it is to be said [that, apart from all intellectual activity, there does exist an ordered universe] in very near potency with respect to order, so that the intellect immediately is forced to form that [i.e. the order]. So the universe by itself is said [to be] foundationally ordered, not however actually and formally does it have the respect of order except from apprehension.[55]

Even with no intellects existing, the order of the universe would still exist in potency in such a way that an intellect immediately would be forced to form the actual relation of order. Hence, the

---

[54] Henry of Ghent, *Summa*, a. 27, q. 1 (i, fol. 162 O); *Quodl.* V, q. 6 (i, fol. 161 I–O). See ch. 3, sect. 4.2.

[55] *Scriptum*, d. 30: 'Et si dicatur quod circumscripto omni intellectu non erit universum ordinatum, dicendum quod immo in potentia propinquissima ad respectum ordinis, ita quod intellectus statim cogitur ipsum formare. Unde universum se ipso fundamentaliter dicitur ordinatum, non tamen actualiter et formaliter habet respectum ordinis nisi ex apprehensione' (fol. 331ʳa; *In I Sent.*, p. 687.2 C).

universe is said to be of itself ordered 'foundationally', i.e. as providing some extra-mental grounds for the formation of the relation of order that actually or formally exists only from the activity of apprehension.

Peter also uses this potential–actual distinction in an attempt to maintain the difference between real relations and relations of reason. According to him, a real relation exists in potency in extra-mental reality, and the intellect is forced to reduce this potency to act. With a relation of reason this is not the case. For example, he claims that if a column is to the right of an animal, that relation of 'being to the right of' is not in potency in the column nor is there anything extra-mentally in the column that forces the intellect to conceive of a relation of rightness.[56]

But it seems this will not do. In the case of taking inventory by counting white file cards, I am not forced to apprehend any indistinction with respect to colour; I may choose to so direct my attention, but nothing forces me. Yet the relations of similarity involved really, though potentially, exist extra-mentally. So also in the case of the column: although nothing forces my intellect to do so, if I choose to attend to the position of the column, I can produce an objectively existing apprehension of the column's position with respect to the other object. I see no reason to deny that in this case the relation exists really, though potentially, in extra-mental reality.

Peter has drawn the distinction between relations of reason and real relations in terms of whether or not the relations exist in potency in extra-mental reality. This in turn is analysed in terms of whether the extra-mental objects have the power or *virtus* to cause the corresponding apprehensions. But he then assumes that in the case of real relations the intellect is somehow forced to produce these apprehensions. This is not, however, consonant with the voluntaristic stamp of his conceptualism.

---

[56] *Scriptum*, d. 30: 'Prima quidem quod relatio non dicitur realis ex hoc quod sit actu in re, sed quia est in re secundum propinquam potentiam, ita quod cogitur intellectus illam reducere in actum non ex aliquo extrinseco sed ex intimis ipsius fundamenti. . . . Ideo namque dextrum in columna est relatio rationis quia dextrum non est in potentia in columna nec aliquid quod sit in columna cogit intellectum ad concipiendam relationem dexteritatis circa eam' (fol. 336^{r}a; *In I Sent.*, p. 698.1 CD). See also fol. 336^{r}b–^{v}a; *In I Sent.*, pp. 698.2 E–699.1 C).

the phantasm and agent intellect and possible intellect are in the power of the will, and this [is so] speaking of the exercise of the act; and so that impression, which the intellect receives from the phantasm and the agent intellect, and the mode [e.g. distinctness] or degree [i.e. intensity] of that impression are under the rule of the will. Therefore, I can voluntarily and intentionally transform an impression from greater to less [with respect to distinctness, intensity, etc.] or vice versa.[57]

Although Peter often criticizes Duns Scotus, he has learned and made his own Scotus' emphasis on the role of the will in our psychological life. I do not see how such an emphasis on the voluntary aspect of our apprehensions can be reconciled with his attempt to maintain the distinction between real relations and relations of reason or with his reply to the objection regarding the order of the universe.

3. Conclusion

Peter's characteristic attempt to mediate between widely divergent positions is seen in his theory of relations. He distances himself from Scotus who claims that a categorical relation is an extra-mental thing really distinct from its foundation. But he also explicitly rejects a position attributed to the Stoics whereby a relation is not an entity, really or objectively existing, distinct from the foundation. According to this position, there is no ontological difference between a relation and its foundation; there is only a verbal difference, the terms 'similarity' and 'whiteness' having different connotations.[58] Rejecting both positions, Peter holds that a real relation exists potentially in real being, only becoming

---

[57] *In II Sent.*, d. 3, q. 2, a. 4: '. . . phantasma et intellectus agens et intellectus possibilis sunt in potestate voluntatis et hoc loquendo quantum ad exercitium actus, et non [*lege*: ideo] subest imperio voluntatis illa impressio, quam intellectus recipit a phantasmate et intellectu agente, sed [*lege*: et] modus sive gradus ipsius impressionis. Ideo voluntarie possum et volo me convertere ad maiorem vel minorem impressionem' (ii, p. 68.2 AB). See Dreiling, *Konzeptualismus*, pp. 112, 121; Prezioso, 'Nominalismo ambiguo', pp. 289–90.

[58] *Scriptum*, d. 30: 'Unde qui opinantur relationem non differre a fundamento nisi ratione termini connotati incidunt in sententiam Stoicorum. Negant enim propriam hypostasim relationis quae in sola habitudine per modum cuiusdam intervalli consistit. Sic igitur patet quod Stoici negaverunt a relationibus et sex praedicamentis proprias quidditates et entitates formales dicendo quod erant sola nomina sive solae denominationes absque hypostasi sive fundamentali ratione' (fol. 332^{r}b; *In I Sent.*, p. 690.1 CD).

actual in objective being in the soul. Sentences of the form '$a\mathrm{R}b$' are true if and only if (i) a and b are really distinct extra-mental things, and (ii) there exists an objective apprehension (of intellect or sense) connecting a and b. As argued at the end of Section Two, I do not see how these truth conditions allow Peter to distinguish real relations from those of reason.

Peter incorporates relations into his more general conceptualist ontology, an ontology in which sound and odour along with time and numbers have no actual existence in extra-mental things, but only in intentional being as apprehended.[59] The extent of his conceptualism is evident in his theory of the categories. For Peter, there actually exist extra-mental things only in the categories of substance, quantity, quality, action, and passion. He still maintains, however, that there are ten and not five categories, since the things of the other five categories exist at least potentially outside the soul and become actual through the activity of apprehension.[60]

Finally, his psychological conceptualist approach should not obscure what I believe to be a fundamental turning-point in the history of the problem of relation: a change in the very way of thinking about relation. The radical novelty of Peter's theory lies in conceiving a relation not as in one subject and 'toward' another, but rather as an entity between two subjects. The traditional medieval view of a relation as an extra-mental accident is abandoned.

As with Peter's teaching on universals, this novel view of relations was disputed by many of his contemporaries. William of

---

[59] *Scriptum*, d. 30: 'Ad secundum dicendum quod Philosophus, II *De Anima*, videtur innuere quod sonus non habeat esse reale sed tantum intentionale et obiectivum in potentia auditiva. Unde dicit Commentator, II *De Anima*, commento CXXV, quod Aristoteles opinatur quod tactus accidat rebus tangibilibus et opinatur quod olfacere accidat odori, sed opinatur quod olfacere est quasi ipse odor, et audibile [*lege*: audire] ipse sonus. Et quasi opinatur quod sensuum quidam sint in capitulo relationis, quidam autem in capitulo actionis et passionis per se, sed accidit eis relatio. Et paulo ante dixerat quod esse odoris non est nisi secundum quod est olfactus. Olfactus autem non invenitur nisi in olfaciente' (fol. 330$^\mathrm{v}$b; *In I Sent.*, p. 687.1 CD). For the existence of time and number, see n. 50 above.

[60] *Scriptum*, d. 30: 'Sed forte dicetur quod praedicamenta debent esse vere realia et per consequens non sunt nisi quinque praedicamenta, scilicet actio et passio, substantia, quantitas, qualitas; reliqua vero sunt fictiva et entia rationis. Dicendum tamen ad hoc quod non oportet omnia praedicamenta habere esse completum extra animam, sed sufficit quod sint extra in potentia et eorum actus per animam compleatur . . .' (fol. 330$^\mathrm{v}$a; *In I Sent.*, p. 686.2 DE).

Ockham, who early in his career posited some form of objective existence, came to reject it, and so also Peter's views on both universals and relations.[61] Peter's influence is seen also in discussions later in the fourteenth century. Gregory of Rimini begins his lengthy discussion of relations by asking 'if any relation be a true thing actually existing outside the soul, or on the contrary every relation be only in the soul subjectively or only objectively'.[62] He immediately singles out Aureoli for criticism, devoting a whole article or chapter to his theory. Gregory denies Peter's novel way of conceiving a relation as somehow between two things, marshalling arguments against him. He denies Peter's distinction between potential/real and actual/objective, for then, Gregory contends, no two things would be actually distinct prior to the mind's activity and all would be one, which is false.[63] At present we do not know how many thinkers sided with Gregory and how many defended Peter. More research is needed to trace the fortunes of the conceptualist theory of relations in the later Middle Ages and its transition into the early modern period when it met with such success.

[61] In addition, contrary to Ockham, Peter does not construe the term 'relation' and terms of specific relations such as 'similarity' and 'equality' as connotative terms; they refer directly to the objectively existing object of the act of apprehension; see *Scriptum*, d. 30 (fols. 319^{r}a–320^{r}a; *In I Sent.*, pp. 663.1 E–665.1 F). Also note that although Ockham posits a relational entity in Christ's human nature to the Divine Word, Peter does not; see *Scriptum*, d. 30 (fol. 332^{v}a; *In I Sent.*, p. 690.2B). Finally, contrary to Ockham and Harclay, Peter holds that God is related to creatures only by a relation of reason; see *Scriptum*, d. 30 (fols. 336^{v}b–337^{r}b); *In I Sent.*, pp. 699.2 D–700.2 D).

[62] *Gregorii Ariminensis OESA Lectura super Primum et Secundum Sententiarum*, ed. D. Trapp and V. Marcolino, vol. 3 (Spätmittelalter und Reformation: Texte und Untersuchungen, 8; Berlin and New York, 1984), distinctions 28–32: 'Primum est, utrum aliqua relatio sit vera res actualiter extra animam existens, an omnis relatio sit tantum in anima subiective vel obiective tantummodo' (p. 81; see pp. 81–91).

[63] *Lectura super Primum*, ibid., pp. 90–1; also: 'Contra hoc autem primo sic: Si nulla distinctio est absque operatione animae, nullae res sunt distinctae absque operatione animae. Consequens est falsum quoniam tunc nec deus et creaturae, nec creaturae ab invicem, nec personae divinae ab invicem essent distinctae, nisi essent ab anima apprehensae. . . . Confirmatur, quia, si non essent distincta, non essent plura; et per consequens non essent plura res extra animam, sed omnia essent unum numero' (ibid., p. 83).

9

Conclusion

IN the late Middle Ages many thinkers debated the ontological status of relations because a number of theological issues needed a coherent and illuminating theory of relation. As a result of this intellectual need, a long-standing and deep problem in the history of Western metaphysics finally received protracted and sustained discussion.

Despite the variety of theories, no one held that real relations are completely mind-dependent; even Peter Aureoli taught that they exist potentially in extra-mental reality. This is not surprising. Given the pervasive Aristotelianism, it would be extremely difficult to deny all extra-mental reality to relations, for the scholastics interpreted Aristotle as explicitly teaching that relation is one of the ten categories of extra-mental being. More fundamentally, both Aristotle's and the medievals' thought is pervaded by the notion of an extra-mental order, whether this be the Greek cosmos or the medieval universe. In the thirteenth and early fourteenth centuries the principal problem was not whether relations have extra-mental reality, but rather what specific type of extra-mental reality is to be accorded them.

In debating this latter point, some scholastics came to change how a relation was conceived. There was a change from what I term 'a traditional medieval view', with its roots in the thought of some prominent Greek philosophers, to a view similar to those of some thinkers of the early modern period of philosophy. Two points of clarification are necessary. First, the vagueness of the term 'traditional medieval view' can be diminished perhaps by saying that though certain thinkers proposed conflicting theories, they agreed on what was required of an adequate theory of relation. When certain other thinkers ceased making these demands, ceased conceiving of a relation in such a way that these requirements had to be met, they quitted the tradition. Second, I do not claim that this traditional view of relation was unique throughout the Middle Ages. As mentioned in the Introduction, the Islamic Mutakallimūn seem to have held quite a different view.[1] But what I present below was the predominant view among scholastics of the thirteenth and early fourteenth centuries, the period in which the change took place.

Notice first that many medieval thinkers believed that there were two demands made on an adequate theory of relation. The first demand is historically conditioned, a product of the pervasive Aristotelianism in the late medieval period. The second is what I might call transhistorical, being present in an adequate theory of relation in whatever era.

The first demand, resulting from a substance–accident ontology, was to treat a real relation as an accident existing in one subject. The second demand was to do justice to a relation's character as somehow involving more than one thing. If one's theory must respond to both of these demands, one conceives of a real relation as existing in one thing, yet depending on and somehow 'referring to' another thing. In scholastic terminology, there are two aspects to the being of a real relation: a being-in (*esse-in*) and a being-toward (*esse-ad*).

The medieval dispute becomes more intelligible if we see the individual theories as various strategies for responding to these two demands. If one emphasizes the first demand, one tends to view a real relation on the model of an inhering accident like whiteness. As something is white by virtue of an inherent accidental form of whiteness, so something is similar by virtue of an inherent accidental form of similarity. A real relation is posited as a theoretical entity with the function of 'relating' the subject to another. On the other hand, if one loosened this first demand, one could conceive of a real relation as not inhering in one thing, but more loosely 'belonging to' one thing. Finally, if one neglected or positively repudiated this first demand and emphasized the second, one could conceive of a real relation in quite different,

---

[1] Indeed, in Ibn Sīnā's discussion of relations in his *Metaphysics* commentary, he claims that most of his contemporaries do not subscribe to what I call 'the traditional view'. More research is needed into the thought of the Islamic thinkers on relations; it seems, though, that Ibn Sīnā's minority view became 'the traditional view' of the later scholastics. See M. E. Marmura, 'Avicenna's Chapter, "On the Relative", in the Metaphysics of the Shifā', in *Essays on Islamic Philosophy and Science*, ed. G. F. Hourani (Albany, 1975), pp. 83–99, esp. 87–9.

non-traditional ways, e.g. as equally 'belonging to' *both* relata or as somehow obtaining between them.

Why did one thinker emphasize the traditional accidental reality of a relation and another its specifically relational character? Although a person's theory of relation is the result of a number of factors, such as the theological problems that motivated the discussion, e.g. problems regarding the Trinity and the Incarnation, the most important philosophical factor is the variety of general ontologies they brought to the problem of relation. In the rest of this chapter, I discuss various theories in the light of the two demands mentioned above, and, when possible, I show how a person used parts of his general ontology to construct his theory.

Thomas Aquinas is squarely in the tradition, insisting on both the *esse-in* and *esse-ad* of a real relation. He repeatedly begins discussing relations by stating that

(T1)   In each of the nine accidental categories there is a distinction between accidental being common to all nine categories and the *ratio* of that particular category

and

(T2)   For each of the nine accidental categories, accidental being is to be in (to inhere in) a subject.

Hence, he maintains the traditional view of an accident as that which inheres (or is apt to inhere). The elegance and economy of his solution lie in the identification of the accidental being (*esse-in*) of a real relation with the accidental being of its foundation. Hence, a real relation does inhere in its subject. The *ratio* of a relation is to be toward another (*esse-ad*); it is an intelligible aspect of that one accidental form that is the foundation. Thomas (with Giles of Rome) gives equal weight to each demand on an adequate medieval theory of relation. This is seen clearly in a key thesis of his theory:

(T6)   The respect toward another *and* the accidental being of a relation are each necessary and jointly sufficient for a real relation.

Henry of Ghent is also squarely within the medieval tradition and like Thomas Aquinas distinguishes two aspects of a real relation. For Thomas these are *esse* and *ratio*; for Henry they are *res* and *ratio*. In both theories the first aspect is prior to, more fundamental than the second, and the contrast between their general ontologies could hardly be clearer: for Thomas that more fundamental aspect is being, for Henry it is the absolute nature or essence, the *res*.

For Thomas, among creatures the being of substance is the primary reality, and it is the cause of its accidents, including relation. For Henry, absolute nature or essence is the primary reality; the Platonic-Augustinian metaphysics of immutable essences takes the place of a metaphysics of being as found in Aquinas. In essential being, substance, quantity, and quality are equally basic; they are all absolute natures, deriving ultimately from the divine ideas. Through God's free act of creation, creatures begin to exist in existential being (*esse existentiae*), a mode of being. In each creature there is an intentional distinction between *what* it is, say, a human being, and *how* it exists, in existential being. So also, like any other created reality, real relations exhibit two aspects which Henry calls *res* and *ratio*. The *ratio* is the mode of being specific to a relation, its being toward another. The more fundamental aspect, the *res* of a real relation, is identical with the absolute nature it is founded upon; and if it is founded upon quantity or quality, the relation also has the mode of being peculiar to these, i.e., to be by inhering in another. Hence, Henry of Ghent attends to both demands on an adequate medieval theory of relation: the relation must exist in its subject and be 'toward' another. In a quite unique and novel way, he answers these traditional demands using his own distinctive ontology of essential being.

Henry of Ghent is the chief representative of the modalist theory of relation and had a number of followers, such as John Quidort (d. 1306), James of Metz (*fl.* 1295–1309), and James's pupil, Durand of Saint Pourçain (d. 1334).[2] One of the more interesting modalists to study would be Durand of Saint Pourçain, who taught that a real relation was a mode of being toward another. He went beyond his teacher James of Metz in applying the modalist theory of relation to his theory of the origin of ideas.

---

[2] For James of Metz and other followers of Henry of Ghent, see Paulus, *Henri de Gand*, pp. 187–91. For John Quidort on relations, see 'The First Quodlibet of Jean Quidort', ed. A. J. Heiman, in *Nine Mediaeval Thinkers*, ed. J. R. O'Donnell (Toronto, 1955), pp. 271–91, esp. 272–4.

In September 1314 he was censured by his fellow Dominicans for holding among other things that the act of knowledge is not something absolute, but a relation, a *modus essendi*. The act of knowledge does not perfect the soul since it is not something absolute added to the cognitive faculty, but only a simple comportment of the soul before an object.[3] At one point in his stormy career, Durand taught that on such a relational theory of knowledge it is not necessary to posit a *species* or an agent intellect. It seems he also taught that universality is not able to exist extramentally, but is a mental product, a relation of reason.[4] Durand's theory of relation colours and co-ordinates a complex of doctrines that his contemporaries termed *opinioness singulares*. A study of this modalist school would be helpful for discovering more completely how relations were explicated as modes and the effect this had on other doctrines.

Unlike his predecessors, Richard of Mediavilla does not distinguish two aspects of a relation, its *esse-in* and *esse-ad*. Although a real relation is based on a foundation, he does not conceive of it as inhering in its foundation. Instead, he conceives of a real relation as a non-inhering accident, and so its character as an accident is changed. The relation is conceived of as slightly cut off or separated from its foundation. In one way, Richard calls it a 'relative thing' really distinct from its foundation, an 'absolute thing'; in another way, a relation is a condition obtaining between two terms. Significantly, both formulations evidence Richard's stress on its specifically relational character over its character as an inherent accident. This is also seen in his insistence that if one is to understand relations adequately, one must not consider only one of the relata, as if one could discover the relation there on the model of an absolute accident that inheres. Rather, one must consider both relata taken together, for a relation is a condition obtaining between two things. Still, Richard tends to talk of this condition as in some way belonging to one subject, though not inhering in it.

Like others before him, John Duns Scotus tries to do justice to both aspects of a real relation. But in his particular solution, he

---

[3] See M. De Wulf, *Histoire de la philosophie médiévale*, vol. 3 (Louvain and Paris, 1947), pp. 17–22.
[4] Ibid., p. 21.

puts more stress on the *esse-in* aspect than any other scholastic. Unlike Thomas Aquinas, Giles of Rome, Henry of Ghent, and Richard of Mediavilla, Duns Scotus accords a categorical real relation its own inhering accidental reality really distinct from the accidental reality of its foundation. His emphasis on inherence is seen in his use of

(Fi)   If *b* properly inheres in *a*, and *a* cannot exist without *b*, then *b* is really the same as *a*

in his response (H) to the charge of an infinite regress.

Regarding his general ontology, Duns Scotus uses his doctrine of a formal distinction *a parte rei* throughout his discussion of transcendental relations as really identical with yet formally distinct from their foundations. His use of natural priority and posteriority of formalities is necessary for his argument (G) in support of (Fi). Duns Scotus, then, with his realist ontology of formalities, is a good representative of a strongly realist theory of relation. Further research should investigate the defence by Walter Chatton (d. 1344) of this realist position, along with John of Pouilly who in 1307 also defended it, specifically arguing at length against the theory of Henry of Ghent.[5]

The later Henry of Harclay distinguishes between two aspects which he calls the 'in-ness' (*initas*) and 'toward-ness' (*aditas*) of a real relation. He says explicitly that for him the term 'relation' signifies toward-ness and not in-ness, and so he emphasizes its specifically relational character over its being an inherent accident. For Harclay, a real relation is a non-inhering condition of one thing toward another. Consequently, a real relation is not said of its subject by intrinsic denomination, as if it were an inherent accidental form. Rather, it is said of the subject by extrinsic

---

[5] Walter Chatton, *Reportatio* I, d. 30, q. 1 (Paris, Bibliothèque Nationale lat. 15887, fols. 62^{r}a–64^{v}a): 'Utrum sit necessarium ponere in universo res relativas.' For John of Pouilly, see 'La Métaphysique de la relation chez Jean de Pouilly', ed. A. Pattin, in *Mélanges médiévistes offerts à Dom Jean-Pierre Müller, O.S.B.*, ed. T. W. Köhler (Studia Anselmiana, 63; Rome, 1974), pp. 415–37. In John's *Quodlibet* I, question 7, which Pattin has edited, John states: 'Sed omnia decem praedicamenta sunt entia extra animam distincta ex opposito, non ex opere animae, ut patet per Aristotelem V et VI *Metaphysicae*, qui ens distinctum contra ens secundum animam dividit in decem praedicamenta. Ergo omnia decem praedicamenta sunt ad invicem distincta realiter seu ex natura rei. Si enim essent divisa opere rationis, tunc non essent entia extra animam. Ex quo sequitur per consequens quod sint res diversae non solum quantitas, qualitas et substantia ad invicem, sed relatio et sex principia et ab invicem et a tribus praedictis' (pp. 419–20).

denomination because of the existence of the term. Hence, something can become really related without changing, for

(T7)   Something changes only if there is a change *in* it

if by 'in' is meant inherence. And

(T8)   *a* comes to be or ceases to be really related to *b* through some change of the foundation that is or is in *a* and/or of the foundation that is or is in *b*

and

(T9)   If the foundation that is or is in *a* changes, then there is a change of *a*; but if only the foundation that is or is in *b* changes, there is no change of *a*, for there is no change *in a*.

   To summarize so far: the divergence in theories can be formulated in terms of three severally necessary and jointly sufficient conditions for a real relation. The six thinkers discussed above agree on the first two conditions, but disagree on the third. Sentences of the form '*aRb*' ('*a* is really related by R to *b*') are true if and only if (i) *a* and *b* are really distinct extra-mental things, (ii) there is a real foundation in *a* for R, and either (iiia) there exists a real relation R identical in being but differing in *ratio* from its foundation (Thomas Aquinas and Giles of Rome); or (iiib) there exists a real relation R, a mode of being intentionally distinct from its foundation (Henry of Ghent); or (iiic) there exists a real relation R, a relative thing really distinct from its foundation (Richard of Mediavilla, John Duns Scotus, and the early Henry of Harclay); or (iiid) there exists a real relation R, a non-inhering condition of *a* toward *b* (the later Henry of Harclay). In (iiic), both Duns Scotus and the early Henry of Harclay held that a real relation does inhere; Richard of Mediavilla taught that it does not inhere.
   William of Ockham and Peter Aureoli do not share this traditional medieval view of relation, and they do not see themselves constrained to respond to both demands on an adequate medieval theory of relation. This can be shown rather clearly by that fact that their theories do not fit into the summary in the last paragraph, the precise reason being that neither subscribes to the second condition, that there is a real foundation in *a* for R. This is

significant, for this condition expresses the medieval view of a relation as existing *in* a foundation.

It is not by chance that in his lengthy discussions of relation Ockham refers to foundations so infrequently, for he positively insists that a real relation does not have a foundation. 'Similarly I say that a relation does not have a foundation, nor is that word "foundation of a relation" found in the philosophy of Aristotle, nor is it a philosophical word.'[6] Aiding him in his move from the traditional view is his systematic use of terminist logic in which relational terms are connotative.[7] Relational terms do not signify an accidental relational form inhering in a subject. Rather, Ockham teaches that according to human reason (unaided by divine revelation) categorical relational terms signify both relata (or signify one relatum directly and the other connotatively), and also connote that the relata exist in a certain way. Hence, Ockham departs radically from his predecessors as summarized above and holds that sentences of the form '*aRb*' are true if and only if *a* and *b* exist in the way connoted by substitutions for 'R'. Further evidence of his departure from the tradition is seen in his denial of condition (i). For Ockham, the relata need not be really distinct; numerical identity is a real relation. And mental realities, such as mental acts, can be really related.

Such novelty could not go unchallenged. Already around 1310 Henry of Harclay had rejected a theory very similar to the one Ockham would later espouse, precisely on the ground that it is incompatible with the nature of a relation.[8] Following Ibn Sīnā, Harclay insists on the second condition above, that a real relation must in some way be in one subject and founded on it. Walter Chatton also criticized Ockham's theory, substituting for Ockham's famous razor his own 'anti-razor': 'I argue thus: an affirmative proposition, when it is verified, is only verified for things: if

---

[6] William of Ockham, *Quodlibet* VI, q. 10: 'Similiter dico quod relatio non habet fundamentum, nec invenitur illud verbum "fundamentum relationis" in philosophia Aristotelis, nec est verbum philosophicum' (O T ix, p. 624:85–8); *Ordinatio* I, d. 30, q. 3 (O T iv, p. 355:6–12); *Summa Logicae* I, c. 54 (O P i, p. 177:12–13).

[7] Others before Ockham had talked of relational terms as connotative. See Thomas Aquinas, *In I Sent.* d. 30, q. 1, art. 2, corp. Richard of Mediavilla follows Thomas in this but is less detailed; see Richard's *In I Sent.* d. 30, art. 1, q. 3, corp. (fol. 267b); d. 31, art. 1, q. 2, corp. (fol. 273b). With Ockham, however, there is a new systematic use of connotative terms to deal with the ontological status of relations.

[8] Henry of Harclay, 'Question', nn. 46–7.

three things do not suffice to verify it, it is necessary to posit a fourth, and so on.'[9] Following Scotus, Chatton argues that a passage from contradictory to contradictory must be accounted for by some real change, a change in what things exist. If at $t1$ it is true that 'The fire does not burn wood', and at $t2$ it is true that 'The fire does burn wood', one must posit a relative entity, the relation of burning, to account for this change.[10]

Significantly, Peter Aureoli maintains that a real relation has one aspect, not two.[11] It is clear that this one aspect is the specifically relational element, for he conceives a real relation exclusively as a condition obtaining between two things. As he says repeatedly, a real relation connects things, is a medium or condition between things. He stresses the specifically relational aspect to such an extent that the traditional *esse-in* aspect is finally abandoned. Sentences of the form 'aRb' are true if and only if (i) a and b are really distinct extra-mental things, and (ii) there exists an objective apprehension (of intellect or sense) connecting a and b.

His abandoning of the *esse-in* aspect of a real relation is closely related to his conceptualism. In other thinkers we have examined, it is the aspect of being an accident that grounds the extra-mental reality of a real relation. This is so since accidents are said to exist with reference to that which primarily exists, and for the medievals what primarily exists is some extra-mental reality. In the ontology of Thoms Aquinas, an accident that is a real relation is caused by and derives its being from that which primarily exists, i.e. a substance. In the ontology of Henry of Ghent, an accident that is a real relation is caused by and derives its being from that which primarily exists, i.e. an absolute nature.

Peter departs radically from such treatment of the *esse-in* aspect: the real relation is not grounded in one extra-mental subject, but in *both* relata as apprehended and existing in objective being. It is the act of apprehension of, say, two white things that is

---

[9] Walter Chatton, *Reportatio* I, d. 30, q. 1: 'Arguo sic: propositio affirmativa quae quando verificatur solum verificatur pro rebus: si tres res non sufficiunt ad verificandum eam, oportet ponere quartam, et sic deinceps' (fol. 63ʳb). See also A. Maurer, 'Ockham's Razor and Chatton's Anti-Razor', *Mediaeval Studies* 46 (1984), pp. 463–75.

[10] See Maurer, 'Anti-Razor', p. 469. Compare Scotus' argument (E) regarding secondary causality, in sect. 1.5 of ch. 5.

[11] See n. 9 of ch. 8.

the condition of possibility and so the foundation for the act of apprehension of their indistinction with respect to colour. It is this latter really existing act of apprehension that has the character of connecting the relata and produces the corresponding objectively existing apprehension, i.e. the relation which also connects both relata.

Peter's novelty—conceiving of a real relation as only existing between two things—enables him to deny it any but a potential extra-mental existence. For Peter has a strong intuition that no extra-mental thing could have this peculiar property of 'existing between'. Rather, the only things that can have this property are an act of apprehension and its object. As a result of this novel conception of relation, Peter is puzzled at the very notion of a relation as an inherent accidental form. He also rejects Henry of Harclay's theory as still a version of the traditional view, for Harclay conceived a real relation as a condition of one thing toward another, a non-inhering accident still in some sense in one of the relata. In sum, with Ockham Aureoli has left behind the terms under which his fellow scholastics felt constrained to construct an adequate theory of relation.

It would be rash to pronounce on the subsequent historical influence of this change, since at present we do not know the course of the debate among others of the period. Just as, for example, some have recently become less certain about the number of genuine followers of William of Ockham,[12] so also we should be careful here. But with a knowledge of some principal protagonists in the controversy, we have a basis for research into other figures of that time. For example, how did early Dominicans, such as Thomas Sutton and Hervaeus Natalis, defend or depart from the teachings of Aquinas on relation? What of the controversies between Hervaeus Natalis and Durand of Saint Pourçain in 1314? With an understanding of the theories of Duns Scotus, William of Ockham, and Peter Aureoli, we can investigate the theories of such figures in the fourteenth century as William Alnwick, Richard Campsall, Adam Wodeham, Robert Holcot, John of Jandun, John Rodington, Thomas Strassburg, Gregory of Rimini, Richard Fitzralf, and many others.

[12] See K. H. Tachau, 'The Problem of the *Species in Medio* at Oxford in the Generation after Ockham', *Mediaeval Studies* 44 (1982), pp. 394–443.

Finally, with the disclaimer about subsequent historical influence, it seems a few brief remarks are in order regarding the
success of the conceptualist view in the early modern period of
philosophy.

Spinoza writes in *Metaphysical Thoughts* (part I, chap. 5,
perhaps directed against the scholastic author Burgersdijck) that
relations are not extra-mental entities other than the relata,
but only simple modes of thought. Aureoli would agree with
Spinoza's charge: if we consider relations as things existing
somehow outside of thought, we render confused a concept that is
clear. In his *Short Treatise* (part I, chap. 10), Spinoza calls relations
entia rationis and 'our own creation'.

Gassendi, after allowing (as all medievals) for the exceptional
case of the Trinity, loses himself in a rhetoric of ridicule against
the Aristotelians and their doctrine of relation.[13] He asks the
readers in good faith to watch a white wall while another is being
built and tell him if they can see the entity Relation approaching
the wall. Echoing Aureoli, he claims it would be a great miracle if
while a new white wall were being built in India, a white wall in
France became clothed as for a festive ball with this new reality. If
ten thousand new white walls were built, the poor French wall
would crumble under the weight of new relations! After citing
the labours of Hercules, he finally (and significantly) asks the
Aristotelians whether a relation is a double entity, that is, whether
it has an *esse-in* and *esse-ad*. But he quickly falls back into rhetoric
demanding how the latent relation in the French wall came to
know so quickly the news from India and sprout forth like a
mushroom?[14] His own doctrine is that a relation is an 'extrinsic
denomination', in itself hardly an illuminating theory. Hobbes
seems to hold that a relation, such as similarity, is not some entity
other than the whiteness. Rather it is a 'comparison', presumably
made by some mind or sense.[15]

Echoes of the medieval debate are present in Leibniz's distinction between a relation as a mental entity common to both relata

[13] Pierre Gassendi, *Dissertations en forme de paradoxes contre les aristotéliciens*, bks. I and
II, ed. and trans. B. Rochot (Paris, 1959), bk. II, ex. 3, a. 12 (pp. 345–9).

[14] Ibid.: '. . . quomodo latens relatio sub pariete audiat et intelligat dealbari parietem in
India, ut proinde statim, ac citius, quam e terra fungus erumpat, emergat, prosiliat, aliaque
similia, quam eris austerus, si risum contineas?' (p. 347).

[15] Thomas Hobbes, *Elements of Philosophy*, part II, c. 11, sect. 6, in *The English Works*,
ed. W. Molesworth (London, 1839–45), vol. i, p. 135.

and as a relational property of one of the relata. He illustrates this with the example of paternity, shorn of its medieval Trinitarian (but not of its biblical) origins: 'I do not believe that you will admit an accident that is in two subjects at the same time. My judgment about relations is that paternity in David is one thing, sonship in Solomon another, but that the relation common to both is a merely mental thing whose basis is the modifications of the individuals.'[16] Following Ibn Sīnā and the tradition, most medievals would agree with the first sentence, but it was Aureoli who drew the further conclusion that relations only exist in the intellect (or sense).

I see certain parallels between Aureoli's theory and that of John Locke. More often than his contemporaries Peter used empirical arguments, stressing the testimony of our senses, and he distinguished himself by using a psychological approach to ontological and epistemological problems. More specifically, his theory of relation is similar to that of Locke, who conceived of a relation as a complex idea resulting from the mind comparing one idea with another.

The Understanding, in the consideration of any thing, is not confined to that precise Object: It can carry any *Idea*, as it were, beyond it self, or, at least, look beyond it, to see how it stands in conformity to any other. When the Mind so considers one thing, that it does, as it were, bring it to, and set it by another, and carry its view from one to t'other: This is, as the Words import, *Relation* and *Respect*.[17]

Locke's psychological explanation of the mind considering and comparing ideas, 'carrying' one to another, is similar to that of Aureoli. Locke held that relations are 'not contained in the real existence of Things, but something extraneous, and

---

[16] Gottfried Leibniz, *Philosophical Papers and Letters*, trans. and ed. L. E. Loemker, Synthese Library, 2nd edn. (Dordrecht, 1969), p. 609. For Leibniz's medieval connection through the late scholastic Suarez (1548–1617), see L. B. McCullough, 'Leibniz and Traditional Philosophy', *Studia Leibnitiana* 10 (1978), pp. 254–70.

[17] John Locke, *An Essay Concerning Human Understanding*, ed. P. H. Nidditch (Oxford, 1975), bk. II, ch. 25, par. 1, p. 319. Also ibid., par. 5: '*The nature* therefore *of Relation*, consists in the referring, or comparing two things, one to another; from which comparison, one or both comes to be denominated' (p. 321); par. 7: 'For, as I said, *Relation* is a way of comparing, or considering two things together; and giving one, or both of them, some appellation from that Comparison, and sometimes giving even the Relation it self a Name' (p. 322).

superinduced.'[18] And in similar fashion to Aureoli, Locke talks of the foundation of a relation as an idea.[19]

Perhaps in the future we shall have a fuller understanding of medieval thinking on relations and so have a better foundation for comparison of medieval and modern theories.

[18] Locke, *Essay*, par. 8, p. 322.

[19] Ibid., par. 1: 'And since any *Idea*, whether simple, or complex, may be the occasion, why the Mind thus brings two things together, and, as it were, takes a view of them at once, though still considered as distinct: therefore any of our *Ideas*, may be the foundation of Relation' (p. 319).

Works Cited

Primary Sources

Avicenna. *Avicennae Perhypatetici Philosophi ac Medicorum Facile Primi Opera . . . Logyca . . .* Venice, 1508.
—— *Liber de Philosophia Prima sive Scientia Divina* I–IV and V–X. Ed. S. Van Riet. In *Avicenna Latinus*. Louvain and Leiden, 1977 and 1980.
Boethius. *The Theological Tractates*. Ed. and trans. H. F. Stewart, E. K. Rand, and S. J. Tester. Cambridge, Mass., 1978.
Gassendi, Pierre. *Dissertations en forme de paradoxes contre les aristotéliciens*, bks. I and II. Ed. and trans. B. Rochot, Paris, 1959.
Giles of Rome. *Egidii Romani in Libros de Physico Auditu Aristotelis Commentaria*. Venice, 1502.
—— *Primus Sententiarum Aegidii*. Venice, 1521.
—— *Super Authorem Libri de Causis, Alfarabium*. Venice, 1550.
—— *B. Aegidii Columnae Romani . . . Quodlibeta . . .* Louvain, 1646. Repr. Frankfurt am Main, 1966.
Gregory of Rimini. *Gregorii Ariminensis OESA Lectura super Primum et Secundum Sententiarum*. Vol. 3. Ed. D. Trapp and V. Marcolino. Spätmittelalter und Reformation: Texte und Untersuchungen, 8. Berlin and New York, 1984.
Henry of Ghent. *Summa (= Quaestiones Ordinariae)*. 2 vols. Paris, 1520. Repr. St Bonaventure, NY, 1953.
—— *Quodlibeta Magistri Henrici Goethals a Gandavo Doctoris Solemnis*. 2 vols. Paris, 1518. Repr. Louvain, 1961.
—— *Quodlibet I. Henrici de Gandavo Opera Omnia*, ed. R. Macken, v. Louvain and Leiden, 1979.
—— *Quodlibet IX. Henrici de Gandavo Opera Omnia*, ed. R. Macken, xiii. Louvain and Leiden, 1983.
Henry of Harclay. *In I Sententiarum*. Vatican Library Lat. 13687, fols. 13^v–97^v; Casale Monferrato, Biblioteca del Seminario Vescovile MS b 2, fols. 1^r–84^r.
—— *Quaestiones Ordinariae*. Vatican Library Borghese 171, fols. 1^r–32^v; Worcester, Cathedral Library F.3, fols. 181^v–215^v; Assisi, Biblioteca Comunale 172, fols. 125^r–131^v, 133^r–136^r, 149^r–153^v.
—— 'Henry of Harclay's Question on the Univocity of Being'. Ed. A. Maurer. *Mediaeval Studies* 16 (1954): 1–18.
—— 'Henry of Harclay's Question on Immortality'. Ed. A. Maurer. *Mediaeval Studies* 19 (1957): 79–107.

—— 'Henry of Harclay's Question on the Divine Ideas'. Ed. A. Maurer. *Mediaeval Studies* 23 (1961): 163–93.

—— 'Henricus de Harclay: Quaestio de Significato Conceptus Universalis'. Ed. G. Gál. *Franciscan Studies* 31 (1971): 178–234.

—— 'Henry of Harclay's Disputed Question on the Plurality of Forms'. Ed. A. Maurer. In *Essays in Honor of Anton Charles Pegis*, ed. J. R. O'Donnell. Toronto, 1974: 125–59.

—— 'Henry of Harclay's Questions on Divine Prescience and Predestination'. Ed. M. G. Henninger. *Franciscan Studies* 40 (1980): 167–243.

—— 'Henry of Harclay on the Formal Distinction in the Trinity'. Ed. M. G. Henninger. *Franciscan Studies* 41 (1981): 250–335.

—— 'Henricus de Harclay: Quaestio "Utrum mundus potuit fuisse ab eterno"'. Ed. R. C. Dales. *Archives d'histoire doctrinale et littéraire du Moyen Âge* 50 (1983): 223–55.

—— 'Henry of Harclay's Question on Relations'. Ed. M. G. Henninger. *Mediaeval Studies* 49 (1987): 76–123.

Hobbes, Thomas. *Elements of Philosophy. The English Works*, ed. W. Molesworth, vol. i. London, 1839.

John Duns Scotus. *Ioannis Duns Scoti . . . Opera Omnia.* 12 vols. Ed. L. Wadding. Lyons, 1639.

—— *Ioannis Duns Scoti Ordinis Fratrum Minorum Opera Omnia.* Ed. under the direction of C. Balić. Vatican City, 1950– .

—— *God and Creatures: The Quodlibetal Questions.* Trans. with introd., notes, and glossary by F. Alluntis and A. B. Wolter. Princeton, 1975.

John Lutterell. *Libellus contra Doctrinam Guilelmi Occam.* In *Die Schriften des Oxforder Kanzlers Iohannes Lutterell*, ed. F. Hoffmann. Leipzig, 1959.

John of Pouilly. 'La Métaphysique de la relation chez Jean de Pouilly'. Ed. A. Pattin. In *Mélanges médiévistes offerts à Dom Jean-Pierre Müller, O.S.B.*, ed. T. W. Köhler, pp. 415–37. Studia Anselmiana, 63. Rome, 1974.

John Quidort. 'The First Quodlibet of Jean Quidort'. Ed. A. J. Heiman. In *Nine Mediaeval Thinkers*, ed. J. R. O'Donnell. Toronto, 1955.

Leibniz, Gottfried. *Philosophical Papers and Letters.* Trans. and ed. L. E. Loemker. Synthese Library, 2nd edn. Dordrecht, 1969.

Locke, John. *An Essay Concerning Human Understanding.* Ed. P. H. Nidditch. Oxford, 1975.

Mill, John Stuart. *A System of Logic Ratiocinative and Inductive. Collected Works of John Stuart Mill*, ed. J. M. Robson, vol. 7. Toronto and Buffalo, 1973.

Peter Aureoli. *Scriptum super Primum Sententiarum.* Vatican Library MS Borghese 329, fols. 1–519.

——*Commentariorium in Primum Librum Sententiarum Pars Prima Auctore Petro Aureolo Verberio Ordinis Minorum Archiepiscopo Aquensi*. Rome, 1596.
——*Petri Aureoli Verberii Ordinis Minorum Archiepiscopi Aquensis . . . Commentariorum in Secundum Librum Sententiarum*. Rome, 1605.
——*Peter Aureoli Scriptum super Primum Sententiarum*. 2 vols. Ed. E. M. Buytaert. St Bonaventure, NY, 1952 and 1956.
Peter John Olivi. *Quaestiones in Secundum Librum Sententiarum*. 3 vols. Ed. B. Jansen. Quaracchi, 1922–6.
Plotinus. *Enneads*. 3 vols. Ed. P. Henry and H.-R. Schwyzer. Oxford, 1982–4.
Quine, Willard van Orman. *Word and Object*. New York and London, 1960.
Richard of Mediavilla. *Clarissimi Theologi Magistri Ricardi de Mediavilla super Quatuor Libros Sententiarum Petri Lombardi Quaestiones Subtilissimae*. 4 vols. Brescia, 1591.
——*Quodlibeta Doctoris Eximii Ricardi de Mediavilla Ordinis Minorum*. Brescia, 1591 (end of vol. 4 of his *Sentences* commentary).
Russell, Bertrand. *A Critical Exposition of the Philosophy of Leibniz*. 2nd edn. London, 1937.
Sextus Empiricus. *Adversus Dogmaticos Libros Quinque* (= *Adv. Mathem.* VII–XI). *Sexti Empirici Opera*, ed. H. Mutschmann, vol. 2. Bibliotheca Scriptorum Graecorum et Romanorum Teubneriana, 1801. Leipzig, 1914.
Simplicius. *In Aristotelis Categorias Commentarium. Commentaria in Aristotelem Graeca*, ed. C. Kalbfleisch, vol. 8. Berlin, 1907.
——*In Praedicamenta Aristotelis. Corpus Latinum Commentariorum in Aristotelem Graecorum*, ed. A. Pattin and W. Stuyven, vol. 5/1. Louvain and Paris, 1971.
Suarez, Francisco. *Disputationes Metaphysicae. Opera Omnia*, vol. 26. Paris, 1866.
Thomas Aquinas. *Opera Omnia*. 25 vols. Parma, 1852–73. Repr. New York, 1948–50.
——*Sancti Thomae Aquinatis Doctoris Angelici Opera Omnia*. Rome, 1882– .
——*On Being and Essence*. Trans. A. Maurer. 2nd rev. edn. Toronto, 1968.
Walter Chatton. *Comment. in I Sententiarum* (*Reportatio*), d. 30, q. 1. Paris, Bibliothèque Nationale lat. 15887, fols. 62^{r}a–64^{v}a.
William of Ockham. *Opera Theologica*. St Bonaventure, NY, 1967– .
——*Opera Philosophica*. St Bonaventure, NY, 1974– .

Secondary Sources

Adams, M. 'Ockham on Identity and Distinction'. *Franciscan Studies* 36 (1976): 5–74.
—— 'Ockham's Nominalism and Unreal Entities'. *Philosophical Review* 86 (1977): 144–76.
—— *William Ockham.* 2 vols. Notre Dame, Ind., 1987.
Balić, C. 'Henricus de Harcley et Ioannes Duns Scotus'. *Mélanges offerts à Étienne Gilson*, pp. 93–121, 701–2. Études de philosophie médiévale (hors série). Toronto and Paris, 1959.
Baudry, L. 'A propos de la théorie occamiste de la relation'. *Archives d'histoire doctrinale et littéraire du Moyen Âge* 9 (1934): 199–203.
Beckmann, J. P. *Die Relationen der Identität und Gleichheit nach J. Duns Scotus.* Bonn, 1967.
Bellemare, L. *Les 'Quaestiones super VIII libros Physicorum', attribuées à Henri de Gand (Ms. Erfurt, Amplon., F.349, ff. 120ʳa–184ʳb): étude sur l'authenticité de l'œuvre; étude et texte des Quaestiones super VIII libros Physicorum, attribuées à Henri de Gand.* 3 vols. Université de Louvain, Institut Supérieur de Philosophie, dissertation. Louvain, 1961.
Blanche, F.-A. 'Les Mots significant la relation dans la langue de saint Thomas d'Aquin'. *Revue de philosophie* 32 (1925): 363–88.
Boehner, Ph. '*Notitia Intuitiva* of Non-Existents according to Peter Aureoli, O.F.M. (1322)'. *Franciscan Studies* 8 (1948): 388–416.
Brampton, C. K. 'Personalities at the Process against Ockham at Avignon, 1324–26'. *Franciscan Studies* 25 (1966): 4–25.
Brown, J. V. 'Abstraction and the Object of the Human Intellect according to Henry of Ghent'. *Vivarium* 11 (1973): 80–104.
—— 'Divine Illumination in Henry of Ghent'. *Recherches de théologie ancienne et médiévale* 41 (1974): 177–99.
—— 'The Meaning of *Notitia* in Henry of Ghent'. In *Sprache und Erkenntnis im Mittelalter*, ed. J. P. Beckmann *et al.* Miscellanea Mediaevalia, 13/2. Berlin and New York, 1981.
—— 'Duns Scotus on the Possibility of Knowing Genuine Truth: The Reply to Henry of Ghent in the "Lectura Prima" and in the "Ordinatio"'. *Recherches de théologie ancienne et médiévale* 51 (1984): 136–82.
Bruni, G. 'Saggio bibliografico sulle opere stampate di Egidio Romano'. *Analecta Augustiniana* 24 (1961): 331–55.
Castañeda, H.-N. 'Plato's *Phaedo* Theory of Relations'. *Journal of Philosophical Logic* 1/3–4 (1972): 467–80.
—— 'Plato's Relations, Not Essences or Accidents, at *Phaedo* 102 b2–d2'. *Canadian Journal of Philosophy* 7 (1978): 39–53.

—— 'Leibniz and Plato's *Phaedo* Theory of Relations and Predication'. In *Leibniz: Critical and Interpretive Essays*, ed. M. Hooker. Manchester, 1982.

Catto, J. I. (ed.). *The Early Oxford Schools*. The History of the University of Oxford, 1. Oxford, 1984.

Clarke, W. N. 'The Limitation of Act by Potency: Aristotelianism or Neoplatonism'. *The New Scholasticism* 26 (1952): 167–94.

Coffey, B. 'The Notion of Order according to St. Thomas Aquinas'. *The Modern Schoolman* 27 (1949): 1–18.

Cunningham, F. A. 'Richard of Middleton, O.F.M. on *Esse* and Essence'. *Franciscan Studies* 30 (1970): 49–76.

Dales, R. C. 'Henry of Harclay and the Infinite'. *Journal of the History of Ideas* 45 (1984): 295–301.

De Wulf, M. *Histoire de la philosophie médiévale*. Vol. 3. Louvain and Paris, 1947.

Dipert, R. R. 'Peirce, Frege, the Logic of Relations, and Church's Theorem'. *History and Philosophy of Logic* 5 (1984): 49–66.

Doncœur, P. 'Le Nominalisme de Guillaume Occam: La Théorie de la relation'. *Revue néo-scolastique de philosophie* 23 (1921): 5–25.

Dreiling, R. *Der Konzeptualismus in der Universalienlehre des Franziskanererzbischofs Petrus Aureoli*. Beiträge zur Geschichte der Philosophie des Mittelalters, 11/6. Münster, 1913.

Duhem, P. *Études sur Léonard de Vinci: Ceux qu'il a lus et ceux qui l'ont lu*. Vol. 2. Paris, 1909.

Ehrle, F. 'Beiträge zu den Biographien berühmter Scholastiker: I. Heinrich von Ghent'. In *Archiv für Litteratur- und Kirchengeschichte des Mittelalters*, vol. 1. Rome, 1885: 365–401.

Emden, A. B. *A Biographical Register of the University of Oxford to AD 1500*, ii. Oxford, 1958.

Felt, J. 'Invitation to a Philosophic Revolution'. *The New Scholasticism* 45 (1971): 87–109.

Frankfurt, H. G. (ed.). *Leibniz: A Collection of Critical Essays*. New York, 1972.

Geiger, L. B. *La Participation dans la philosophie de S. Thomas d'Aquin*. 2nd edn. Paris, 1953.

Glorieux, P. *La Littérature quodlibétique de 1260 à 1320*. Vol. 1. Kain, 1925.

Gómez Caffarena, J. 'Cronología de la "Suma" de Enrique de Gante por relación a sus "Quodlibetos"'. *Gregorianum* 38 (1957): 116–33.

—— *Ser participado y ser subsistente en la metafísica de Enrique de Gante*. Analecta Gregoriana, 93. Rome, 1958.

Greive, H. 'Zur Relationslehre Wilhelms von Ockham'. *Franziskanische Studien* 49 (1967): 248–58.

Hartshorne, C. *The Divine Relativity.* New Haven and London, 1948.

Hintikka, J. 'Leibniz on Plenitude, Relations and the "Reign of Law"'. In *Leibniz: A Collection of Critical Essays*, ed. H. G. Frankfurt. New York, 1972: 155–90.

Hocedez, E. *Richard de Middleton: Sa vie, ses œuvres, sa doctrine.* Louvain, 1925.

—— 'Gilles de Rome et Henri de Gand sur la distinction réelle (1276–1287)'. *Gregorianum* 8 (1927): 358–84.

—— 'Gilles de Rome et saint Thomas'. *Mélanges Mandonnet* 1 (1930): 385–409.

Holzer, O. 'Zur Beziehungslehre des Doctor Subtilis Johannes Duns Scotus'. *Franziskanische Studien* 33 (1951): 22–49.

Horten, M. *Die philosophischen Systeme der spekulativen Theologen im Islam.* Bonn, 1912.

Koch, J. 'Neue Aktenstücke zu dem gegen Wilhelm Ockham in Avignon geführten Prozess'. *Recherches de théologie ancienne et médiévale* 7 (1935): 353–80; 8 (1936): 79–93, 168–97.

Kossel, C. 'Principles of St. Thomas's Distinction between the *Esse* and *Ratio* of Relation'. *The Modern Schoolman* 24 (1946): 19–36; (1947): 93–107.

—— 'St. Thomas's Theory of the Causes of Relation'. *The Modern Schoolman* 25 (1948): 151–72.

Krempel, A. *La Doctrine de la relation chez saint Thomas.* Paris, 1952.

Lindner, B. *Die Erkenntnislehre des Thomas von Strassburg.* Beiträge zur Geschichte der Philosophie des Mittelalters, 27/4–5. Münster, 1930.

McCullough, L. B. 'Leibniz and Traditional Philosophy'. *Studia Leibnitiana* 10 (1978): 254–70.

MacDonald, S. 'The *Esse/Essentia* Argument in Aquinas's *De ente et essentia*'. *Journal of the History of Philosophy* 22 (1984): 157–72.

Macken, R. 'La Temporalité radicale de la créature selon Henri de Gand'. *Recherches de théologie ancienne et médiévale* 38 (1971): 211–72.

—— 'La Théorie de l'illumination divine dans la philosophie d'Henri de Gand'. *Recherches de théologie ancienne et médiévale* 39 (1972): 82–112.

—— 'La Volonté humaine: Faculté plus élevée que l'intelligence selon Henri de Gand'. *Recherches de théologie ancienne et médiévale* 42 (1975): 5–51.

—— 'Hendrik van Gent (Henricus de Gandavo): Wijsgeer en theoloog'. *Nationaal Biografisch Woordenboek*, vol. 8. Brussels, 1979: cols. 377–95.

—— 'Le Statut de la matière première dans la philosophie d'Henri de

Gand'. *Recherches de théologie ancienne et médiévale* 46 (1979): 130–82.

—— 'Les Diverses Applications de la distinction intentionnelle chez Henri de Gand'. In *Sprache und Erkenntnis im Mittelalter*, ed. J. P. Beckmann *et al.* Miscellanea Mediaevalia, 13/2. Berlin and New York, 1981.

——*Bibliotheca Manuscripta Henrici de Gandavo*, ii. In *Henrici de Gandavo Opera Omnia*, vol. ii. Louvain and Leiden, 1979.

——(ed). *Henri de Gand (d. 1293), maître en théologie à l'Université de Paris, archidiacre de l'évêché de Tournai: Dates et documents*. *Henrici de Gandavo Opera Omnia*, vol. iv (forthcoming).

McPherran, M. 'Matthen on Castañeda and Plato's Treatment of Relational Statements in the *Phaedo*'. *Phronesis* 28 (1983): 298–306.

Maier, A. *Codices Burghesiani Bibliothecae Vaticanae*. Studi e Testi, 170. Vatican City, 1952: 373–4.

—— 'Zu einigen Sentenzenkommentaren des 14. Jahrhunderts'. In *Ausgehendes Mittelalter: Gesammelte Aufsätze zur Geistesgeschichte des 14. Jahrhunderts*, i. Storia e letteratura, 97. Rome, 1964.

Mandonnet, P. 'La Carrière scolaire de Gilles de Rome (1276–1291)'. *Revue des sciences philosophiques et théologiques* 4 (1910): 480–99.

—— 'Les Premières Disputes sur la distinction réelle entre l'essence et l'existence 1276–1287'. *Revue thomiste* 18 (1910): 741–65.

Marmura, M. E. 'Avicenna's Chapter "On the Relative", in the *Metaphysics* of the Shifã'. In *Essays on Islamic Philosophy and Science*, ed. G. F. Hourani. Albany, 1975.

Martin, G. *Wilhelm von Ockham: Untersuchungen zur Ontologie der Ordnungen*. Berlin, 1949.

—— 'Ist Ockhams Relationstheorie Nominalismus?'. *Franziskanische Studien* 32 (1950): 31–49.

Martin, R. M. 'On the Metaphysical Status of Mathematical Entities'. *The Review of Metaphysics* 39 (1985): 3–21.

Matthen, M. 'Plato's Treatment of Relational Statements in the *Phaedo*'. *Phronesis* 27 (1982): 90–100.

Maurer, A. 'St. Thomas and Henry of Harclay on Created Natures'. In *III Congresso internazionale di filosofia medioevale*. Milan, 1966: 542–9.

—— 'Ockham's Razor and Chatton's Anti-Razor'. *Mediaeval Studies* 46 (1984): 463–75.

Mohan, G. E. 'The *Quaestio de Relatione* Attributed to William of Ockham'. *Franciscan Studies* 11 (1951): 273–303.

Nash, P. W. 'Giles of Rome: Auditor and Critic of St. Thomas'. *The Modern Schoolman* 28 (1950): 1–20.

—— 'Giles of Rome'. *New Catholic Encyclopedia*, vol. 6. New York, 1967.

194 *Works Cited*

O'Briant, W. H. 'Russell on Leibniz'. *Studia Leibnitiana* 11 (1979): 159–222.

Owens, J. 'Quiddity and Real Distinction in St. Thomas Aquinas'. *Mediaeval Studies* 27 (1965): 1–22.

Passmore, J. *A Hundred Years of Philosophy*. London, 1957.

Paulus, J. *Henri de Gand: Essai sur les tendances de sa métaphysique.* Paris, 1938.

Pelster, F. 'Heinrich von Harclay, Kanzler von Oxford und seine Quästionen'. In *Miscellanea Francesco Ehrle*, i. Studi e Testi, 37. Rome, 1924: 307–56.

Pelzer, A. 'Les 51 Articles de Guillaume Occam censurés, en Avignon, en 1326'. *Revue d'histoire ecclésiastique* 18 (1922): 240–70.

Prezioso, F. A. 'La teoria dell' essere apparente nella gnoseologia di Pietro Aureolo, O.F.M. (1322)'. *Studi francescani* 22 (1950): 15–43.

——'Il nominalismo ambiguo di Pietro Aureolo'. *Sapienza* 25 (1972): 265–99.

Rucker, P. P. *Der Ursprung unserer Begriffe nach Richard von Mediavilla: Ein Beitrag zur Erkenntnislehre des Doctor Solidus.* Beiträge zur Geschichte der Philosophie und Theologie des Mittelalters, 31/1. Münster, 1934.

Tachau, K. H. 'The Problem of the *Species in Medio* at Oxford in the Generation after Ockham'. *Mediaeval Studies* 44 (1982): 394–443.

Teetaert, Am. 'Pierre Auriol'. *Dictionnaire de théologie catholique*, vol. 12, cols. 1810–81. Paris, 1935.

Weinberg, J. *Abstraction, Relation, and Induction: Three Essays in the History of Thought.* Madison and Milwaukee, 1965.

Weisheipl, J. *Friar Thomas D'Aquino: His Life, Thought and Works.* Washington, DC, 1983.

Wilhelmsen, F. D. 'Creation as a Relation in Saint Thomas Aquinas'. *The Modern Schoolman* 56 (1979): 107–33.

Wilson, G. 'Henry of Ghent and René Descartes on the Unity of Man'. *Franziskanische Studien* 64 (1982): 97–110.

Wippel, J. 'Aquinas's Route to the Real Distinction: A Note on *De ente et essentia*'. *The Thomist* 43 (1979): 279–95.

——*The Metaphysical Thought of Godfrey of Fontaines.* Washington, DC, 1981.

——'The Reality of Nonexisting Possibles according to Thomas Aquinas, Henry of Ghent, and Godfrey of Fontaines'. *The Review of Metaphysics* 34 (1981): 729–58.

——'The Relationship between Essence and Existence in Late-Thirteenth-Century Thought: Giles of Rome, Henry of Ghent, Godfrey of Fontaines, and James of Viterbo'. In *Philosophies of Existence Ancient and Modern*, ed. P. Morewedge. New York, 1982.

Wolter, A. B. *The Transcendentals and their Function in the Metaphysics of Duns Scotus.* Washington, 1946.

Wong, D. 'Leibniz's Theory of Relations'. *The Philosophical Review* 89 (1980): 241–56.

Wood, R. 'Adam Wodeham on Sensory Illusions with an Edition of "Lectura Secunda", Prologus, Quaestio 3'. *Traditio* 38 (1982): 213–52.

Zavalloni, R. *Richard de Médiavilla et la controverse sur la pluralité des formes.* Philosophes médiévaux, 2. Louvain, 1951.

Index

absolute accidents 16, 18, 21, 22, 27,
    49–54, 63–4, 66, 72, 73–4, 90,
    113, 117
absolute nature 15–16, 43, 45, 47, 48,
    49–50, 55, 57, 74, 76, 95, 177,
    182
absolute power 107, 109–10, 125
action and passion 7, 17–19, 35, 105,
    107–8, 172
Adam Wodeham 162 n.
Adams, M. 82 n., 119 n., 162 n.
Anselm 102, 129 n., 147
Aristotle 1, 5, 6–10, 14, 24 n., 26, 33,
    40 n., 62, 63, 66, 72, 76, 77 n., 85,
    86, 120, 128 n., 132, 133, 143, 146,
    174, 181
    Physics V, c. 2: 8–9, 19–21, 23, 28, 87,
        102–3, 129, 147, 155
    Metaphysics, V, c. 15: 6, 17–19, 33, 144
Augustine 1, 41, 57, 59, 81 n., 115, 140,
    143
Averroes 153
Avicenna, *see* Ibn Sīnā

Balić, C. 98 n., 99 n.
Baudry, L. 120 n.
Beckmann, J. P. 70 n.
Bellemare, L. 40 n.
Blanche, F.-A. 13 n.
Boehner, Ph. 149 n., 162 n.
Boethius 50–1, 94 n.
Bradley, F. H. 10
Brampton, C. K. 147 n.
Brown, J. V. 41 n.
Bruni, G. 26 n.
Buytaert, E. M. 150 n., 151 n.

Castañeda, H.-N. 4 n.
Catto, J. I. 98 n.
Clarke, W. N. 38 n.
Coffey, B. 13 n.
creation as relation 37–8
Cunningham, F. A. 59 n., 61 n.

Dales, R. C. 98 n.
De Wulf, M. 178 n.

Dipert, R. R. 3 n.
divine ideas 44, 46, 50
Doncoeur, P. 119 n., 134 n.
Doucet, V. 99 n.
Dreiling, R. 150 n., 153 n., 157 n.,
    158 n., 159 n., 171 n.
Duhem, P. 59 n.
Duns Scotus, John 1, 11, 25, 32, 40, 55,
    67, 68–97, 98–101, 103, 104–6,
    108–9, 111–12, 115, 117–18, 119,
    120–2, 123–5, 125–8, 130–2, 141,
    145–6, 147, 149 n., 153, 156, 157,
    171, 178–9, 180, 182
Durand of Saint Pourçain 177–8

Ehrle, F. 40 n.
Emden, A. B. 98 n.
essential being 11, 41, 44–6, 47, 49–50,
    87, 95, 96, 169, 177
existential being 46–7, 49–50, 177

Fabro, C. 38 n.
Fakhr al-Din al-Rāzī 9–10
Felt, J. 32 n.
formal distinction 69, 81, 82–5, 98 n.,
    122, 127, 146, 179
Frege, G. 3

Gál, G. 98 n., 99 n., 146 n.
Gassendi, P. 184
Geiger, L. B. 38 n.
Giles of Rome 26–9, 41, 46, 55, 57, 58,
    61, 66, 67, 69, 87, 92, 152, 176, 179,
    180
Glorieux, P. 60 n.
Godfrey of Fontaines 61
Gómez Caffarena, J. 41 n., 42 n., 44 n.,
    46 n., 47 n., 48 n., 50 n.
Gregory of Rimini 173
Greive, H. 119 n., 134 n.

Hartshorne, C. 32, 38
Henninger, M. 98 n., 99 n.
Henry of Ghent 1, 11, 40–58, 61, 62–3,
    67, 69, 70, 71, 73–4, 76, 77, 78,